Budget Travel

by Geoffrey Morrison

for
dummies®
A Wiley Brand

Budget Travel For Dummies®

Published by: **John Wiley & Sons, Inc.,** 111 River Street, Hoboken, NJ 07030-5774, www.wiley.com

Copyright © 2024 by John Wiley & Sons, Inc., Hoboken, New Jersey

Media and software compilation copyright © 2024 by John Wiley & Sons, Inc. All rights reserved.

Published simultaneously in Canada

For general information on our other products and services, please contact our Customer Care Department within the U.S. at 877-762-2974, outside the U.S. at 317-572-3993, or fax 317-572-4002. For technical support, please visit https://hub.wiley.com/community/support/dummies.

Wiley publishes in a variety of print and electronic formats and by print-on-demand. Some material included with standard print versions of this book may not be included in e-books or in print-on-demand. If this book refers to media such as a CD or DVD that is not included in the version you purchased, you may download this material at http://booksupport.wiley.com. For more information about Wiley products, visit www.wiley.com.

Library of Congress Control Number: 2023951015

ISBN 978-1-394-21295-8 (pbk); ISBN 978-1-394-21297-2 (ebk); ISBN 978-1-394-21296-5 (ebk)

SKY10062803_121523

Contents at a Glance

Contents at a Glance

Table of Contents

Introduction

Picture yourself relaxing on a tropical beach with white sand and azure waters. Picture yourself exploring the cobblestone alleyways of an ancient city. Picture yourself on horseback among a herd of zebras. If you could go anywhere in the world right now, where would it be? What's stopping you?

If you're like most people, the answer is money. The good news is, travel doesn't have to be outrageously expensive. *Budget Travel For Dummies* shows you how to keep costs low and still have an adventure you'll remember forever.

You can discover not only how to make your next trip more affordable but also how to make all travel so easy and inexpensive you're able to head out and explore again and again and again. You can find out not only how to budget money for a trip but also how to budget the true rarest of resources: time.

There's a whole world of adventure out there. Let's go explore.

About This Book

This book is the culmination of ten years of extensive and extended travels in addition to ten-plus years before that making many, many travel mistakes. I've written about travel for *The New York Times*, *Forbes*, and numerous other publications, all while traveling through 60 countries, 50 states, and during months of continuous adventure. There are numerous personal anecdotes throughout these pages, and I've included advice from other travelers I've met on the road.

Topics covered in this book include

>> Getting the most bang for your traveling buck

>> How to pack for any trip and save on luggage

>> Budget-friendly lodging and dining all over the world

>> How to get the best price on airfare

>> Common travel blunders to avoid

>> And more!

I've organized the book to flow from initial planning, to booking flights and accommodations, to packing, then on to things you'll need to keep in mind while you're traveling. Feel free to bounce around, though!

Foolish Assumptions

The foolish assumptions are actually by me about you! While writing this book I've had an idea in my head about who you are, with the hope that I can pre-answer any questions you have and write about things you want to know. Broadly speaking, I had two types of people in mind for this book. First, someone who's new to travel. Second, someone who has traveled but wants to travel a lot more. In both cases, of course, they're on a tight budget. More specifically, you're

>> Someone who wants to travel, perhaps for the first time, and you can't figure out how to afford it.

>> Someone who has the time to travel more, but not the money.

A few more general assumptions:

>> Most of my advice can apply to solo travelers as well as couples and families. I've made specific callouts when that's not the case.

>> My advice throughout is for adults of "all ages." There's no upper or lower limit on travel, budget or otherwise.

>> My advice isn't gender specific. I am a man, but I've had lengthy conversations with women (friends and fellow travelers) and have made sure to include their advice throughout this book.

Perhaps most importantly, I don't believe in gatekeeping travel. If you're 80 and want to see elephants in the wild, 20 and want to stand on the battlefield of Thermopylae, or 50 and want a selfie atop the Eiffel Tower, do it. It's all an adventure, and you should follow your heart. My goal is to help you afford it — not just that next trip, but the one after, and the one after that, and the one after that . . .

Icons Used in This Book

Throughout the book, I use a handful of icons to point out various types of information. Here's what they are and what they mean:

REMEMBER

This is an important point that's key to budget travel or travel in general.

TIP

I've traveled a lot and I've found a lot of ways to make it easier. These tips should help you too, though they're often more situational.

WARNING

Basically the negative version of a "Tip," something that might cause an issue or is worth avoiding if possible.

FIND ONLINE

This icon points out helpful online resources as well as items you can find on the resources page at www.dummies.com/go/budgettravelfd.

Beyond the Book

I've put together an online resources page to help you get the best prices on flights, find the right accommodations, and more. Here's what you can find:

>> Direct links to the best booking websites

>> Links to trusted (by me) gear review sites

>> Visa, passport, and other important travel info

Just go to www.dummies.com/go/budgettravelfd. Be sure to bookmark the site so you can easily find it later.

Where to Go from Here

Everywhere! No, seriously. The world is a lot smaller than it seems. Go wherever seems interesting to you, assuming it's in your budget and welcoming of visitors.

Where you should go *in this book* is an easier question. You can certainly read it chapter to chapter, cover to cover, if you want. There's certainly lots of info throughout (I hope!) and even if it's a section you're not sure you need, there might be some nuggets in there that you weren't expecting.

Alternately, you can bounce around. If you just want to know about booking cheap flights, finding the best place to stay, or what to pack, you can dive into those chapters directly. There's no Budget Travel Extended Universe you'll need to research to get the most out of each section. If there is something I explain better elsewhere in the book, I make a note of it.

If you're new to travel, I would say starting with Chapters 1 to 3 is a good idea. They'll give you a framework about what travel in general and budget travel specifically can be. They include a lot of "best practices" that will help throughout your adventures.

If you're a more advanced traveler and just want to know some key ways to save money, Chapters 4 and 5 are two important chapters to help keep your costs down.

Lastly, if you're really advanced and want to know about how to travel for weeks, months, or longer, start with Chapters 11 and 12.

Thanks for reading. I hope your next adventure is epic!

Chapter **1**

Wanting to Travel at Any Cost

dventure — that's what travel means to me. Whether it's exploring the streets of Vienna, floating in the clear blue waters of Fiji, or hiking through a rainforest, it's all an adventure. Travel can be a weekend away upstate, or a multi-month journey around the world. Big budget or small, long or short, travel can make you feel alive, rejuvenate your psyche, and give you memories you'll cherish for a lifetime.

The trick, of course, is being able to afford it. Don't worry, though. I'm here to help you become an avid traveler whatever your budget.

FIND ONLINE

Be sure to check out www.dummies.com/go/budgettravelfd to find any web addresses mentioned in the chapter as well as links to other fun and useful sites.

Ditching the Notion That Travel Has to Be Expensive

You don't need to be rich to travel. I mean, sure, it'd be great to hop on your private jet, get whisked away to your private island, and enjoy a feast prepared by your private chef. If you've got a line on how to do that, I'm all ears. But I'm not waiting around to hit that lottery. I've traveled for months at a time on a limited budget. How limited? Less than many people spend on rent, even to gorgeous locations like the one in Figure 1-1.

Geoffrey Morrison

FIGURE 1-1: It's possible to travel on a budget just about everywhere!

The fact is, the way most people travel is significantly more expensive than it needs to be. I've heard people who were convinced that a trip to Europe can't cost less than $4,000 plus airfare. I've heard people dismiss entire countries because they think it will cost too much. Most upsetting, I've heard from far too many people who think that *all* travel is "too expensive," despite having an income higher than mine.

This is one of the few times in this book I'm going to be judgmental: Most people are wrong about travel. It doesn't have to be expensive. It can be affordable enough that most people, with a little planning and savings, can travel anywhere. While I don't have just one secret that allows this (that would be a pretty short book!), there are a variety of simple adjustments and "best practices" in this book that can greatly reduce the cost of every aspect of your adventure.

My goal is to show you not only how you can afford your next trip, but also how to use the skills you'll learn to have one after that, and one after that, and fully embrace the goal of adventure. Because no matter where you want to go, the way to get there is budget travel (hey — that's the title of the book!).

Deciding Where to Go

By *far* the best way to be able to afford travel is picking your destination carefully. This, above all other tips and tricks, will save you the most money. Or to put it another way, your money goes a lot farther in some places than in others. Don't get me wrong, if you've got your heart set on seeing the lights of Paris or the sun setting over Serengeti, there are ways to make that affordable, too.

If you just want to get *out there*, to go somewhere you can't read the signs and no one knows your name, you can find a variety of options similar to the popular places where you can enjoy a comparable experience at a fraction of the cost.

For example, Tokyo is one of the most expensive cities in the world. If you're looking for the hustle and bustle of a huge city, along with some amazing varieties of food, Taipei is significantly more affordable. London is another hugely expensive city, but if you're looking for history and atmosphere, Lisbon has that Old World feel and is easier on the budget.

Not every place has a less-expensive option. If you have your heart set on Paris, France, then Paris, Texas, is not going to work. The Luxor in Las Vegas is not the same as Luxor, Egypt. It's a big world out there, though, and there are adventures to be had all over. If your budget is limited now, you can get out there, explore, and make some memories right away without having to save up for three years for just one short trip.

With any luck, you'll have more money in the future to venture into more expensive places. Or even better, you'll discover from this book and your initial budget travels how to become such a clever and frugal traveler that you can spend days and weeks in even these expensive places, with a budget that seems impossibly low right now.

TIP

For now, if you're not set on a location, several flight booking sites (more on these in Chapter 4) can show you what the cheapest flights are from your closest airport. The best deals might be a less-visited and less-expensive location.

If you're not sure where to go, the following sections should help you narrow down the best destination for your next adventure.

What kind of experience are you looking for?

Some types of travel are more affordable than others. If it's your dream to spend weeks on safari in southern Africa, that's going to be difficult to do on the cheap. If you want to try every restaurant and café along the river Seine, you're going to need deep pockets.

What is it about the location that appeals to you? If there's some personal reason, that's great. But if it's just "I want to see X," it's worth asking yourself what it is about that specific location that's drawing you there. If it's to see something unique about that location, the Eiffel Tower or Iguaçu Falls, go for it. If it's just to be on a beach, to climb a mountain, or explore an unfamiliar city, there are lots of inexpensive and still incredible options.

Of course, you don't have to have a reason. I'm absolutely not trying to talk you out of seeing what you want to see. I've certainly done plenty of "touristy" trips myself (see Figure 1-2 for just one example), and I don't think there's anything wrong with that. Even if it's just "I want to take a picture on the Great Wall of China," don't let anyone talk you out of it. I've certainly gone on trips for worse reasons. I once took a series of trains from northern England to Spain because I thought it'd be funny and make a good story. It was, it did, and I won't do it again.

REMEMBER

If your budget is extremely limited, though, and you just need to get out and see the world, figuring out what you want from travel is the first step in figuring out what locations can satisfy that desire, and more importantly, which of those are affordable.

FIGURE 1-2: The picturesque village of Hallstatt, Austria is a UNESCO World Heritage Site and gets thousands of visitors a day. It's gorgeous, but so are many other less-visited towns in the area.

Ideas for first-time travelers

It's a big world out there. That's exciting, but also daunting. If you're new to travel, the whole idea can be intimidating. It's awesome if you have an endless list of places you want to see and things you want to do, but don't feel the need to tackle all of it at once. The idea of budget travel is not to be cheap but choosy so that you can make travel sustainable on your budget. Rather than breaking the bank for a singular "trip of a lifetime," the goal is to take as many trips as often as possible throughout your lifetime, creating countless memories over many years.

Hopefully, you can narrow down your dream travel list to what you want to see the most. Don't let anyone make you feel guilty about what's on this short list. If you want to take a selfie in front of the Leaning Tower of Pisa or eat sushi at a fish market in Japan, you do you. It's all an adventure and as long as you treat the locals with respect and you have fun, who cares what your former roommate's brother's partner's jealous cousin has to say about it.

REMEMBER

Throughout this book I give you tips that should help you wherever you want to go, but I want to give you this piece of advice now, before you get your heart set on any one place: start slow. If this is your first trip of hopefully many, stick to one place, and ideally, a place that's not overly challenging to visit.

I'm not here to yuck anyone's yums, but for novice travelers I generally recommend places that are well-known tourist destinations. This partially goes against my advice of going where the tourists aren't, but there's a line to be walked for sure between affordability and accessibility. Perhaps the cheapest destination isn't as easy to navigate as a slightly more expensive option. On the other hand, the easiest destination could be the most expensive for getting around, while one a bit cheaper could prove nearly as easy.

What do I mean by "easy"? Tourist-friendly destinations will have the infrastructure to help you out if something goes wrong, many people will speak English, and it will be fairly simple to get around. Cities might be entirely walkable or have an extensive metro system. Grocery stores and inexpensive eateries will be plentiful. Stores will take your credit cards, or it will be easy to find a cash machine.

Later, when you've got a few trips under your belt, feel free to go somewhere you'll never hear English, no one takes credit cards, and the hotels are a room in some guy's garage. Some of the best adventures in my life have been to places where I've vibrantly stuck out like every inch of the bald, bespectacled weirdo that I am. It's great! It's just not something even I could have handled at the start of my extended travels.

Of course, I realize many live life according to the credo that says being out of your comfort zone is the only way to live. At least, that's what all the posters, candle holders, bathmats, and pillow cushions at IKEA tell me. I don't disagree, but there's being out of your comfort zone, and there's being out of your comfort zone. If you're new to travel, maybe bushwacking through a swamp five hours from the nearest town isn't the best way to start.

So find your own way and your own adventure, but as someone that's done this for a while, there's no shame in starting small. In fact, starting small is an amazing gateway into something epic.

TIP

If you're not set on a specific destination, there's no harm starting with places where you speak the language. There's endless fun being in places where you don't, but for a first overseas adventure, it's okay to start with at least one thing you're familiar with.

Don't try to do everything at once

WARNING

By far the biggest, and often expensive, mistake new or infrequent travelers make is trying to cram in everything, everywhere, all at once. If you've been saving for months and only have two weeks to travel, it's understandable you want to see everything possible. But this is a recipe for disaster. I discuss more about planning in Chapter 2, but it's crucial to start pushing back on your own intentions before you've set anything in stone. Narrowing your focus to one place or area will not only save you money but will also make your trip better overall. Wanting to see every capital in Europe during a two-week vacation is not a tenable plan. One or *maybe* two is a far better start.

I made this mistake for many years, and it never ended well. I'd be disappointed I didn't see certain things, I'd be rushed seeing the things I did see, and through it all, nothing but stress.

Here are a few things to keep in mind now:

>> You'll always see less than you want to.

>> The more you try to do, the more expensive the entire trip.

>> Quality time with a few things is almost always better than mediocre time with many things.

>> Flexibility is the best gift your planning self can give your traveling self.

TIP

There's nothing wrong with a to-do list. They're great! Just don't expect to do it all. Prioritize and plan, with the intention of changing as you go.

Focusing on Less So You Can Enjoy More

When you're looking at a series of dates in the future, it can be easy to think you have more time than you actually do. Everything always takes longer than you expected. Take a step back. What city have you visited the most? Could you explore it all in a day or two? There's no reason to think you could do the same while on vacation. If your itinerary involves something like "We'll spend an hour here, and then an hour here . . ." stop. You're almost certainly trying to do too much.

Dialing back the number of things you want to do will not only save you money and stress, but it will also let you be in the moment and enjoy the things you're actually doing. In the above example, what if you get to the first location and want to spend more than an hour there? What happens then?

I'm not saying pick only one thing to do each day, though that can be fun, too. I'm saying don't plan on seeing five cities in ten days or four museums in an afternoon. You'll always be on the go. Doesn't that sound like work? Generally, I try to spend at least three days in any location and limit my daily to-do list to just a few things. Sometimes three days isn't enough and a few things is too much, but it's a safe place to start.

Keep transit to a minimum. Planes, trains, and automobiles are fun, but unless your intention is to enjoy the transit itself as part of your adventure (and for what it's worth, I do), then the time spent in transit could be better spent enjoying yourself in that place you just left.

TIP

Multi-city travel agendas are perilous. I'm not saying don't do it, but you should be cautious. Far too much could go wrong, and it's possible you'll be seeing the inside of a vehicle more than the place you're visiting.

Planning less is one of the greatest challenges for any lover of travel. Whether it's wanting to get the most out of a hard-earned dollar or not wanting to waste precious vacation time, everything in your being is going to want to plan as much as possible. Here's why you should resist that urge.

The challenge of planning to do less

This is all crazy, right? Who am I to tell you your five-day, 14-city adventure isn't going to be legendary. Well, I've traveled a lot, all over the world (60 countries and counting), and in all my years of travel, every time I've tried to do a lot, it has gone poorly, and every time I've tried to do less, it has been amazing.

I get it, though. There's immense pressure for an expensive trip to be perfect. I call this "The Curse of 'Once in a Lifetime.'" I hate the phrase "once in a lifetime" because it's often absolute nonsense and a toxic way to think about travel. Going to Europe for two weeks? Not once in a lifetime. Seeing a zebra in South Africa? Nope. Hiking Angel's Landing at Zion National Park to watch the sunset? Okay, that one is definitely once in a lifetime for me because there is no way I'm doing that hike again.

What I'm saying is it's vital to push back against the idea that your next trip is the only trip you'll ever take. If you don't see something this trip, you can go again. The whole idea of budget travel, in my mind, is to make travel inexpensive enough that you can do it over and over again. Not, "I went to Europe once for two weeks," but instead, "I went to Europe last year, and I'm going again this summer." Not, "I saw a zebra in South Africa," but instead, "I saw a zebra in South Africa, and I'm going to Zimbabwe next spring."

If you embrace the mindset that there will be a next time, it can greatly reduce the stress in needing to see everything possible in one go. Sure, it would be great to do everything on your list during one trip, but if it's at the cost of always feeing rushed and not enjoying any of it, what's the point?

And if you do miss something then — oh no — you'll have to go back. How terrible. Better start looking at flights now.

How to narrow your focus (one city, not five)

Make a to-do list. Apps like Keep on Android and Notes on iOS let you create a list and have access to it from any internet-connected device. Make a huge list! Go nuts! But as you do, figure out what's most important. You're never going to see it all. You'll probably only see a fraction of it and that's absolutely fine. What is it you *really* want to see or do? What are the core memories you want to create on this specific trip. As you add something new to the list, slot it in above things you currently find less interesting. Soon enough you'll have a list that's in a rough order of things you want to do from most interesting to least.

Now that you have this semi-ordered list, pick the things you absolutely have to do. Maybe this final curated list is just a few things. If it's just one thing, that's even easier! Try to keep this "must-do" list as short as possible. It will make your trip far more manageable and less expensive. If you're able to do everything on your core list, you'll still have the rest of the list for ideas. With any luck, you'll find other cool things to do once you get there.

If you're having trouble moving things down your priority list, check out online reviews. Take these with a big ol' grain of salt, though. People love complaining, especially online. Even US National Parks get bad reviews sometimes, and these are some of the most beautiful places on Earth. That said, the text of the reviews might give you an idea what it's like, which can be helpful. Maybe some spot is actually always crowded with tourists, or cheap souvenir shops, or something else that isn't readily apparent from photos and write-ups.

For instance, I went to an incredibly famous castle in Scotland and found out after I got inside that it was barely older than my house. The whole thing was built from a nearly bare rock in the early twentieth century. Sure, it looks great in pictures, but knowing it's barely older than my parents sure took the shine off it.

TIP

There's also nothing wrong with keeping things on your to-do list for a potential future visit. Enjoy your first visit at a reasonable pace, and then you'll know what you want to do and how to get there for your next visit.

Travel days eat into your adventure

For example, let's assume that like most Americans, you have two weeks of vacation. You want to see as much as you can on a trip to Europe. You want to spend a few days in Paris, a few days in Amsterdam, a few days in Berlin, and a few days in London. It's going to be great.

Except, it's not. That's going to be brutal. Anyone who has been to Europe is going to think the above itinerary is crazy, and yet I've met people who have tried. Best case, each transit between cities mentioned above is a day. Some less, some more. So for your 14-day trip, that's one day on each end flying and at least four days to each city. Throw in one where you're jetlagged and miserable, and suddenly your 14-day trip is actually seven. So you have roughly one and a half days in each huge city to see everything you want to see.

It's a difficult decision, but you should try to minimize travel days on any trip, although I discuss some exceptions Chapter 4. For the most part, however, unless the transit is itself part of your trip (night trains, ferries, and so on), try to avoid it.

WARNING

It's easy to make the mistake of not leaving enough total time for a specific journey. That one-hour flight isn't really one hour. It's probably closer to six hours door-to-door when you include getting to and from the airport, security, and so on. Don't expect to do much on transit days other than transit, even if it seems like a short trip.

Budget Travel that Doesn't Feel Like Budget Travel

In all my years of traveling on a budget, I almost never felt like I was traveling on a budget. I've stayed at beachfront resorts in Fiji for $30 a night (as shown in Figure 1-1). I've explored Japan from Wakkanai to Nagasaki eating the most amazing food for less than $50 a day. I've stayed for weeks in the most expensive cities in the world, and I've done it again and again year after year.

So when I say "budget travel" I'm not talking about the quality of the adventure. I'm talking about getting the most adventure you can for your specific budget. That doesn't always mean spending the least amount possible. It's about spending the least amount to get the most enjoyment.

That's what you'll discover through the rest of this book. How to save money and selectively spend money to get the best travel possible on whatever budget you have, from the mountains (like those in Figure 1-3) to the ocean and everywhere in between. Not just for your next trip but to also make travel financially sustainable so you can enjoy regular adventures for years to come.

TIP

It's okay to selectively spend more to get a specific experience you want. You'll find ways throughout this book to save money on the less important things, so you can spend more on the cool stuff.

FIGURE 1-3: Time to find some adventure!

Chapter **2**
A Fist Full of Dollars (And Euros and Yen)

When many people hear the words "budget travel" they probably imagine dank and dripping hovels, eating saltines with no salt, and staring longingly as better-off travelers enjoying catered meals and 1,000-thread-count sheets. Get that idea out of your head. It's possible to travel anywhere on a budget and have an epic time doing it.

Sure, the more money you have the more options you have, but putting off travel until you have a less limited budget might mean you're not traveling for years — or maybe ever. The best time to travel is now and there's no reason to wait. (Well, almost no reasons, but more on that in a moment.)

Money isn't most people's favorite subject, but you need it to travel. So in this chapter, I talk about how much you'll need, costly traps to avoid, and how to save up for the trip of your dreams.

WARNING

As incredible and potentially life changing as travel can be, don't go into debt to do it. Travel is one of the most important things in my life, but I'm still the first to tell you it's a luxury. I am always aware how lucky and privileged I am to be able to travel as much as I do, and I think that's an important perspective regardless of how much one travels. So save what you can and plan that epic trip, but if you can't save as much as you want to, don't feel bad. Put your actual needs first and don't get a new credit card just to max it out on flights and hotels. If you saddle yourself with tons of debt now just for one trip, that means you probably can't afford another trip down the road. Another trip, or worse, something costly and more vital.

What's a Realistic Travel Budget?

This might seem hard to believe, but you should be able to visit just about any city in the world for less than $50 a day. In some places you'll find it difficult to spend $50 even eating at restaurants for every meal. In others, it might be tight with sandwiches and tap water. This is not including the flight, of course, but I talk more about that in Chapter 4.

Generally, that $50 is per person. However, some costs can be shared. It might be cheaper to buy some foods in bulk, lowering the per-person cost. A hotel room for one person is very expensive, still expensive but less so for two, and fairly affordable for four. Starting your budget at $50 per person, per day, though, is a great place to start.

TIP

A bit of a spoiler, but a big part of how you can make a budget of $50 per day work is hostels. I know, I know, you're thinking I'm crazy. Your first thought about hostels is probably that they're, at best, a foul hole that even cockroaches avoid. Your second thought may bring up a series of horror movies that have done to hostels what *Jaws* did to sharks. Although I go into it more detail in Chapter 5, you should know that I once shared your view of hostels, and I was wrong. I've stayed in hostels all over the world and in most places I prefer a hostel over a hotel. In fact, most hostels I've stayed in are better than hotels that cost two to three times their price. In most places hostels are safe, clean, and a great way to meet people. You can use other ways to get your budget below $50 a day, of course, but staying in hostels is one of the easiest and best ways to do it.

Travel can be more affordable than you think

When you think of an expensive location, what comes to mind? Common answers are probably Tokyo or London. How about beachside on a tropical Pacific island? You'd certainly be right about all three. There are lots of potentially expensive places to visit. I mention these three because I've stayed in all of them for under $50 a day. In Tokyo, that's staying at my favorite place in Japan. It's on the west bank of the Sumida River, with a view from several of the beds of the Skytree and the iconic Asahi Group Office Building. In London, it's a hostel where I met one of my best friends. The hostel in Fiji was only a few steps from the beach. Not bad for $50 a day, right?

Now, I don't want to oversell it. In the cases of Tokyo and London, it was far more of challenge to eat well while staying under $50. That's not steak and sushi every night. Often lunch would be pre-made sandwiches from Tesco or onigiri from Family Mart. Though to be fair, in the case of the latter I'd probably eat those for lunch even if I was rich. Dinner might be an inexpensive take-away or restaurant or, even more cost effective, making something at the hostel bought from ingredients at the local market.

There were, of course, a few times when even I couldn't stay under the $50 mark. If you want to stay in Venice in the summer, for instance, that's going to be costly. One of the most expensive places I've ever visited was Dubrovnik, Croatia, during the peak of *Game of Thrones*. If you're not familiar, Dubrovnik was the stand-in for the fictional capital city of King's Landing on that long-running show. Everything in the real city was expensive. The hostel was $40 a night for a 12-bed room and all the food was amazingly expensive. That's what I get for going to what was probably the most touristy location in the world at the time.

Other times, in other locations, even eating at restaurants for every meal I couldn't come close to spending $50.

REMEMBER

My hope is that this information changes your perspective on how inexpensive travel can be. Sure, $50 a day is by no means cheap, but it's significantly better than spending $200-plus a day that I've heard people claim to be the bare minimum to travel.

Why $50 a day is a great place to start your budget

If you're new to travel, $50 gives you a specific number to aim for, especially if you have plans to travel in the future but you're not sure of the location yet (which is great!). I say $50 because that's a good average. Depending on where you're going, you might need more, or less, but $50 is a nice even number to begin your planning. So for a two-week trip, that's $700 plus airfare. Conceivably, and again this depends on where you're going, you could do an entire trip for less than $1,500.

What does travel life look like on $50 a day?

Accommodations

Roughly half of your budget will be going to your accommodation. Hostels, as I mentioned, are the easiest way to do this. Even if you're traveling as a couple, a hostel will almost always be cheaper than a splitting a hotel. There are other options I'll talk about in Chapter 5, like splitting an Airbnb or couch surfing, but for now we'll say $25 is going toward some sort of place to sleep. You can spend less, for sure. I stayed in an immaculate and cozy hostel in the heart of Lisbon for $20 a night. I've stayed in some great hostels for as low as $15 a night. Prices will vary depending on where you're going and when, but $25 is a good average for now.

Food

Next up is food. One of my favorite things to do while traveling is trying out local restaurants. This can be expensive though. Ideally wherever you're staying has a kitchen. Most hostels do. This is another easy way to save money. Buy groceries and cook your own meals. Pasta goes a long way and is cheap everywhere. Some fresh bread and local cheeses have served me well all over. Generally, though, you'll have enough in your budget to eat one local meal every day — like a local fast food chain or some epic street food. If you're spending less on accommodation, you'll have more money for food and "other," the category you lump everything else into that you want or need to spend money on.

The rest

I classify everything else as "other" since it's impossible to say what you'll need or want to spend money on. Many museums around the world are free as is exploring where you are. A local metro ticket is likely a few dollars a day, but it's worth it so you can see everything you want to see. Sure, some things can be expensive, but that doesn't mean you have to avoid them. Your budget is simply a daily average. You may spend more or less of that $50 each day, so you can splurge on an expensive item one day by staying under budget another day.

For example, as of this writing, a ticket to the top of the Eiffel Tower was $30. That's more than half a day's budget! But you're not doing that *every day*. So one day you might enjoy walking around (free) and be under budget, and the next day you can buy a ticket for an epic view from the top of the tower.

Like I said, $50 is a good place to start. If you aim for that, save up for that, but end up going a little over, that's okay. Just don't go too crazy. When you're home, you're hopefully saving for your next trip, not paying off your previous trip with interest.

TIP

If you know you want to do something expensive, like sky diving, scuba diving, surf lessons, Michelin-star restaurants, car rental, and so on, make sure that cost is included in your budget. Maybe that means you need to save more than a $50-a-day average, but maybe not.

Airfare considerations

I've got a whole chapter (see Chapter 4) dedicated to figuring out ways to save on airfare. It's a big chapter because airfare is the single biggest expense of any trip. It could easily be more than half your total budget. There isn't any one single thing you can do to save money on airfare. There are lots of little things you can do, though, and those little things can add up.

TIP

A few broad tips to keep in mind if you haven't skipped to Chapter 4 already.

>> Weekends and the summer are the most expensive times to fly. Ideally, avoid both.

>> Airline points, via flown miles, credit card perks, and so on, can be great but *only* if you use them regularly. Once every few years is not regularly.

>> Some websites let you see historical prices for different routes. You can also set up alerts for price drops.

>> There's surprisingly little profit in airline seats, which is to say, the same route isn't going to be radically different in price across different airlines.

Unexpected costs

I hope that all your travels go smoothly. May the wind be at your back, as they say. Chances are, everything will go as planned. In all my years of traveling, I can only point to a few times where everything went pear shaped. And when it does, it can do so in a hurry.

How do you budget for the unexpected? Well, you can't. You can, however, be prepared. I talk about the pros and cons of credit cards a little later in this chapter, but this is one of the best reasons to have one. It might be an emergency cab to the airport, a random trip to the clinic to wrap a busted ankle, or a bus ticket out of a spot you were sure would be awesome but was, in fact, decidedly not awesome.

Having an emergency fund in an account is great, but I doubt most people can afford to have a few thousand dollars sitting around. I'm no financial planner, but having that much money just sitting in a checking account is probably not an ideal use of money for anyone.

I usually keep the equivalent of $20 to $50 in local currency on me, despite paying for most things with a credit card. This covers the lesser surprises, including finding out after a meal or cab ride that *oops*, they only take cash. It's also great to have cash on hand to tip, which is appreciated just about everywhere. As your trip winds down, if you haven't spent your cash reserves, you can do so instead of charging things for the last day or at the airport. That way you don't have to convert it back to your home currency (and lose money in the process).

Although you can't plan for the unplanned expenses, you can consider what situations often lead to unexpected costs. That way you can either change plans, change a booking, or try to get the fees reduced. All of which is vital to keep the costs down for any trip. Airline and other ticket fees are a common trap. Hotel "resort" fees are a new common tactic, where you have to pay extra to the hotel directly after you've already paid for your booking online. Airbnb's "cleaning" fees are infamous for often costing as much as the booking itself. I like paying for ride shares and taxis via an app because the cost is known. I'm sure many, maybe most, cab drivers around the world are honest, but you have no way of knowing who is and who isn't when you just need a ride to the airport at 6 a.m.

Hope for the best, plan for the worst, as they say. There's no way to plan for everything, though, so don't stress about it too much. Throughout the book I make sure to call out situations where you need to be wary of prices. Best case, decide with a merchant or driver on a price ahead of time and stick to it. Easier said than done, of course. After that, having some way to pay for an emergency, ideally a credit card, is the best safety net.

TIP

One of the best reasons to have a credit card for travel is for an emergency. Having travel insurance (more on this in the section, "Protecting Yourself and Your Belongings with Insurance," later in this chapter), is another way to make sure you don't go into debt because something unforeseen happened.

Saving for Travel

No one should go into debt to travel. My idea for budget travel in general is being able to afford an adventure on just about any budget. Maybe you need to save for a few months, or longer, but with the right saving plan and the right cost-saving tricks, you should be able to travel where you want, when you want without going into debt to do it.

Avoid racking up significant credit card debt, spending ages to pay it off, and being left with a lingering financial regret that you traveled at all. My hope is that you can save up for a bit, have a grand adventure, save up for a bit, have *another* grand adventure, and on and on. It's definitely possible. I've done it for years. Many people do.

Credit cards absolutely have their use. They can open doors, and through their perks, they can allow for either cheaper travel or more luxurious travel for the same price. Paying things off with their insane interest rates, though, is a recipe for going into significant debt that's hard to get out of. It's great to think that in the future you'll have more time and more money, and maybe you will, but don't bet your future financial health on it.

TIP

Approach credit cards with caution, and remember that the interest you pay carrying a balance each month is money you're not spending on travel (or anything else).

Saving money now saves stress later

It's all about balance. If you've saved up the aforementioned $50 a day for your next trip, that means by the time you leave, your trip is basically paid for. Yes, you've saved for quite some time, so you want your trip to be worth it, but at that point it's not "costing" you anything. It's money you've already made and saved with the specific purpose of travel.

The alternative, and one that's far too common, is to finance a trip on a credit card. You're relying on your future self to pay for your current self, instead of having your past self pay for your current self. There's nothing wrong with using a card to pay for certain things, even if you don't have the cash on hand to pay it off at the end of the month. Just don't go overboard. I've certainly had trips where I've missed my budget and needed to pay it off after I returned home, but it's not a great feeling. Especially since every dollar not paid off at the end of that month will accumulate interest, meaning whatever I bought with that money actually cost even more than it did when I initially purchased it.

So for me, I greatly prefer having the majority of a trip paid for ahead of time so I have that $50 a day saved up to use as I go.

Automatic savings

By far my favorite trick for saving money is never saving money. Okay, that sounds weird. Let me explain. Most banks will let you set up an automatic withdrawal or transfer to a savings account. For me, I'd rather the cash just not be in my checking account so I'm not tempted to spend it.

This is, of course, easier said than done. I hate those financial "gurus" who say things like "stop ordering lattes and avocado toast and you can afford a house." This is either a wild overestimation of what people spend money on, cluelessness as to what things actually cost, or a cynical attempt to ridicule a specific group to make themselves seem clever. I have no such illusions. Saving money is hard when you don't have much money to spare. Making a budget and sticking to it was the only way I was able to afford travel for a long time. More on this in a moment.

Check your current bank and see what they offer in terms of savings accounts and automatic transfers. Some might offer you a bonus to set something up, but usually these come with laughable terms like "Deposit $100,000 and we'll give you a gift card worth $5!"

Choosing travel over other things

If you don't have a big budget, that money has to come from somewhere. That somewhere almost certainly isn't going to come from skipping coffee. Coffee is magic, and I don't think anyone should skip it. However, saving for travel usually means making something else less of a priority.

When I first started my extended travels, many people would ask how I was able to afford it. I can't blame them for being confused. I was traveling for months at a time, while most of them hadn't traveled at all in years. I wasn't, and still am not, rich. I wish I was. That'd be *way* easier and a much shorter book of advice.

The trick, initially, was living very cheaply. I was driving a 12-year-old, paid-off car. I had a roommate. I didn't buy fancy clothes (though some would argue I erred too much the other way in this category). Watches, jewelry, things that other people spent money on, I didn't. This isn't preaching austerity. I just prioritized travel over other things. If someone wants a new and fancy car, that's great! But to me in those shiny wheels I just see months of travel lost and a monthly cost that will burden any budget for years.

I'll freely admit that I had and have the advantage of being able to work from anywhere. I've been a freelance writer for over a decade. I certainly wasn't living on some lavish salary (or any salary for that matter). Being freelance afforded me the time to travel, but it was only through careful budgeting that I was able to pay for travel.

REMEMBER

Figure out your spending priorities. If you want a new car, a better apartment, and so on, that's fine, but to travel more you need to prioritize saving for that over other things.

Living cheaply so you can travel

I'm always shocked how few people have a budget. I'm a huge nerd, and I love spreadsheets, so when I first started traveling

I made a list of all my expenditures, my consistent (if often irregular) income, and had a good long look at where I could save money. There are endless apps and websites that can compile this for you if you don't know your "=SUM" from your "A2:A20." Whatever your preferred technology, the basic steps for budgeting will be the same:

1. **Make a budget.**

   List all your daily, monthly, and yearly costs. Rent, insurance, phone/internet, every subscription, everything.

2. **Trim.**

   Where can you cut costs? Is there a cheaper phone plan? Do regularly watch every streaming service you pay for?

3. **Save money.**

   Even costs that seem set in stone, like car insurance and internet might have cheaper plans available the company conveniently "forgot" to mention. It's worth spending time to really dive into all your costs. You might be surprised how much money you can save each month.

Part of this will be making decisions about your future budget. Do you need a more expensive (or cheaper) apartment? Is it cheaper to repair your car or should you get a new one (not the point but as a car guy, it's almost always cheaper to repair).

One of my favorite YouTube channels, Sailing Uma, follows a couple that bought a 40-year-old sailboat, fixed it up, and have been sailing it around the world for nearly a decade. Before they started they had no knowledge how to do any of that. Their big saying? "Don't buy a couch." That's how you afford a lot of things. Either not buying "stuff," or getting by on cheaper versions.

Every piece of advertising shown to you on your phone and TV is designed to get you to spend money. Buy something new because the new version is better. Get this other expensive thing because it's shinier. Do you need that new sprocket or cog? Maybe yes. Maybe you just want it. That's all fine. There's no right or wrong answer. But if you want to travel, and I mean travel *a lot*, then that has to be one of your top priorities, if not *the* top priority. Live cheap, travel more. Easier said than done, for sure. Just an important perspective to keep in mind.

Cash? Credit? Both?

Credit cards, like bears, are dangerous and should be avoided. Even so, I have several (not the bears). They're an extremely useful tool and I wouldn't travel without them, but they can snowball out of control. So start with the idea that credit cards are bad and can get you in a lot of trouble so that you approach them with caution and use them wisely.

Many of you reading this already have credit cards. Hopefully you've learned about their potential evils without going into too much debt.

If you're new to the world of credit cards, they can be exceptionally handy while traveling. They often add a layer of safety between you and your money. They often have perks that can make travel easier. Some include a modicum of travel insurance that isn't as good as the real thing (see "Protecting Yourself and Your Belongings with Insurance," later in this chapter) but might fill in some gaps in your other coverage.

The old saying of "cash is king" is becoming less and less the case. Some places are moving away from cash entirely, and many activities you'll want to do while traveling require a credit card.

So as much as I hate to say it, you should probably look into getting a credit card.

REMEMBER Credit cards are a tool, but don't use them to finance anything, especially travel.

The pros and cons of cash

The viability of using cash on a trip varies a lot depending where you're going. Some places use it extensively, others barely use it at all. Having at least some local currency on hand can reduce your anxiety knowing that if something comes up you've got some way to pay.

Cash is dangerous, though. Tourists are targets of pickpockets and thieves worldwide. If you're careful you're not likely to get hassled, but it can happen. If it does, now you're out a big chunk of your budget with no way to get it back. If a thief steals your credit card it's a hassle for sure, but as long as you report it to your credit card company right away, you probably won't need to pay for any fraudulent purchases. Some credit card companies will even overnight a new card to you anywhere in the world.

As mentioned earlier, it's wise to have some cash on hand when you travel, even if you're not using it to pay for most things. Sometimes there are tourist fees at hotels/hostels that can only be paid in cash. Some places require a deposit for keys/keycards. Many places appreciate (or expect) a tip. Street vendors might only accept cash. Some public toilets cost money to enter. So even if you're headed somewhere that's famously "cashless," you should have at least some local currency on hand. The equivalent of $20 to $50 should cover you for most situations.

ATMs, aka cash machines, are common around the world. In some places they're even free. Well, they're sort of free. Now here's a novelty that will shock most Americans. They're free in that the ATM itself doesn't charge you money. Of course, your bank will almost certainly charge you. These fees can add up, especially if you're relying on cash to pay for things but don't want to carry the equivalent of hundreds of dollars everywhere you go.

There are a small number of debit cards that don't charge these kinds of fees. Some even re-imburse you if the ATM you use charges you a fee. I opened a secondary checking account at a bank that offers one of these debit cards. I only have a few hundred dollars in it, and transfer money over from my main account when needed. I don't even bring that main account's card anywhere. With this other account I can use just about any ATM in the world for free, and if something happens, I'll only lose the relatively small amount in that one account.

WARNING

Converting currency will always cost you money, and in some places, cost you a *lot* of money. Don't withdraw lots of your home currency and then convert it as you go. If you only want to pay for things in cash, it's cheaper to convert it once at a place with a decent rate than incur a fee every few days when you run out of the local currency.

Spotting scam ATMs

You know how in nature the brightly colored animals are often the deadliest? Think of ATMs the same way. The more flashy the signage pointing toward them, the more likely they are to take your money.

Which is to say, if you see an ATM in a touristy area *avoid it*. It's almost certainly not owned by a bank and will charge you significant amounts of money to withdraw cash. What's significant? How about trying to take out the equivalent of $50 and getting charged $10 or more? That's 20 percent of that day's budget just to get cash. Take out cash five times in a trip and that's like losing a full day of travel.

Best bet? If you really need an ATM, find a local bank and use theirs. Worst case, the fees won't be any better. Worst, worst case, if the ATM eats your card you at least have an actual company to harass to get it back. Best case? It's free.

Some newer cash machines allow you to tap, instead of inserting your card. This is safer on just about every level. If the machine has that option, use it.

The pros and cons of credit

I'll admit up front that 80 to 90 percent of my spending on an average trip is via credit cards. It's safer, easier, and their various perks are handy. I say "average" because sometimes that number is flipped. I've spent months in Japan, and it was surprising how few places took credit cards at the time.

For years the most annoying, and unintentionally amusing, aspect to using US-based credit cards abroad was our reliance on signatures. Signing receipts just isn't a thing in most countries. This has changed for the better in recent years with just about all US cards finally embedding NFC "contactless' tech inside the cards so you can just tap to pay. For the most part, this is infinitely better than watching a waiter stare at his pay terminal in confusion, and then try to find a pen. I carried pens for this purpose for years. This tap-to-pay convenience extends to using your phone, which I talk about later in this chapter in the section, "The convenience and safety of using your phone instead."

Certain activities specifically require a credit card. Renting a car is a big one. Most hotels also require a credit card. In both cases they'll hold some amount of security deposit, which gets removed when you return the car or check out. Some companies may allow you to use a debit card for this purpose as well, but many won't.

Then there are credit card perks. Airline-branded credit cards often allow things like free baggage checks, early boarding, and extra miles/points when you use the card. Some cards let you convert their points to miles at several different airlines, especially handy if you need to fly an airline that's not your usual choice. Most travel-friendly credit cards won't charge foreign transaction fees (see "Using credit cards that don't charge foreign transaction fees," later in this chapter).

The biggest perk, of course, is if you get wrongly charged, you can contest it with your credit card company. I've rarely needed to do this, however. Theoretically, you can do it if you've paid with your debit card, but in this case, your actual cash is gone until you get it back. With credit it's just a small part of your overall limit and maybe a little interest if the charge remains on your bill for a while.

TIP

Most banks and credit card companies have clever algorithms and teams of actual people keeping an eye out for fraudulent charges. Which is to say, you probably don't need to tell them you're traveling. They have a record of the hotel and airfare, for instance, so they know what's up. That said, it's worth checking if your card company is that "smart." The info will be on their website.

The main issue with credit cards is the fees. Many of the better travel credit cards have annual fees. If you don't travel often, these fees vastly outweigh the card's perks or benefits. The biggest "fee" is the interest incurred if you don't pay off your entire balance each month. The interest rates on credit cards are outrageously high. If you're not careful and carry a balance month-to-month you're going to pay a lot.

To oversimplify this a bit, let's say you charged $3,000 for a big trip on a credit card with a 20 percent APR. You'll be paying $50 if you don't pay that off before the end of the billing cycle. If you pay $1,000 on that before the end of the next billing cycle, you'll get hit with another $33 in interest. It's frustratingly more complex than even that, with interest compounding daily, a different calculation if you already had a balance, and so on. Ideally, pay off the entire balance each month. Easier said than done, of course, but paying as much as you can is second best, and *never* just pay the minimum.

WARNING

Really, though, the biggest potential problem with credit cards is an intangible one. If you get approved for some amazing credit limit, do you have the self-control not to use it? Credit card debt is pernicious and a frustrating way to limit your future travels.

Using credit cards that don't charge foreign transaction fees

Banks love fees. Anything they can do to make your money their money, they're going to do it. As a traveler, one of the most common you'll find is the dreaded "foreign transaction fee." These are a charge by the card company for the privilege of using your card outside of your home country. It makes everything you purchase a little more expensive, which adds up.

Fortunately, there are lots of options for cards that don't charge foreign transaction fees. Most credit cards that promote themselves as a travel card, including most airline-branded cards, won't charge a foreign transaction fee. Check your current cards, or any card you're considering. Foreign transaction fees are best avoided if at all possible.

The insidious charge option that steals your money

WARNING

If you buy something in a store or pay for your meal or lodging, in most foreign countries, you'll be presented an option to "pay in your home currency." Don't do it! This is pretty close to a scam, not by the shop owner exactly but by banks and credit cards.

The option seems logical. To save you from getting charged a foreign transaction fee, you can instead choose to be charged in your home currency. Except you pay a nominal "fee" for this convenience *and* you're given the worst possible currency conversion. These fees and conversions could end up costing you a lot of money over the course of your trip.

Instead, just get a credit card that doesn't charge foreign transaction fees and choose the local currency when you use it. You might still get a mediocre conversion rate, but at least there won't be any fees on top of it.

REMEMBER

If you're given the option to pay in local or home currency, always choose local as long as your card doesn't charge foreign transaction fees.

Some cards are bad for travel

Generally, I like to avoid calling out specific companies, positive or negative, but this is one instance where I must. There are some credit cards that just aren't good for travel. To be clear, I have no financial incentive to promote or disparage any of these companies. With that said, here we go.

If a merchant accepts credit cards, they probably take Visa and/or Mastercard. Both companies claim to be accepted in over 200 countries. That's pretty much every country on earth. That's not to say they're universal. You won't be able to use your Visa or Mastercard in literally every store in the world, but they're definitely the most likely ones you can use. Usually if a store takes one of these as payment, they take both, though not always.

American Express just isn't as widely accepted internationally. It's possible you might visit a country where it's commonly accepted or maybe even stumble upon a random merchant that does, but for the most part, you are much better off having a Visa or Mastercard.

Discover used to be in the same boat as American Express, but in the last few years they've partnered with several payment networks that aren't common inside the US, like JCB, UnionPay, and others. As of this writing, Discover claims acceptance in stores across Europe, Asia, South America, and parts of Africa and the Middle East. They do warn, however "Some locations may not display acceptance decals, so always try presenting your card when paying." This could lead to confusion if the shop owner doesn't recognize Discover. If you don't speak the language, you might have difficulty explaining that no, this card really does work even though it looks like it shouldn't.

Since Discover isn't as simple and as commonly accepted as Mastercard and Visa, a card with one of the latter logos will likely be easier to use while traveling internationally.

Unforeseen fees can eat into your budget

Throughout this chapter we've talked about fees. Banks aren't the only ones that like fees. There are fees for everything. Hotels often charge a "resort fee" that's added to your bill when you check in.

Airlines have countless fees, which I talk more about in Chapter 4. Your mobile phone provider will probably charge you fees to use data while you travel (more on that in Chapter 8). Each fee in itself might not be a lot — a few dollars here, a few dollars there. They add up, though — maybe to the cost of a meal, maybe several meals, maybe a night in a hotel.

The only way you can avoid these fees is to remain diligent. Everything you plan on using during a trip that interacts with the internet or a specific company, check before you travel to find what kind of fees they charge.

I mention as many fees as I can think of throughout this chapter and this book. It will only take an hour or so to check your own accounts before you leave. It could save you some money you could spend on literally anything else.

The convenience and safety of using your phone instead

Nearly all modern phones have the ability to tap to pay. It's called "contactless," and the two biggest apps to enable it are Apple Pay and Google Pay. You should absolutely set this up before you travel.

The idea is this: You register a credit card with one of the aforementioned apps. Then, when you're ready to pay, you unlock your phone and tap it to the "point of sale" device, aka the place you'd usually swipe or insert your card. This interaction is encrypted, and the merchant doesn't actually get your credit card number.

This is more secure than using your card directly because you have to unlock your phone for it to work. Signing a receipt was never secure, US credit cards rarely had PINs, and even if your face was on the back of your card, how often do people look? The back of my card says "*CHECK ID*" and maybe 20 percent of the time was I ever asked. Now the card never leaves my wallet. I just use my phone.

In some countries, contactless payment can be found just about everywhere. In other countries, not so much. In some countries the app isn't even available on the phone. However, it doesn't cost anything for you to sign up, and having it is hugely convenient at home and abroad. Most credit cards have the ability to tap for payment as well, though this isn't as safe as using your phone.

 Sign up for your phone's contactless payment app. It's safe, fast, and far more secure than using your physical credit cards.

Protecting Yourself and Your Belongings with Insurance

One of the worst things to happen to me while traveling was getting robbed on a night train in Italy. My friend and I were headed from Taormina in Sicily up to Rome. This involved a train ferry, which was cool in its own right. Sometime after the ferry, but before Rome, someone entered our cabin and took our stuff. We didn't notice until the morning because the train was exceptionally loud, and they left our bags, just removed our valuables.

My groggy and half-awake brain had registered the door opening and closing, but I had thought she had gone out to use bathroom. She thought I did. I lost all my camera gear, headphones, and most heartbreakingly, a battered but beloved classic iPod that had been discontinued years before.

The next day was upsetting and disturbing. The train steward was willing to help, and he brought me to his boss who gave me a look like I'd asked him to lift the Colosseum to find a unicorn. "What about the cameras?" I asked. He laughed in my face. They didn't work "of course." The Roman train station police were even less help, despite me making it clear that literally all I wanted from them was a report for my insurance that said it happened. He did this begrudgingly and told me that in the future I should "look after my stuff better." When I flushed red in fury, he shrugged and said "such is our country." Great, now he made me feel bad.

All told, my sleepy inattention in Italy cost me my DSLR, 2 lenses, a Kindle, some great headphones, a 360 camera I was reviewing, and the aforementioned iPod. Luckily, they didn't grab my noise canceling headphones and laptop, which were on the bed next to me. Still, it totaled a few thousand dollars in gear.

How much of that did I get back from insurance? Basically nothing. Travel insurance rarely covers electronics, and, if they do, it's for a paltry amount. Despite that, I strongly recommend travel insurance and get it for every trip. Why? Because it can cover you for far more costly misadventures, and it has for me. It can also cover you for issues with flights, weather, illness, and more. There are always risks, but being covered for whatever you can offers great peace of mind and can seriously help you if something really goes wrong, not just someone taking your replaceable stuff.

Getting small, TSA-approved locks for your luggage is a good idea, but if someone wants your stuff it will barely slow them down.

TIP

The necessity of insurance (personal experience)

The *second* worst thing to happen while I was traveling was breaking my leg in Vina del Mar, Chile. I was ten days into what should have been three months, and due to some sporadic flights and Carnival plans with my friend, I had booked tickets and accommodations to Brazil and later to Easter Island. Due to the time of year and the infrequent flights, it was all quite expensive.

Not two days later I was walking on a beachside sidewalk, something caught my eye, and my right leg slipped off and planted in the sand two feet beneath the level of the concrete walkway. I rolled back and *pop pop*, I heard both the bones in my other leg crack. So that was the end of that trip.

But I still had to get home. I was staying in Valparaíso, which thankfully was just an inexpensive cab ride away. Lucky for me the hostel owner was bilingual and took me to a local clinic where I got X-rays and a temporary cast. The doctor told me that I needed to stay off my leg immediately because if the crack in my tibia got any worse I'd need permanent pins. So I decided to fly home to heal up and wallow in self-pity on my own couch. The international airport in Santiago was over 90 minutes away. That was a long cab ride, but thankfully not too expensive. Once at the airport and checked in, however, I felt like a celebrity, whisked through security and immigration in a wheelchair.

Once home, however, I was faced with the somewhat daunting and absolutely time-consuming task of canceling and trying to get back the money I'd spent on everything I'd booked.

Here's the amazing part. I got back nearly all of it. A few of the flights, despite being "non-refundable" were in fact quite refundable with a valid medical excuse. The rest I got reimbursed via my travel insurance. The money I got back for this one incident more than "paid" for every other time I've bought travel insurance and didn't need it.

There are different levels of travel insurance from a variety of different companies. but generally speaking, the cheapest plans will just cost a few dollars a day and cover you up to a certain amount in canceled bookings, missed flights, some medical issues, and so on (see Figure 2-1).

OneTrip **PREMIER**	OneTrip **PRIME**	OneTrip **BASIC**
The best coverage for dream vacations and remote destinations	Our most popular plan for family vacations, cruises and tours	The economical choice for domestic & international travelers
$172 per traveler	$109 per traveler	$80 per traveler
$172 total cost	$109 total cost	$80 total cost
SELECT	SELECT	SELECT
Plan and Pricing Details (PDF)	Plan and Pricing Details (PDF)	Plan and Pricing Details (PDF)
Epidemic Coverage Endorsement ✓	Epidemic Coverage Endorsement ✓	Epidemic Coverage Endorsement ✓
Trip Cancellation **$2,000** per insured	Trip Cancellation **$2,000** per insured	Trip Cancellation **$2,000** per insured
Trip Interruption **$3,000** per insured	Trip Interruption **$3,000** per insured	Trip Interruption **$2,000** per insured
Emergency Medical **$50,000** per insured	Emergency Medical **$50,000** per insured	Emergency Medical **$10,000** per insured
Emergency Transportation **$1,000,000** per insured	Emergency Transportation **$500,000** per insured	Emergency Transportation **$50,000** per insured
Baggage Loss/Damage **$2,000** per insured	Baggage Loss/Damage **$1,000** per insured	Baggage Loss/Damage **$500** per insured

FIGURE 2-1: Three plans from Allianz, one of the larger travel insurance companies, and some of what each one covers.

Also, it's worth noting that some countries and some tours require you to have travel insurance. A handful of countries require you to buy it through their government. Some of these rules are holdovers from COVID-19 restrictions, but not all. Most likely the airline will prompt you to supply this information when you book your ticket. It's worth double checking before you get to that point, though.

Don't assume your current health insurance covers you

I've been the first American several people had ever met, or at least, gotten to know well enough to ask the *real* questions. And there's always two questions that all of those people wanted to ask to their first American. The first question is about guns, which I am unqualified to answer and *way* beyond the subject matter of this book.

The other question is about healthcare. Nearly every other country offers their citizens some amount of healthcare. It's unfathomable to most people that I have to pay several hundred dollars a month for my health insurance and still often have to pay out of pocket for any services. I had to pay several thousand dollars out of pocket for a week-long stint in the ICU (a story too long to get into here) and most non-Americans upon hearing that story asked, "You didn't have insurance?" No, foreign friends, that was *with* insurance.

This tangent has a point, however. Don't assume your health insurance, no matter where you get it, covers you while you're traveling. It almost certainly doesn't. Luckily, in most countries, healthcare is far cheaper than it is in the US Even so, you still have some amount of money you'll have to pay if something happens. You're probably not going to be able to bargain with them to charge your insurance instead of your credit card.

While travel insurance can seem like an unnecessary cost, it's almost certainly covering you for things you're not otherwise covered for.

What travel insurance covers, and what it doesn't

As I alluded to at the start of this section, travel insurance probably isn't going to cover things getting stolen, especially electronics. There are specific callouts for electronic equipment with high deductibles and low reimbursements. Most other types of insurance, like homeowners insurance, have similar restrictions against stolen electronics.

That's not to say you shouldn't get it. The money I got back from my ill-fated South America trip was several times more than I would have gotten back without insurance.

There's also the aspect that is less pleasant to talk about but is a key part of the coverage: evacuation. It's highly unlikely you'll ever need to use it, but nearly all travel insurance will cover the cost of evacuating you from an area due to medical or other reasons. Aliens invade Australia and you need to bug out? Good thing you got travel insurance. This is a lighthearted example, but the reality can be quite ugly.

Generally, travel insurance doesn't cost a lot, and if you're travelling for any length of time, it's probably worth it. I'm all about reducing stress during travel, and this is a way to do that. At the very least, it's worth looking into before you leave.

Lastly, it's worth noting what the US State Department has to say about it: "The US government does not provide insurance for US citizens overseas. We do not pay medical bills or unexpected costs. We highly recommend that you purchase insurance before you travel."

Chapter **3**
Plan Less for More Fun

used to plan everything. Before any trip, I'd have every night booked and every activity timed out. I knew where I needed to go, when to leave, and how to get there. I'd even print out maps with step-by-step directions on the off-chance I couldn't find my way. So trust me, I get the desire to plan. But I was wrong.

Imagine you have your heart set on a trip to someplace sunny. You've got a week scheduled for the beach, with snorkeling, scuba, surf lessons, and more. After that, a week in the jungle, checking out the flora and fauna, hiking, and seeing the treetops. Everything's going to be perfect. Except, when you get there, the beach is covered in tourists, and the ocean is too rough to swim. What then? Or almost worse, it's serene and the most perfect place you've ever been, and you have to leave to go to a jungle the hotel clerk describes as "very buggy." You're locked in no matter what happens. How much will you have to spend to change your plans? Is it even possible?

You have to walk a fine line when planning. You of course want to have the trip of your dreams, but it's impossible to ensure that everything happens exactly as planned. It's better to plan way less. I'm not saying don't book anything (though that can be amazing), but only booking part of your adventure allows for flexibility that can save your trip, save you money, and make for an unforgettable experience.

Go to www.dummies.com/go/budgettravelfd for a handy list of links to the web addresses mentioned in this chapter, as well as other helpful resources.

FIND ONLINE

Planning Less Reduces Stress

This is probably the most counter-intuitive statement most people have ever heard about travel: Planning less reduces stress. Every frequent traveler I've met, though, agrees with me. I wouldn't have believed it myself had I not had a series of situations where I wished I'd planned less. Since then, the less I plan the better. It can be that way for you, too.

The best way to think about travel planning is you're trading your current stress for future stress. I can totally understand the desire, months before your trip, to do every you can to make sure everything goes smoothly. The thing is, it's almost impossible for everything to go smoothly because there are so many factors, like weather, that you can't control. So plan to be flexible with those inevitable detours because your ability to adjust can make or break an adventure.

There are two key steps to making this work:

REMEMBER

>> First, build flexibility into your plans so you're not booked wall-to-wall for your entire trip. That's a recipe for disaster.

>> Second, get comfortable with a few key apps and techniques to let you easily adjust your plans so you can book travel and lodging on the go. I talk about both of these steps throughout this chapter.

I used to be an extensive planner and I was wrong

I can highlight what I mean about planning less with a story from my own adventures. It was my first trip to Australia, at the beginning of when I started traveling for most of every year. I was still figuring it all out, and not particularly well. In a fit of panic, the kind familiar to most of you I'm sure, I went on a booking spree. First I booked a few days in Melbourne, then a few days in Brisbane, and then I'd fly up to Singapore to join a two-week guided trip through Malaysia and Thailand (read more about guided trips in the section at the end of this chapter, "Recognizing the Drawbacks of Guided Tours, Cruises, and All-Inclusive Resorts"). At the time, all the bookings — flights, hostels, hotels, and more — put my mind at ease. I had the next few weeks "sorted" and I could, for a moment anyway, relax.

Then in Melbourne I fell in with a group of amazing people. We had an absolute blast — but then I had to leave while they stayed. That happened *again* in Brisbane, and again I had to leave right as things were getting great. Then the two-week trip I thought would be the highlight turned out to be the opposite of what I'd expected for a variety of reasons.

I learned my lesson. Don't book too far in advance. This paid off only a few months later when I found myself in a tiny hotel in Cherbourg, France, with a sliver of a view of the ocean that was one of the most peaceful places I've ever been in my life. I had booked for two nights. I changed it to 4 the next morning. Then a full week the next day.

How planning less actually reduces stress

Since I've been on both sides of the planning/no-plan issue, I completely understand how alien this seems. Most people, especially those who don't travel often, can't imagine not planning as much as possible. I understand the anxiety of not knowing. I understand the anxiety of leaving certain things to chance.

I'll be the first to admit that given the nature of my job, and how I've designed my life, I have the luxury and privilege of time. So if I can't get a specific flight, or if I miss a daily ferry, it's not a crisis. Like I mentioned before, there's a line to be walked between how much you need to do to reduce your current stress without adversely affecting your future stress. There's no right answer to that question, it's going to depend on a lot variables.

In my mind, you want to be as stress free as possible during your travels so you can enjoy where you are and be in the moment. It's natural to think that booking everything beforehand is the way to ensure that happens. What your current self can't know is what your future self will feel in that place, in that moment. There's the beach scenario I mentioned earlier, but there's also all the incidental stress caused by your past book-everything self. The rush to get a train that was harder to find than you anticipated.

The traffic that was unexpectedly heavy so you're rushing to see everything and only getting a few minutes at each location.

You can study Google Maps all you want, but it's impossible to know ahead of time that the 15-minute walk from your hotel to the museum actually takes over an hour because the shops along the way are amazing, you need just one more fresh croissant, and you find a street so gorgeous you need to take some more pictures. Don't misunderstand, I think you absolutely *should* do all of those things and more! The key is making sure you have the time to do it. To me, enjoying yourself, your traveling self, is the most important thing.

TIP

If this is all too much of a leap, consider taking a few small steps in this direction and see how it is. If you've got three days planned in a city, maybe don't schedule anything for one of them. Take a day to just wander. Some of the best days I've ever had traveling was leaving the hostel in the morning with no goal other than "lunch" and just spending the day being in a place. It can be magic.

Trading current stress for future stress

TIP

My core advice is to plan the first few days and the last few days. That way you're at least covered for the first and last chapter of your travel story. If you like the place you're staying, see about adding a few more days. Maybe you'll find a better part of town to stay in or want to try a different town or country. The possibilities are endless.

Beyond those basic guidelines, there are a few things that are definitely worth planning ahead of time. I'm not a lunatic — even I plan sometimes. Here are some things that are worth planning:

>> Anything that has timed entry or requires advanced booking (for example, the Sagrada Familia, as shown in Figure 3-1, or some popular museums)

>> A specific or unique tour (or any small group tour that could get booked up)

>> Specific or unique lodging (a treehouse in Scotland or a beachside bungalow in Fiji)

>> Infrequent ferries, trains (especially night trains), or buses

>> Rental cars (these are a huge expense and best avoided if possible)

FIGURE 3-1: Looking straight up at the remarkable ceiling of the Sagrada Familia cathedral in Barcelona, Spain.

Then there's the many things that you can probably leave to figuring out during your trip.

» Ferries, trains, and buses with regular service throughout the day (knowing there's an identical train one hour after your chosen train can be a *huge* stress reducer during your stay)

» Most museums and famous landmarks (though check when they're open)

» In most areas, lodging for every day of your trip

» Pretty much anything that's unlikely to sell out every day

In many cases, there won't be any difference in price booking things day-of (or close to it). A train at 6 p.m. likely costs the same, maybe less, than one at 5 p.m. Entrance fees to most touristy places are usually fixed, though sometimes there is a discount for booking ahead of time. If you're curious, check the price as if you were there today versus a few weeks from now. Just keep in mind there are often price differences across different weekdays and seasons.

TIP

Most countries don't require you to know where you're staying during your entire visit, but some do. It's worth checking the country's tourist information page.

Traveling Without a Plan
(Yes, It's Possible!)

My personal record is booking an international flight less than 24 hours before it left. This sounds impulsive, but it wasn't. I knew where I wanted to go and vaguely when. I just hadn't booked the ticket because I hadn't settled on the exact day I wanted to leave.

The key is having a list of things you want to do but keep the specific dates and times vague. I find this helps me alleviate the stress of "what if I miss something." When I'm thinking about a trip, I'll keep a to-do list, or add bookmarks in Google Maps saved to a list for that specific adventure.

Don't get me wrong, I have shown up to places without even a list. I just show up and see what happens. I consider that a bit advanced for most people though. It's best to at least have something in mind.

TIP

Note apps, such as Keep on Android and Notes on iOS, are a real help. No matter where you are when you think of something — for me it's invariably 3:30 a.m. mid-slumber — you can add it to a list you can access anywhere. You can also bookmark cool posts in Instagram and TikTok with things you've seen and want to try.

I've traveled for months without a schedule

On my second Australia trip, after I learned the hard way planning too much there the year before, I planned nothing. I had a hostel booked for the first few days, and then nothing for the three months I was planning on staying. It was exhilarating and for the most part, stress free. I didn't even start packing until the day before my flight. My to-do list included seeing some friends I'd met the year before, driving the Great Ocean Road, learning to scuba dive on the Great Barrier Reef (lots of "greats" in Australia I realize), and more.

One of my favorite trips ever was to Japan. I had the advantage that I'd been there before for work, but I hadn't visited on my own just to explore. I had six weeks and all I had booked was the flight and hostel for the first few days. Japan is one of the easiest countries to explore this way. The trains are always on time and run all day, nearly all signs are also in English, and there always seemed to be someone around if I needed assistance.

For me, the greatest benefit of a lack of planning is giving yourself the time to follow interests in the moment. Having the flexibility, and the mindset, to change on the fly is vital. I don't think that comes easily for most people, especially when you're spending a lot of money and using up precious vacation days.

The comment I hear most often when I talk about minimal planning is that it must cost a fortune. Generally, no. I discuss flights more in Chapter 4, but for the most part it's less about when you book your ticket and more what days and months you're flying. Weekends, big holidays, and so on are more expensive than midweek, off- and shoulder-season flights. The flight is typically the single largest expense for any trip, and it's definitely worth trying to find the best price. Usually, though, the difference is more like 20 to 30 percent not 100 to 200 percent. For a $700 flight, that's $175. Worth saving? Absolutely. Would you pay that much to have less stress and more fun on your trip, especially if you can save that much in other spending areas? Just something to consider.

Checking ticket prices over time is a great way to see how much difference this timing works. Google Flights and some other websites and apps let you see this and compare it to past prices. For instance, as I'm writing this, I could book a flight to London tomorrow for around $1,050. In three months, the middle of summer, that same flight is $1,000. In six months, early autumn, $800. Lower, for sure, but is that because it's six months away or because fewer people are interested in flying to London in September? Backing up one month, to mid-August, the flights cost $900. Google Flights shows you if these prices are higher or lower than typical.

Which is all to say, the prices will vary but not by as much as you might think. Worth considering, but not a dealbreaker.

There's (almost) always lodging available

Most destinations have a lot of places to stay, between hotels, hostels, Airbnb's, and so on. I've never not been able to find a place. That said, if you're trying to stay in New Orleans during Mardi Gras, Munich during Octoberfest, or any number of other widely known events, it's going to be difficult to find something.

In terms of budget travel, though, your money will go a lot farther not visiting places like that during the peak times they're popular. The price difference between peak and off season, or even my favorite, the "shoulder" seasons between the two, can be significant. What's a shoulder season? It's the time between the off season and the "on" season: early spring or late autumn for a place popular in the summer, for example. Prices are lower and it's less crowded.

Now true, if you're booking days or hours in advance, maybe you can't get the exact hotel you wanted, or the best room in a hostel you like, but isn't the adventure the point, not where you're sleeping? Sure, you want it to be safe and clean, but that's pretty easy. You shouldn't want to spend lots of time in your hotel room anyway.

Personally, I find spending lots of money on hotels a strange way to waste money. I've stayed in some pretty expensive places in my life, but none offered a fraction of the experience I've gotten walking around a city for free. If your goal is to be pampered in a five-star resort, that's fine. It's just not quite the kind of thing I'd do on a budget. I'd rather spend that money on literally anything else (not least of which, another trip!).

Apps that help you navigate and more

Given the rapidly changing nature of technology, it's impossible for me to know what the best travel apps are by the time you read this. I'm going to name a few that have helped me over the years, and hopefully their longevity continues and they help you out as well.

For them to work best you'll need data on your phone or tablet while you travel. You shouldn't expect Wi-Fi everywhere you go. I talk more about that in Chapter 8.

>> **Rome2Rio:** This app and website has helped me countless times. The idea is rather simple: You put in two locations, and it gives you all the options of how to get from one to the other. By land, by sea, by air, they'll show pretty much every possible option. They push harder for you to book something through one of their partners than they used to, but the core functionality is free. See Figure 3-2.

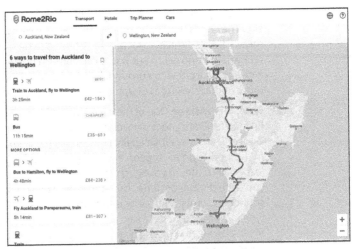

FIGURE 3-2: An example route from Rome2Rio between Aukland and Wellington, New Zealand, showing bus, train, and air options.

>> **Maps:** I'm partial to Google Maps, but Apple Maps has come a long way. You probably use one all the time. Take a moment to learn how to download the maps for a location so you can use them offline. Even if you have mobile data in the country you're visiting, it's inevitable you'll suddenly lose signal the moment you actually need it. In many cities these apps can help you navigate metro systems, too.

>> **Uber:** I try to avoid Uber for a variety of reasons, but it can come in handy when you need it. Available in 70 countries, it's worth checking if they're active where you're headed. It might be cheaper than a taxi, and it can be easier than trying to explain to a taxi driver where you're headed (take a picture of your hotel and its sign either way!). Many countries have apps for the local taxis, often advertised on the side of taxis themselves.

>> **Local scooters and bikes:** Many cities have rental scooters and e-bikes available to help you get around. The scooters especially are controversial, due to how many have littered the streets. In some places they can be expensive, so don't count on them as your only transport in a city. They can be a great way to explore, though. Just read up on local laws and customs before you ride.

- **Orbitz/Expedia/Kayak/et. al:** I don't have a favorite booking site. The prices tend to be roughly the same across all of them. There's almost never any secret deals to be had. Find one you like and get to know it. It can come in handy booking a new hotel from your current flea-infested one. Find out more about booking in Chapter 5.

- **Google Translate:** One of the most important apps you can have to facilitate your navigating through any country is Google Translate. While English is basically the lingua franca of the world and most people working in tourist hotspots (especially if they're younger) can speak it to some degree, you should never assume someone does. You shouldn't count on it either. With Google Translate not only can you type in what you want to say, and it will translate it, but in most languages you can speak to the app and the other person will then hear a computerized voice say what you said in their language. That's not all. With most languages the app has the ability to translate signs, menus, and other written words using the phone's camera, translating words in real time, so on your phone it looks like the sign/menu is in English. It's creepy and exceedingly helpful.

  That said, learning a few phrases can go a long way to endearing yourself to the locals. "Please" and "thank you" are good to know in any language.

  Most places call a bathroom a "WC," so that's handy to use just about everywhere.

Not all will go according to your lack of plan

It's entirely possible that the flight you want, the boat you need, the window seat you craved, won't be available. The fact is, that's always going to be the case. No trip is perfect. It can't be. As the saying goes, don't let the perfect be the enemy of the good. If the point of travel is to see new places and enjoy new things, let that be the overriding rule. Accept that it's impossible to control every aspect of a trip, and make the best of the situation you're in. Maybe that means you'll get one less day at your dream destination, but it might also mean you'll get to avoid wasting a week at one it turns out you hate.

As I've mentioned before, I think the phrase "once in a lifetime," can be toxic for an adventure. It puts far too much pressure for something to be perfect. There are plenty of things that are truly once in a lifetime, but visiting a country or city shouldn't be thought of that way.

See as much as you can, sure. Try to check off as much on your list as you can. But if you miss something, you can always go back. That's the core idea behind budget travel. Making it affordable enough that you can do it again, and hopefully, again, and again, and again.

The Drawbacks of Guided Tours, Cruises, and All-Inclusive Resorts

It probably doesn't surprise you that I'm, in general, against guided tours, cruises, and all-inclusive resorts. Without exception these are all very expensive ways to travel. That much is easy to see. Subjectively, they're also not a great way to see the location you're visiting.

There are, of course, exceptions. It's going to be pretty difficult to get to Antarctica without a cruise. Maybe it's not a good idea for your first trip up the Amazon to be alone in a canoe. If your whole family is going on some trip and the only way grandpa will go is if he can sit in a lounge chair staring at the sea sipping a beverage with a little umbrella, then sure, why not. Go for it. Just keep in mind that your money can be more efficiently spent elsewhere.

Well, maybe except the drinks with little umbrellas. Those are great.

Unless there's a view you want to enjoy, don't eat in famous tourist spots. Walk a few blocks in any direction and you'll find something cheaper and almost certainly better. Better yet, ask a local where they eat.

Pre-planned, packaged vacations are not cost effective

I can see the appeal of a single price that covers your entire trip. One number, you can take it or leave it, that covers everything. No surprises, right? Except, who's to say you couldn't have gotten a cheaper hotel that's just as good? Who's to say you couldn't find a better walking tour after you arrived? You almost certainly can find better food.

By combining all the costs into one, most companies can add in a profitable buffer in the name of convenience. As an example, Figure 3-3 shows the package cost for two people to London, UK, from a well-known US company, priced at the time of this writing for the following late spring. Most travel companies don't post package prices online, requiring a phone call. Even this one doesn't list individual costs, only the package price. The Self-Booked column is the same trip (hotel, flight, and so on), priced online by me for the same travel days, but booking it all yourself. This gives you an idea about the potential markup with package "deals." The Budget Option is the same flight, which did happen to be the cheapest, but staying in a private room at a high-end hostel in central London. The transportation prices are for roughly two weeks of Underground travel for two people. With the package deal, transportation to and from the airport is via a private car. Booking it yourself, it's the fast but expensive Heathrow Express (booked in advance). The budget option is a separate ticket for the Underground — cheap but slow. The activities cost is "included" as a credit with a tour company in London. You might be able to find better ticket prices, or only do certain activities, so this is an unknown cost. I included it as a fixed amount in the two other options for consistency.

	Package "Deal"	Self-Booked	Budget Option
Flight	???	$1,210	$1,210
Lodging	???	$4,070	$1,826
Transportation	???+$100	$54+$100	$30+$100
Activities	$400 Credit	~$400	~$400
Total	$6,453	$5,834	$3,566

FIGURE 3-3: A cost comparison of a package deal versus the same trip self-booked and an alternative budget option.

The package pricing isn't nefarious; it's simple business. If you're okay paying for that convenience, that's fine. But because you're reading Budget Travel For Dummies, I don't think paying large sums of money for convenience is your goal.

If it's "included," you're paying for it

Part of the appeal of many of these package deals is the all-inclusive nature of it. This is something I've heard from multiple people who like these types of vacations. I think they're missing the fact that these meals and drinks are a part of the price you're paying. They're not free.

In many, if not most, parts of the world, you can get an amazing meal for a fraction of the price that you're pre-paying in a package. One of my favorite places I've ever eaten is a tiny shop in Taipei, Taiwan where a bowl of noodles with spicy sesame sauce and peanut flour cost $3 including a Coke. It's easy to eat cheaply in most cities. You can read more about that in Chapter 9.

Even if you're getting a "deal" on meals or drinks in a package, there's no guarantee the food itself will be any good and the drinks not watered down. This is anecdotal for sure, but I've stayed at a few all-inclusive resorts in my life, in Mexico, Antigua, and Barbuda, and several others. The food was mediocre at each one.

It also creates a mindset that you're wasting money if you go out to find better food and drinks somewhere else. In a way, you would be. You're paying for the same meal twice. Along the same lines, it's natural to want to over-indulge with the unexceptional food to "get your money's worth."

You rarely get to see the real location you're visiting

When you travel as a large group (whether on an immense cruise ship or as part of a guided tour), you may not get a sense of the area's true culture.

WARNING

The worst offender of this is cruises. These massive ships distort the reality of every place they visit. Hundreds, if not thousands, of people disembark in the morning, swarm the streets, crowd the shops, then disappear back onto the ship at sunset. The streets, shops, even restaurants, in order to survive, have to adapt. They change their menus, wares, and especially prices. I don't fault people for making a living, but it changes a place, and these cruise ship deluges often do more harm than good.

This is why many people call certain locations "touristy," as a pejorative. These locations are catering to the clientele they're getting. It might seem like that influx of tourist cash is a good thing, but if you talk to the locals, you'll find out it rarely is. People visiting on cruise ships spend a fraction of what someone does who stays in town for a few days.

I've been in cities where, at night, it's quiet and mostly locals. Then during the day, it's wall to wall people angrily and loudly speaking English. It was, to put it mildly, a different vibe. Personally, that's not the kind of adventure I'm looking for.

You won't meet the locals and travelers from other countries

Cruises and big group tours are inherently self-selecting. You'll spend your entire trip with people who wanted that specific trip and could afford it. In my years of traveling I can count on two hands the number of Americans I've met. Instead I've met and been lucky enough to befriend Brits, Brazilians, Australians, Austrians, Germans, Swedes, and more. Meeting locals is awesome, as is meeting people from all over the world, with wildly different lives than yours, who share an interest in the place you're visiting.

Lightly guided tours: The potential exception

There is a class of guided tours that I call "lightly guided." I'll carve out an exception for these. I've done three, the last was actually the two-week trip I mentioned at the start of the chapter that cured me of being a planner. The first two were great though.

Broadly speaking, these lightly guided tours involve a guide shepherding you to a destination, giving you a list of things you could do, and that's it. The guide will help with translations and logistics but isn't there to give you a "tour." They're typically locals, so they'll know a lot about the culture. The group itself is usually small, a dozen people or less.

There's no hard line between a tour like this and a more typical guided tour. It's a spectrum, with the other end being strict timesheets of activities, huge, packed buses, and zero choice of things to do.

I'll also carve out an exception for single day trips/activities, as well as multi-hour walking tours. These can be great fun without restricting your entire trip. They can be a way to meet people, as well as do things that you might not be able to do on your own such as a trip up an active volcano, a behind-the-scenes tour of some famous buildings (skipping the lines), and so on. These can be well worth the money and time.

TIP

If you're new to travel in general, lightly guided tours can be an excellent bridge to get you to a place where you're comfortable traveling by yourself. I still keep in touch with several people I met on these trips and consider several close friends.

I'm not endorsing these companies, but two that offer trips I've described are Intrepid and GAdventures. I did trips in Africa and Asia with the latter, and while it's not the way I travel anymore, at the time it was great fun.

Overall, though, any package trip is going to be expensive compared to booking your own adventure.

Chapter **4**

Now Boarding: Finding the Right Flights

would love to be able to tell you there's one simple trick to save money on flights. Many an article, book, and video claim to be able to do that. The fact is, there isn't a secret website, a magical time window, or crazy hack that lets you get $1,000 flights for $100. I wish there was! That's just not how the airline business works.

However, there are things you can do (I guess you can call them "tricks and hacks") to minimize what you pay. Generally speaking, the difference in the lowest and highest price you'll pay for most flights is more like 25 percent, often less. Airlines are surprisingly efficient businesses and are highly competitive. So even comparing the prices across multiple airlines, over multiple websites, the major routes aren't going to vary too much in price.

What I talk about in this chapter are sort of "best practices." Tools you can use to seek out not just the best possible price but also to give you guidelines to shorten the amount of time you spend searching, knowing you're starting with the best perspectives in mind.

Booking Flights Yourself versus Hiring a Travel Agent

I used to think going to a travel agent was a generational thing. None of my friends, nor most people I've met, had ever used one. I grew up in the Age of the Internet so I was more than comfortable seeking out flights and hotels on my own using any number of websites.

I've met a few people who seemed shocked by this, and not just older, usually less internet-savvy people. For some people, the idea of booking everything yourself is, I guess, daunting or a bad idea. To be honest I've never gotten an explanation that made a lot of sense to me.

What I do understand is the potentially daunting nature of traveling if you don't do it a lot. An entire city, perhaps multiple cities, full of endless choices about where to stay, how to get there, what seats to pick on the flight (see Figure 4-1) and more. Outsourcing that research to someone else certainly has a value if you're not comfortable doing it yourself. This is *Budget Travel For Dummies*, though, and you'll almost always be able to get the same, or better deals, booking yourself.

Geoffrey Morrison

FIGURE 4-1: Window seats are my preference. Why risk missing views like this of some Alaskan mountains?

Do you need a travel agent?

Do you *need* a travel agent? No. You can book pretty much every kind of trip, just about anywhere in the world, by yourself. You can research an area, find cool things to do, check out hotels, hostels, and more, all from the comfort of your couch.

Do you *want* a travel agent? Generally speaking, a travel agent can probably do this kind of research for you. For many destinations, they probably know lots of places to stay and things to do. They can book all that for you so you don't have to think about it.

REMEMBER

One important factor to consider is most travel agents make money for this service. That's fine, it's their job. But whatever they're making from this service could be money you spend elsewhere. They also might be getting a commission for selling you a specific package, a specific tour, and so on. The "deal" they get you might be the normal price if you were to book it yourself.

Or to put it another way, you're paying for a service on top of your trip. That service might save you time, but it almost certainly won't save you money. Just keep that in mind.

What is your time worth?

This is the best way to look at travel agents. They're spending time so you don't have to. Usually, you'll pay a premium for this. That premium might be paid to them directly for their service, or it might be found in hidden costs in hotels and flights that you could have gotten cheaper.

There is a value, which is why travel agents still exist in an age where you can book everything online. I can certainly understand the anxiety of booking travel to someplace new, especially if you're new to travelling. Which is to say, don't feel bad if you want to just offload everything to a travel agent, but you should definitely learn how to do it yourself so you can save money on your next trip.

TIP

If you have time, it's almost always better to book things yourself.

Costs and trust

Most travel agents are doing a job they hopefully like with the goal of getting others a trip they'll enjoy. As in every industry, there are almost certainly bad apples. Trusting your travel agent is crucial, not just for your own enjoyment, but also to make sure you get the best prices.

If you've never used an agent before, read as many online reviews as you can. Even if you want to have someone else book your whole trip, you should at least do this level of due diligence to make sure others have had a satisfactory experience. Chances are, if they're still in business these days, they probably have solid word-of-mouth from former clients.

It's also good to research prices for flights and accommodations where you're headed. If you can find a hotel for $100 a night that looks okay but they say the cheapest in that city is $150, that should give you pause. Maybe they're right? Maybe the one you found is actually in a bad area, but it's good to know that going in.

And once you get used to checking prices on that kind of thing, you'll be ready to book everything yourself for your next trip!

TIP

If possible, double check any flights, tours, or accommodations an agent books for you to see if you could have gotten them cheaper. Maybe it can't help you for this trip, but you'll know for the next one.

Booking Flights

I don't have a favorite booking site. It's a myth that one site secretly has better prices than another. They're all going to be within a few dollars of each other. This is the opposite of what you're told by all the marketing for every booking site. The fact is, airlines run on surprisingly narrow margins. As in, there's not as much profit in each ticket as you might think. So you're not going to find one site offering a seat for $500 and another offering the same seat on the same aircraft for $200. As an example, Figure 4-2 shows price differences across several popular booking sites, plus the cheapest flight option's own site for a round-trip flight from New York to Tokyo.

	Booking	Expedia	Kayak	Orbitz	Skyscanner	Airline's Website
Price:	$1,077	$1,104	$1,047	$1,104	$1,054	$1,104

FIGURE 4-2: The price for flights doesn't vary much between booking sites.

Feel free to check on your own, though. I find the best option is to settle on a single website that has an interface you like, and that lets you find what you want easily and without hassle. Some offer handy charts to help you decide what days to fly, nearby airports, and so on. That's crucial.

It's crucial because the absolute best way to save money on flights by *far* is this: flexibility. I'll talk about this more in a moment, but if you're not set on specific days, or a specific airport, you can save hundreds on every flight.

It's worth checking an airline's own site for prices. Usually they'll be similar, but sometimes they might be a little cheaper.

TIP

When to book flights

There's a myth, maybe it was once true, maybe it wasn't, that there was some secret time during the week where airline prices "reset" and for a brief magical moment, they were cheaper. If that was true once, it isn't now. Every airline is a 24/7 business fully automated and with algorithms applied to the micro-cent.

With some airlines, and some routes, there can be some differences in prices if you book a certain number of days or weeks ahead of time. This isn't a set amount, nor is it set for every airline. Generally, a few weeks ahead will be cheaper than day of, but there are a lot of variables.

Multiple booking websites will let you set up price alerts too, so if the price drops they'll let you know. Just don't get scared if it suddenly goes up. If you know the average, it will probably revert to that.

TIP

When to fly

The biggest price changes happen across all airlines, and it's directly because of demand. As you research prices you'll see this effect. The variable is time. The most consistent drops and spikes in ticket prices have to do with seasons and days of the week. On some routes, even the time of day is important. Save money by flying when other people don't want to.

Some sites, such as Google Flights (shown in Figure 4-3), have a price history feature that lets you compare the current price to past prices to give you an idea of the average range.

TIP

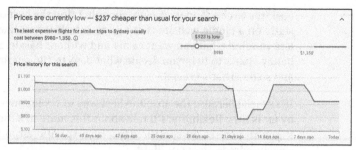

FIGURE 4-3: Check out a flight's price history to determine the most affordable time to travel.

Early morning and late evening flights are often cheaper, because fewer people want to fly during those times. Depending on the route and destination, Tuesdays, Wednesdays, and sometimes Saturdays are often cheaper, since more people fly on Fridays, Sundays, and Mondays for work or weekend getaways. June, July, and August are always expensive for the same reason Thanksgiving week and the second half of December are: Lots of people are traveling.

So flying mid-week in the late spring is almost always going to be cheaper than flying on a Friday in August. This is one half of why it's crucial to remain flexible. I understand this is easier said than done. Many of you probably have to book vacation days months in advance. Maybe this won't help if you're already locked in, but it's something to keep in mind, if possible, when you're requesting time off in the future.

For example, flying out Thursday night might save you money at the cost of a personal day on Friday for a vacation the following weeks. Ideal? Possible? Perhaps not, but it's worth looking into if your vacation days are limited or rigid.

Most booking websites and the aforementioned Google Flights offer date grids that show you different prices if you move the departure and arrival dates around. A couple of days either way could save you hundreds.

Where to fly

Did you know London has six international airports that all claim to be "in London"? Only two are in a borough of London. One has London in its name, but it's 42 miles away and in a different county. This is surprisingly common. There are only so many hours in a day, and every airport adheres to strict regulations for how many flights can arrive and depart every hour. For popular destinations, there are only two ways to deal with demand: increase prices or open additional airports. Often, airports and cities do both.

These smaller airports often offer cheaper flights, at the cost of some slight inconvenience getting to your actual destination. Usually they're connected to the city they serve by public transportation. This might mean a fast and efficient subway; it might mean a bus. It varies.

However, it's a fantastic way to save money. (As an added bonus, these smaller airports are often less busy and have shorter security lines.) Broaden your search. Even if one of these nearby airports doesn't have a convenient flight, go a little farther. Instead of London, how about a few days in Dublin then flying a cheap regional airline to get you to London, saving you money overall. Many countries and regions have airlines like this. Then there are trains. For example, Osaka is connected to Tokyo by one of the most efficient high-speed rail systems in the world. Check prices for both.

Some locations offer highly subsidized flights to incentivize you to stay over for a day or more. Iceland has done this for decades. Cheap flights with long layovers in Reykjavík offer enough time for you to explore this small and delightful city before continuing on to the rest of Europe.

Generally, I'm a proponent of simplifying an itinerary, and this definitely makes it more complex. You'll also have to add in the transport costs getting you to your actual chosen destination, so it doesn't always work. However, it could mean either saving hundreds or seeing an additional location on your trip essentially for free.

The more flexible you are in when and where you fly, the cheaper you'll be able to get a flight.

A huge exception

All the booking advice in this chapter is predicated on one thing: competition. The vast majority of airline routes are serviced by more than one airline. This, in theory, keeps prices down as the airlines compete with each other.

However, there are some routes where there's only one airline. Worse, that airline might only fly on certain days. In this case, the flights are going to be very expensive. A common instance of this is small islands, be it in the Pacific, Caribbean, or really anywhere there's a small population on an island large enough for an airport. The most trouble I've ever had with my "don't book too far in advance" mindset was trying to island hop in the Caribbean. Flights between islands were usually on tiny planes that booked up quickly. Despite the trouble, I still had an amazing adventure and wouldn't change a thing if I do it again.

Occasionally, less popular routes will be subsidized by the local government. When there's one fight a week on an airplane with ten seats, though, you're probably not going to get a bargain. Just something to keep in mind while you're planning possible destinations. Islands can offer some incredible adventures, but often they're expensive ones.

Searching in incognito mode

Web browsers like Chrome, Edge, Safari, and others, have a mode labeled something like "Incognito," "InPrivate," or "Private Browsing" mode. This mode blocks websites from installing something called a "cookie" on your computer that lets it know if, among other things, you've been there before. Pretty much all websites do this, and usually it's not a big deal. Sometimes, if you visit a site repeatedly to check prices, they might show you prices that are higher than what they show to someone who has never visited before. The idea is if you're checking prices all the time, you're motivated to buy. Why not charge you more if you're so interested.

Does this actually happen? It's rather impossible to say. A particular website might do it now, and then stop. Another might not do it now but start doing it later. Generally, I'd put this in the same category of "received wisdom" as the "magical moment in the week prices are lower." However, the technology is already in place for any company to start doing this at any moment.

My advice is don't worry about it up until you're ready to book your tickets. Then take a couple of minutes to open a browser in that mode and check the prices for your exact flight. Chances are they'll be the same. But if not, you can log in and proceed with the purchase in the incognito browser.

If you really want to go to the next level, a VPN (virtual private network) can mask where you're located, so you can surf an airline's website from their own country. Probably not worth the extra hassle, especially if you've never heard of a VPN before this. If you're trying to book a flight on a regional airline from outside that region, it's worth checking. As in, the airline charges the residents of their own country one price and people booking from outside the country a different price. There are a variety of reasons why this could be.

I've checked this before and only noticed a difference a couple of times. For instance, booking a flight from Brazil to the US while in Brazil was one price, the same fight booking from the US was a lower price. Does it happen often? No. When it does happen, is it a big difference? Also no, but again, it's worth checking if you're tech savvy and want to spend the time.

Using third-party booking websites

Any website that's not run by the airline themselves is a third party. There are tons of these booking websites, like Expedia, Kayak, and Orbitz. They compile all, or almost all, the available flights between the destinations you choose on the dates you want to fly. I'm going to guess you're quite familiar with them.

For the most part, their prices are going to be the same, or nearly the same, as what you'd find booking directly from an airline (see Figure 4-2 earlier in the chapter). There are exceptions. Some airlines don't allow their flights to be listed on sites like these. For example in the US, Southwest Airlines doesn't show up in searches on most third-party sites. It would be impossible for me to review every booking and search website and maintain any semblance of usefulness. Even regularly updated websites that do this are almost immediately out of date. Booking websites come and go, gain and lose functionality, or are bought by some other person or corporation and become something different. Throughout this section I've tried to stick to categories of websites, or those that have been in business for a long time. Hopefully this will prevent you from shaking your fist at the page and saying, "Geoff, how could you have not mentioned WakeMeUpForMeals Dot Com? It's the *greatest website ever!*" Perhaps so, but I can't see in the future, and for that I apologize.

Which is to say, there are countless websites out there with the goal of saving you money, often by giving them a little bit of it by buying tickets through them. That's fine, but in the end the only way you'll actually save any money on flights is a little bit of your own research and remaining flexible on time and location. Any website that helps you do that, in a way that you find helpful, is a good one.

Does it hurt to also check an airline's own site or book through them directly? Nope, and it's certainly worth checking if there's a price difference. It's unlikely there will be, and if there is one, it's probably negligible. Some airlines might offer perks if you book directly through them though, like lower baggage fees or early boarding. Personally I've never had an issue booking through a third party for a flight, but there's something to be said about only dealing with the airline and not some other party.

WARNING

It's worth noting that Booking, Kayak, and Priceline are all owned by one company called Booking Holdings. Expedia, as well as CheapTickets, Ebookers, Hotwire, Orbitz, and Travelocity, are owned the Expedia Group. So if you want to check prices on multiple sites, make sure they're at least owned by different parent companies.

Google Flights

Throughout this chapter I've mentioned Google Flights. It's one of the few websites I'm outright recommending. As you'd hope from the search giant, the ways that you can search for flights is unbelievably handy. You can see what the price of the flight has been in the past. You can see in an easy-to-understand graph what the prices are for specific days in the future (see Figure 4-4). You can see how future prices compare to historical averages. Perhaps coolest of all, you can put in your home airport, when you want to fly, and it will show you how much it will cost to fly anywhere in the world on or around those dates.

Google isn't the first to offer many of these features. Some sites offer something similar. The breadth of the data and the simplicity of the interface make this the one site of its kind that I go back to regularly.

Dates   Price graph

Departure   <   >

◆ Cheapest
Compared with other prices shown

Sun May 19	Mon May 20	Tue May 21	Wed May 22	Thu May 23	Fri May 24	Sat May 25	◎	Return
$954	$851	$954	$954	$1,042	$1,059	$1,062	Sun Jun 2	∧
$954	$851	$954	$954	$1,042	$1,059	$1,028	Mon Jun 3	∨
$911	◆ $826	$919	$919	$1,017	$1,028	$998	Tue Jun 4	
$911	◆ $826	$919	$919	$1,017	$1,028	$998	Wed Jun 5	
$919	◆ $826	$919	$919	$1,017	$1,034	$1,037	Thu Jun 6	
$925	◆ $826	$925	$925	$1,023	$1,037	$1,037	Fri Jun 7	
$946	$851	$954	$954	$1,042	$1,059	$1,023	Sat Jun 8	

Cancel   OK

FIGURE 4-4: A sample calendar that shows price differences depending on what day you depart and what day you return.

I won't claim Google is completely neutral in all this. Far from it. They offer this service because they think they can make money on it. That said, you don't book most flights on Google's own site. Once you've found your flight, it directs you to that airline's own website and you book through them. Some flights are labeled "Book on Google" where you do exactly that. Either way, Google is getting some piece of this pie, but if the prices are the lowest you can find, that doesn't matter. Expedia, Orbitz, and all the other booking sites also get a piece of the purchase price.

TIP

As of this writing, Google is testing a price guarantee feature if you book through their site. If the price of the ticket drops between when you buy and when you fly, they'll pay you the difference. It will only be available on some flights from the US, and you have to have a US address. Worth checking for when you're booking, at least for a slight peace of mind about ticket prices.

My only concern is that Google gleefully cancels apps and services on a regular basis. Flights has been around for a while, so hopefully it's here to stay.

Average prices over time

One of the best ways to figure out if you're getting a good price is to check its average price over time. A number of websites do this, including Google Flights. Did your flight cost $900 a few weeks ago, or $1,500. If you're looking at $500 tickets, is that a deal or a price gouge?

As handy as this is, there are two problems. The first is one that Wall Street likes to say about investments: Past performance is not indicative of future results. Just because a ticket cost $500 six months ago doesn't mean it costs that now, or in the future. There are infinite variables that can change the price. The second problem is sometimes mentioned on the site but worth considering if it isn't. Let's say it's currently the spring and you're booking summer travel. The price of a ticket three months ago, in the middle of winter, isn't particularly relevant.

Sites show what the cost of tickets are in a few months, but it's not set in stone. Sudden spikes in gas prices could increase ticket prices. Or some unforeseen global pandemic (you know, totally theoretically) could crater demand and drive prices down, who knows. Aliens could arrive and offer cheap trips to the moon. Who knows what that would do to prices. I bet they still wouldn't offer free checked luggage though.

So generally, checking prices over time is a handy tool, but it's just one of the tools in your deal-searching arsenal.

Spending a little more to fly at better times or get shorter flights

I know the idea of spending more on a flight seems incongruous for this kind of book, but there are situations where it's beneficial. The cheapest flight might leave at 6 a.m., for instance. That means you'll generally need to get to the airport around 4 a.m., which means you'll need to leave around 3 a.m., getting up at 2 a.m., and do you really think you'll be able to fall asleep at 8 p.m. while you're excited for your adventure? I sure couldn't. Not losing a night or being a zombie the next day due to lack of sleep is worth spending a bit more to me. Being sleep deprived on your vacation is only good if it's due to having too much fun, not because you didn't sleep before a flight.

Along the same lines, maybe you can find a flight that involves multiple or long layovers. Do you want to lose a day or more of your vacation in transit just to save a few dollars? Maybe yes, maybe no, but it's worth considering.

A big consideration, especially in Europe, is where the flight actually lands. I mentioned above how many cities around the world are served by multiple airports. If you saved a bit of money flying into an airport over an hour outside of the city, is that extra hassle and time worth the savings? Should you pay more so you don't have to add hours to your trip after you land just to get to your destination? Again, not saying you shouldn't, but it's worth checking all the options.

Which is all to say, there's more to consider than just the dollar value.

Time is the most valuable resource we have. Sometimes spending a little more money to have more time is absolutely worth it.

Pros and cons of one-way tickets

I love one-way tickets. I've flown for years booking one-way. Often this is because I tend to just keep going in my adventures. On a recent trip I hopped my way from Australia to Bali, then on to Qatar and Europe, then to Iceland and back home. I didn't have specific dates I was leaving for most of those legs, so I couldn't book them all ahead of time even if I wanted to. Another version of this is having an exact return date, but you're not sure where or what part of a country you'll be leaving from.

The cost difference to do this usually isn't as big as you'd expect. If a round trip ticket is $1,000, a one-way might be $600. That's not always the case, however, so careful research ahead of time is crucial. A one-way ticket from London to LAX, for instance, costs more than a round-trip ticket. Also, some countries require you to have a way *out* already booked when you arrive. They don't care if you're going back or going forward, but they want to make sure you're going somewhere.

Early in my extended travels I didn't realize some countries require this ticket out. I tried checking in to my flight to New Zealand from Australia, and when the airline employee asked about my return flight, I said I didn't have one yet. Her face had a mixture of surprise and concern. She apologetically informed me I couldn't check in without a ticket out of New Zealand. Hey, we all learn things sometime, right? No problem. I stepped to the side and booked a ticket back to Brisbane a few weeks in the future. Cost me the same amount if I'd booked it a few weeks earlier, and once I showed her the booking, I was on my way. Total time lost to this mistake was just a few minutes.

Now, typically, when I figure out when I want to leave, I'll book the flight to my next location. Then, before I leave, I'll book the flight or train out of that location if that's required. This offers the flexibility I need, while still keeping everything legal for the immigration officials. I have no interest in upsetting them. Traveling as much as I do is already abnormal. No need to throw up additional flags.

If you're booking one-way, search for "proof of onward travel" plus the country you're visiting. You might not need a flight out — a ferry or bus might do — but some proof of a plan might be required. This is especially the case for island countries. If you have a "weaker" passport, you might be questioned about this more often.

This booking-as-you-go isn't something I'd recommend to an inexperienced traveler. As you grow your travel skills, it's something to consider and can be extremely fun. Check out Chapter 3 for more about traveling without a plan.

Then there's the concept of "skiplagging" or "hidden-city ticketing." The idea is to book a flight to a cheap destination that has a layover in an expensive destination. For instance, a flight to Amsterdam that stops in London might be cheaper than a flight directly to London. You get off the plane in London and stay, saving money. This is only possible if you're flying without checked baggage and on a one-way ticket, since the airline will cancel the rest of your reservation since you didn't show up for one segment.

Generally, I advise against this. There's some question about the legality, with a variety of lawsuits in different countries. Many of those cases were thrown out or settled in favor of the passenger, but do you really want to get sued by an airline? Even beyond the legality, an airline could just decide to punish you with a ban or a cancellation of your frequent flier account. They've actually done this. In the most basic sense, you're doing something the airline sees as costing it money, which is true, and they're not going to like that. Will you get away with it? Maybe. But personally, I don't feel like angering a billion-dollar corporation that holds the yoke to getting me somewhere else in the world.

Don't expect huge discounts or deals

If you got the best deal on a flight, booking it on the absolute cheapest day possible, the price wouldn't be hugely different than if you booked it on its worst, most expensive day. For the average $1,000 ticket, the difference might be a few hundred either way, but rarely half or double. Don't get me wrong, if you can save money on the flight, you absolutely should. It's the biggest single cost of any trip. If you're waiting and waiting for the prices to drop and it's stressing you out, know that most of the time it's not going to be radically different.

Setting up price alerts and checking sites like Google Flights for prices over time should give you an idea what the general price is, letting you book when it seems best. Just know that some magical sale bringing a $1,000 flight down to $100 just isn't going to happen.

Choosing between Budget Airlines and Major Carriers

All airlines can be classified into two broad categories: major carrier and budget. There's some overlap in those terms, but for our purposes, they're helpful distinctions. In the US, major carrier airlines are United, American, and Delta. In most countries it's the "flag carrier," often owned or subsidized by the country's government. If the airline's name has a country in it, it's probably that country's flag carrier.

Usually, but not always, major airlines will have the biggest fleets of aircraft, the most available flights, and offer the most perks. To pay for all the equipment and personnel, their ticket prices are often higher. There are exceptions, of course. Southwest Airlines is one of the largest airlines in the US, but they're also a budget airline.

Budget airlines, instead, usually have smaller fleets of aircraft, fewer flights overall, and far fewer perks. Often, but not always, they're regional airlines. While a major airline probably has entertainment screens at every seat, budget airlines often don't. Major airlines might give you a snack or meal on a flight, budget airlines usually don't (unless the flight is quite long). Budget airlines also often fly odd hours to save on airport fees, leaving very early or very late in the day.

When people complain about an airline's myriad fees, often these are from budget airlines, though major airlines are rarely much better. So yes, you could book a $100 flight on CattleCar Airsteerage, but you'll need to spend $20 to pick a seat, $30 to add luggage, $10 for the bathroom, $50 for a seat cushion, and $100 not to get stuffed in an overhead bin. Some of those fees are fiction, but which ones?

Is it worth flying a budget airline? Given the title of this book I bet you'll be surprised by my answer: depends. The worst flights I've ever taken were on budget airlines. The complaints about flying I hear from friends, family, and fellow travelers are almost always related to budget airlines. In order to squeeze a tiny bit more profit out of a surprisingly narrow profit margin, budget airlines go above and beyond to take as much as possible out of the flight.

On one hand, it's a few hours in the sky so who cares? Take a nap, wake up in a different part of the world. So yeah, spend as little as possible. On the other hand, I am not a small human, and after getting folded like origami into a seat designed by sadists, deprived of food and water for seven-plus hours, I'm going to be a touch cranky. Cranky is not how I like to start an adventure.

For shorter flights, which to me is anything less than six hours, I don't think spending more for better service is worth it. I will pay to pick a window seat because, yeah, flying is still cool to me and I want to look out the window (see Figure 4-5). But I'll suffer through my knees rubbing against the seat in front of me for a few hours to save a few hundred dollars. Longer flights though? I'll usually go for something I know will be more comfortable. This is why I use airline points to book a more comfortable seat, when possible. More on those later in this chapter.

TIP

You'll often pay a bit more to get the service and convenience of a major airline, but most budget airlines offer reasonable service for their lower prices.

Behind the scenes (airline costs)

This might come as a surprise, but there's actually very little, if any, profit in that $700 airline seat. Airlines make the bulk of their profit on everything other than your ticket. They haul cargo, they sell ads during the in-flight movie, they charge massive amounts for business and first-class seats, they have loyalty programs generating profit non-stop from credit card and other deals — oh yes, and those endless, endless fees. The competition is so fierce among airlines that they all run at or sometimes below the line just to get the seats filled.

FIGURE 4-5: You never know what gorgeous views you'll see from the window seat, like Old San Juan with the ocean beyond.

This is mostly because all airlines have significant costs. There's the airplane itself, either the purchase or the ongoing lease. There are maintenance and fuel costs. There are airport costs both in terms of the aircraft and everything in the terminal. There's the crew, of course, as well as everyone else that works for the company. The list goes on.

In no way should you think I'm describing these costs to provoke pity. Airlines are a business, and if they can't figure out how to work their balance sheet to continue, they should sell to someone who can. All I'm saying is if one airline is offering a ticket for $1,000, chances are none will offer the same flight for $500 unless there's some huge difference between the service they're providing.

How much cheaper, really?

If you're flying a long-haul international route, the choice is going to be a little easier. Typically those routes are only covered by large airlines. Over the years a handful of budget airlines have tried to do budget long-haul service, and they've all failed. If gas prices go up a little, their margins are ruined, and they go out of business. You might be able to find one of these airlines during its active years and save some money, but don't count on it.

For domestic routes it's a bit different. Especially in the US, parts of Asia, and Europe, budget airlines are big business. Flying one of these airlines might save you 20 percent or more. That's not bad, but when you're looking at $250 versus $300 but you need to leave at 5 a.m., can't pick your seat, and have to fly an airline your friends have all vowed to "never fly again," is that $50 really worth it? Maybe, maybe not. Then again, that $300 for the larger carrier might also not let you pick your seat and might have scores of people who will never fly them again either. There are no easy answers.

Hidden costs and penalties

WARNING

I will never, ever, fly RyanAir ever again. It's one of the largest budget airlines, they fly all over Europe, and after the experience I had with them, they'll never get more of my money.

After a particularly busy day, I forgot to check in early for a flight. My friend and I arrived two hours before its scheduled departure, expecting to check in at the airport like any other airline. We weren't allowed. Instead, we had to pay $65 *each* for the privilege of them printing us tickets. This was more than half the price of the ticket where we'd already added the fees for better seats and checked luggage.

If this sounds weird, it's because it is. You're not required, in most cases, to check in before you check in. You should, clearly, and I normally do, but here it was just another way to squeeze a little bit more profit wherever possible.

This is why there are so many airline fees. Airlines know there's only so low they can charge for a seat, so they have to make money elsewhere. Sure they could just charge more and include those things, but then no one would click on their airline to fly because the prices were "too high." It's not a great system. It is what it is.

Accumulating miles/points

The other benefit to choosing a major airline is the ability to accumulate airline points. These, usually along with an airline-branded credit card, will let you get free upgrades and cheaper or free flights. That's a benefit for sure, but perhaps not as much as it seems. I discuss this more in the section, "The 'Value' of Credit Card Points."

The "Value" of Credit Card Points

I'm a big fan of credit card points for travel, but I also generally advise against them. They're a terrible, terrible value, especially if you don't travel regularly.

My two main credit cards give me either 1.5 or 2 points per dollar spent depending on what I'm buying. I can use these points to book travel or get flights/upgrades on my usual airline. For business and bookkeeping reasons, nearly every bill and charge in my life gets put on one of these cards. As a result, I have enough points each year to fly business class somewhere, with enough left over for a few other flights.

Don't do this. If you only travel once a year, you are infinitely better off getting a "cash-back" card that gives you a percentage of all your purchases back as credit or cash. Put this in a savings account dedicated to travel. The points, as fun as they are, are a bad value.

What points can do for you

If they're such a bad value, why do I still like them? Well, there's an emotional aspect to them I can't deny. I like the idea that everything I buy is going, in some small part, toward my next trip. There's also the undeniable "treat yourself" fun of flying business class. Definitely not "budget," but it's one of the few things I splurge on. When I have the available points and have enough left over for a free flight somewhere, I figure why not. I'll be the first to tell you it's far better to use points for actual free flights.

Tangential to the points is the card itself. Many come with perks like free luggage, early boarding, and airport lounge access. Are these worth the annual fee? If you travel a lot, absolutely. But again, if you're only traveling once a year, will you really get enough use out of that approximately $100 annual fee? If you don't care about the perks, probably not.

They also only really work if you regularly fly that card's airline. I live in Los Angeles, and it's a major hub for United. I can get pretty much anywhere in the world with them. So it's no surprise my credit card points go towards them, and I fly them regularly and accumulate points via flown miles. Is that loyalty? I guess. I've flown better airlines. It is convenient, for sure.

If you don't live near a major airline's hub, or only fly the cheapest option (both are totally fine, by the way), airline points are less useful. Sign up for them, for sure, as it never hurts to accumulate points. But getting multiple cards for the various airlines you fly will cost a lot in annual fees and take forever to accumulate enough points to spend.

What they can't do for you

Used and accumulated carefully, points can help reduce the cost of travel, but not by as much as it seems. Have you ever heard the expression "the house always wins?" This is about casinos, but I'm going to appropriate it to airlines and hotels. The only reason companies offer these programs is because they feel they can make money from them, or at the very least, not lose money.

Let me put it this way. All airline loyalty programs are designed to be underused by the average traveler. Everyone thinks they're getting a good deal, but most people aren't. They're leaving perks and discounts on the seatback table, so to speak. Worse, you spend years accumulating enough points for a free flight, only to find out the cost for the flight in points has gone up.

The ever-depreciating value

Loyalty program points are what's called a "depreciating asset." As in, the longer you hold onto them, the less they're worth. If you have 100,000 points at an airline, every year those 100,000 points are worth less. Every year, airlines increase the points required to buy a ticket, thereby reducing the value of your points. If you're hoping to save up 30,000 points for a "free" ticket next year, by the time you've saved them up it's entirely possible the ticket will cost 40,000 or 60,000. Gone are the days of fixed-point costs for flights. Now they change just like actual ticket prices.

Let me lay out a hypothetical. Let's say you spent $10,000 on your credit card in a year, and that card gave you 1.5 points per dollar spent. That's 15,000 points. That's about half a free domestic flight with most airlines. If you had a card that gave you 2 percent cash back, you'd have $200. Still not enough for a flight, right? Except that $200 is 200 actual dollars, not imaginary currency that could be reduced in value or completely disappear at the whim of one company.

If you travel a lot, especially if you fly regularly with a specific airline, *and* you're able to charge and pay off most or all of your bills via a credit card, *and* you've found a card that offers perks you'll use, then they're worth considering. For most people though, especially infrequent travelers or those just starting out, approach with caution. They can be beneficial, but for most people they are not.

Spending More to Save Time

In travel and in life, the most valuable resource you have is time. This book is about "budget travel," but to me, time is something you have to budget as well. This might seem antithetical to the theme of a book about saving money, but I will gladly spend more money if there's a worthy savings of time.

This is impossible to quantify in any objective way, but I want to put it in your head that my goal with this book is to get you the best adventure you can afford, not "the cheapest travel possible." These are subtly, but importantly, different. If spending $1,200 results in a legendary adventure and $1,000 gets you one that's only okay, I'm going to recommend the $1,200 option. I'll still talk about the $1,000 if you want to go that route, but there are situations where spending a little more is worth it.

You should ask yourself: How much is an hour worth? If you only have two weeks to travel, is spending 15 hours on a bus worth saving $100 versus one hour flying? I'm not saying it is, and I'm not saying it isn't. There are too many variables. I just don't want you to get too swept up in saving every penny at the cost of losing time on an adventure you can't get back. There's a fine line to be walked here, and there's no right answer. The travel is the point, correct? Not specifically saving the most money. Just something to keep in mind.

If you're checking luggage it's far less likely an airline will lose it on a direct flight.

A hotel near transit or your "must-see" locations

My first post-college adventure as an "adult" was with some friends who were still in college. None of us had money. We checked every destination possible to find the cheapest. How nice Google Flights would have been back then. The cheapest flight we could find was to Amsterdam. We had given ourselves a day to think about it, since during the time we were researching the cheapest flight was to Ulaanbaatar. Now *that* would have been a different trip.

So Amsterdam it was. The cheapest hotel we could find was outside the city limits, so we booked it. It meant we spent an hour every morning, and an hour every night, on the train. We weren't exactly early risers (I'm still not), so we had a limited amount of time to explore the city. I didn't enjoy myself as much as I probably should have due to the constant pressure of train timetables.

These days, I'm far more careful about where I book my lodging. There's a constant calculation about walking distance, local transit locations, accessibility to food or groceries, and more. Does this mean I end up spending more? Not usually, thanks to what you'll learn about hotels and other places to stay in Chapter 5. I will spend more, however, if there's a savings of time or hassle.

Often, a better location can save you money in addition to time. For example, let's say you're looking for a hotel for the night before a flight. A cheap hotel outside of town might be $100 versus one near the airport that's $150. Easy choice, right? Except the one near the airport will probably have a free shuttle, and you might need to spend $75 on a taxi from the cheap hotel.

In many cities, the metro system has different zones that cost different amounts. If your hotel is just over the line in "zone 2" and everything you want to see is in "zone 1," perhaps you're paying more in fees and time than had you stayed in a slightly more expensive hotel in "zone 1."

These are just some of the ways that spending more isn't actually spending more. A slightly higher cost in column A to save money in column B.

Trains over buses

In nearly every country, the cheapest form of public transport is a bus. In many countries, long distance buses are quite nice, with reclining seats, a bathroom, and regular stops for food and snacks. They are, however, very slow.

The question becomes, is it worth saving a few dollars to lose a day on a bus, or should you spend a little more and take a train. Throughout Europe and parts of Asia, high-speed trains are quite prevalent. They can be pricey, but if you get an extra day to explore versus a day on a bus, how much is that worth?

There's no specific answer here. I love trains, but I've had some great bus journeys, too. You'll often get to see more of the countryside on a bus than on a train, since high-speed rails are by necessity fairly sequestered from the surrounding area. That depends on where you are, of course, which is worth researching ahead of time. If it doesn't break your budget, I say spending a bit more on a train is worth it since if gives you more of the most valuable resource: time.

A moment to relax

Don't underestimate the benefits of having a moment to do absolutely nothing. This is by far the thing that inexperienced travelers and excessive planners forget to incorporate. Feeling stressed and rushed all the time is no way to enjoy being somewhere new.

Is it worth spending more so you don't have to rush to catch a connecting flight? Is it worth spending more to take a direct high-speed train versus a multi-transfer all-day affair?

Throughout this book one of my main pieces of advice is to slow down. I completely understand wanting to fit as much as possible into the limited time you have, but in doing so you'll often enjoy it all less. If you're constantly worried about making it to the next event, the next location, the next whatever, what time do you have to just enjoy being where you are?

IN THIS CHAPTER

» **Examining the pros and cons of different types of accommodation**

» **Understanding why hostels aren't what you think**

» **Discovering the easiest way to save money on lodging**

» **Finding alternative places to stay**

Chapter **5**

Where to Lay Your Head

You've gotta sleep somewhere. That's just biology. Ideally, you'll be able to find someplace quiet and cozy. If not, hopefully you can find someplace that's at least clean and safe. After airfare, lodging is the next biggest cost for travel. It's also one of the main ways most people waste money. Sure, fancy hotels can offer a much-needed respite from the workweek grind, but unless your goal is specifically to stay at a tropical resort, you're better off staying elsewhere.

The good news is, there are ways to save *a lot* of money. I've had days where I've spent more on food than where I slept, and I was able to sleep soundly and well.

When you're traveling on a budget, it's best to look at all lodging as a necessary but unfortunate cost. A place to leave your bags, sleep, and shower. That's it. All the rest is just decoration. Spend the money on something else. Here's how.

FIND ONLINE

Be sure to check out the links to web addresses from this chapter, as well as other helpful resources, at www.dummies.com/go/ budgettravelfd.

Accommodation Basics

I'm all about saving money, but when you're traveling for months at a time like me, your tolerance for bad beds and noisy neighbors goes way down. Fortunately, finding someplace comfortable doesn't usually require spending a lot.

The first shift in your mindset is to move away from the idea that fancy hotels are the only way to travel. That idea seems oddly and widely common. Not only is it wrong, it's also a waste of money. If the point of travel is to see someplace new, the inside of a hotel isn't it. Sure, there are some impressive-looking hotels all over the world, but once you get past the cool lobby, you're still just paying a lot of money in a place that you shouldn't be spending a lot of time.

TIP

With few exceptions, I'm primarily looking for some key things when it comes to places to stay. None of them are the star rating or the name above the entrance. In no particular order, I'm looking for

>> A great location

>> A place with good reviews

>> A great price

Secondly, I look for a place that has on-site laundry facilities, but I talk about that trick in Chapter 7.

You'll note there are some popular things missing from my list. I don't care if a place has a pool. I don't care if there's a restaurant or a masseuse. These things have their place, of course, but with a limited budget, you're better off spending your money on experiences unique to the area, exploring the location, or leaving some money in reserve for your next trip.

The fact is, expensive hotels are a waste of money. Is a gorgeous hotel more gorgeous than the sunset over the plains of Spain? More gorgeous than the view from the Burj Khalifa? Wouldn't it be better to spend the hundreds of dollars you'd spend on a hotel on more travel days, or travel days at all?

REMEMBER

Beyond a clean, comfortable bed and, hopefully, a warm shower, there isn't much more a budget traveler needs. With that mindset, you can save significantly on every adventure.

Comparing various accommodation types

Broadly speaking, travel accommodations come in three forms:

>> Hotels

>> Hostels

>> Rentals

You could throw in couch surfing and camping too, though those are a bit different. I'll talk about couch surfing in a section later in this chapter appropriately called, "Couchsurfing." Camping is a bit more challenging since you'd need to find a place to rent it, bring your own gear, or buy it when you arrive. I've done the latter and it can be fun, but unless camping is something you do regularly, it probably adds more of a challenge than is really necessary.

Over the years I've stayed in some of the nicest hotels in Asia, Europe, and the US I've also stayed in some absolute dives that only lacked rats because even they wouldn't risk it. I've stayed in hostels on six continents that ranged from "ehhhh" to incredible. I've even stayed in some Airbnb's that promised epic city views (that didn't) and others that claimed to be "cozy with views of the sunrise" that wildly undersold their awesomeness.

Which is to say, I've slept around. Wait, no. That sounds weird. I should say, I've slept in a lot of places. That sounds better. Here are some of the positives and negatives of the various types of accommodation you'll find. Obviously, these are fairly broad, as there are millions of establishments, but these generalizations should give you an idea about each.

Pros and cons of hotels

Hotels, and I'll include motels in the same category, tend to be professionally run facilities with fresh towels and bed sheets when you want them. You have your own room and bathroom, and usually the door is well secured with a deadbolt and a latch. Many hotels have TVs, safes, and air conditioning. You can book most through any number of third-party websites or directly from the hotel's own site.

Hotels are expensive, easily the most expensive places to stay in any area. A huge part of your budget will be going to a place that, at its core, is just somewhere to sleep. Cheap hotels are often under cleaned, with lumpy beds, loud air conditioning, and slow-draining showers. They can be gross, and still cost a lot of money. Lastly, they're not particularly communal. So, if you want to meet people while you're traveling, it's more difficult.

Pros and cons of hostels

Hostels tend to run the gamut between mom-and-pop-run places and larger, more corporate facilities. Typically, you have your own bunk in a shared "dorm" room with a shared bathroom, though some hostels have private rooms, too. Most hostels have lockers for your stuff. Most also have fully equipped kitchens with refrigerators you can use to store groceries, and common areas where you can relax and meet new friends. Best of all, they're often one of the cheapest options for travel.

Unless you pay extra for a private room, you're sharing a dorm and bathroom with strangers. Usually this is fine, because they're all strangers to each other, too, but sometimes this might be loud or otherwise annoying. While the best hostels are cleaned as often, or more often, than hotels, some aren't. There's just as wide a range between good hostels and bad as there are good hotels and bad, but the former is somewhat offset by the far lower cost compared to a hotel.

I talk more about hostels in the section "The Secret to Inexpensive Lodging: Hostels (Wait, Keep Reading!)" later in the chapter.

Pros and cons of Airbnb and similar rental/homestays

Airbnb and similar sites/apps like Vrbo, Homestay, and others, let you rent out a room, apartment, or entire home. These can range from a guest bedroom in a suburb to a penthouse suite in the heart of the city. Generally, you'll start your stay with clean sheets and towels, but you'll need to do your own laundry if you want more during your stay. There's a near infinite variety of what you might get from one of these stays, and you might have access to a kitchen or any number of perks that make your stay more like home (or a cooler version of home). Potentially, they can offer a unique experience for similar or less money than a hotel.

You're renting a space from another person. That might be fine, or it might not. You might be promised one thing and find out when you arrive it's something different. I've had that happen about 35 percent of the time when I've tried Airbnb, which is rather ridiculously high. Prices also vary widely, and there are often tacked-on fees that make the whole endeavor more expensive than it first appears. Worse, there usually isn't immediate support if something goes wrong. I have a section later in this chapter about some of the horror stories I've had renting via Airbnb and some other reasons why it's not as great an option as it once seemed.

TIP

The worst places I've ever stayed were hotels, but I've stayed in some ratty hostels, too. The only reason I don't rate the latter lower is because a bad hostel is at least cheap compared to a bad hotel.

Finding the best location

Google Maps, or your favorite navigation app, is a huge help in finding the perfect place to stay. How far is it from public transit? Can you walk to the things you want to see? What's nearby? The Street View feature can give you an idea what the neighborhood looks like. Is the place you're considering cheap because it's in a sketchy area? Is it cheap because there's nothing around for miles in every direction?

I spend a lot of time finding the best location option, far more than what hotel has the best "amenities" or other perks. I'm not willing to spend money on a larger room, but I am willing to pay slightly more if it will save me time by being in a better location. As far as hostel locations, I'll generally weigh the location 40/60 to the rest of the apparent quality of the hostel. Which is to say, I won't stay in a bad hostel in a good area, but if one is a little worse than another option, but in a better location, I'll often go for the better location.

As I said before, there are other considerations beyond the lowest price. I'm not saying to splurge on a hotel/hostel just because it's a little closer to something you want to see, but there is a calculation between saving you time and spending money. If spending an extra $10 can save you a few hours walking, or let you get cheaper tickets on the metro, or get you a free shuttle to an airport, these are things worth entering into the overall "calculation."

Similar prices across the web

Much like airfare, hotel prices are often very similar or identical across the various third-party websites like Expedia, Kayak.com, Booking.com, and so on. That's largely because many of these seemingly different sites are in fact actually owned by either Expedia Group or Booking Holdings.

There are some differences and exceptions, though. While the same room at the same hotel is probably going to be roughly the same price, you might find different options on different sites. Booking.com, for example, often has hostels and Airbnb-style home and room rentals, too.

It's also worth checking what the price is on the hotel's own website. Some hotels might discount their fares slightly for those who give them money directly, not the remainder after a booking website takes their cut. If you don't mind making phone calls (I hate it), you might even try calling the hotel and being friendly with the front desk staff. Might be hard to do if you don't speak the language, but it's worth a shot. There might also be a discount booking through a smartphone app vs your computer.

TIP

Hotel points, via credit cards or loyalty programs, are a worse use of your time and money than airline points and programs. If a hotel is large enough to have such a program, it's almost certainly too expensive for true budget travel. You're better off using cards that give you cash back, or if you're a frequent traveler, focus on airline points.

The Secret to Inexpensive Lodging: Hostels (Wait, Keep Reading!)

If you've never stayed in a hostel, I'm positive you have the wrong idea about them. I base this on countless conversations with people who look at me in horror for even suggesting staying in a hostel. The fact is, staying in hostels is by far the easiest way to save money on travel. Not only that, hostels can be some of the most convenient and fun places to stay all over the world.

Perhaps I should start with a broad description of what constitutes a "hostel." Generally speaking, hostels have shared rooms and a shared bathroom. They could have as few as two beds, and as many as a few dozen. Usually, though, they sleep four to eight people in a room, often with bunk beds. Most hostels will have different room sizes as well, so if you prefer a smaller room with fewer people, but don't mind spending a little more per night, that's an option. Most hostels will supply under-bed, or nearby lockers for your stuff, and the better hostels have lights and power plugs at each bed.

Just like hotels, there are good hostels and bad hostels. The difference is a bad hotel still costs a lot of money. Also just like hotels, there are multiple review and booking websites, so it's easy to find the best hostel in an area.

Figure 5-1 shows a fairly typical hostel dorm room. Note the pull-out lockers under the bed. Some hostels have curtains for each bed, and most have a light and power outlet. Some have nicer décor; others are plainer.

Geoffrey Morrison

FIGURE 5-1: This hostel room in central London is on the small side for a four-bed room.

I've stayed in hundreds of hostels across every continent except Antarctica. My favorites I've stayed at multiple times. I've made several close friends at hostels, and many more travel friends that I've adventured with for a few days and then we've gone our separate ways. I did all this starting in my 30s.

Hostels are for everyone, and easily the best option for budget travelers. They're great either solo or couples/groups. Even families with children under 18 can save money with hostels compared to hotels, as many will let you book either a private room or every bed in a bunk room. I wouldn't have believed how great hostels were before I started staying in them regularly, but now I've stayed in so many amazing hostels, met so many incredible people, and had so many wonderful experiences, I regret not staying at them earlier in my travels.

Throughout this chapter I explain in more detail why hostels are such a great option. I'll also give you some tips for finding a good hostel and some advice for your first stay of hopefully many.

Staying in hostels can be a fun, safe way to travel inexpensively.

This is the secret no one tells you

Hostels are incredibly common throughout the world. In the US, and a few other countries, they have an almost hilariously bad, and incorrect, reputation. Part of this is because of a series of eponymous horror movies, but that was more a symptom than the actual problem. I think the negativity about hostels was handed down via a sort of received wisdom from parents. They stayed in bad hostels in their youth and warned their children away from them. Yet, in the decades since they stayed, there has been a huge change in hostels.

Regardless of the reason, this is often the hidden secret to saving money on travel. Instead of paying $100 or more for a hotel, you can spend $25 or less for a hostel. Just like hotels, you can almost always find ones that are clean and in great locations.

Hostels are a big reason why I can spend less than $50 a day to visit just about anywhere in the world. Sure, there are ways to spend less on hotels, but not this much less. You could couch surf, but hostels are almost always safer than staying with a stranger.

Hostels aren't what you think

What's your first reaction to the word "hostels?" Do you think of a dirty, crowded, smelly place? Do you picture an unsafe bunkhouse full of sketchy denizens? How about a beachside budget resort in Fiji? How about a spotlessly clean, airy and modern facility in the middle of Taipei? How about cozy memory foam mattresses, or comfy plush couches in front of a fireplace, or relaxing in a glass geodesic dome under the stars on the Isle of Sky.

Hostels run the gamut, just like every other accommodation. Is it possible that you'll bunk with some stinky weirdo? Yes. Is possible you'll meet a new best friend? Also yes. Is it most likely you'll have a clean and quiet place to stay with some fellow budget-minded travelers? Almost certainly.

Hostels aren't just for young adults

It's a misnomer that hostels are only for young adults. While it's true that some hostels have an upper age limit, the vast majority do not. The opposite, in fact. Almost all only allow adults over the age of 18 to stay in dorm rooms (more on staying with kids in hostels later in the chapter).

When I first started staying in hostels, I was 35. I was rarely the oldest person in the hostel. Often, I wasn't even the oldest in my room. At one hostel in France, I was the *youngest* person in my room. By half!

With hostel booking apps and websites, it's easy to find out if there's an age limit. It's pretty rare, though. These same apps and websites can also give you a general idea about the vibe of a place. There are party hostels, for sure, but in most areas there are more quiet and subdued hostels for people not interested in pub crawls and day drinking. If every picture a hostel posts is of 20-somethings drinking, that's a solid clue to what it's probably like to stay there.

That all said, hostels absolutely skew younger. The average age will vary, but under 25 is most common. If you're traveling up the east coast of Australia, for instance, all your roommates will be 18-year-old Brits on their first solo vacation and Germans on a gap year.

Hostels skewing younger makes sense, of course, since people that age combine the enviable attribute of having the time to travel, with the frustrating lack of funds to do so. As long as you're polite and courteous to those around you, most people staying in hostels aren't going to care how old you are.

What's a high-end hostel?

One of the biggest changes in the last decade or so is the increasing number of high-end hostels. These are exactly what they sound like: Accommodations that are practically luxury, boutique hotels. The only difference is shared rooms. These hostels will have elaborate and stunning common areas and usually pair that with ultra-comfortable beds.

As you'd guess, these high-end hostels come with high-end prices. One example in Venice, literally across the canal from St. Marks, can cost upwards of $100 a night just for a bed. There goes your budget. But if you absolutely want to stay in Venice — admittedly, that is an amazing experience — even a cheap hotel on some remote canal can be many times that price (or just stay in nearby Mestre which is cheaper and just a few minutes by train).

Generally, though, the prices are still far more reasonable compared to hotels. Is it worth splurging on an epic hostel in the perfect location for approximately $40 a night? When a crappy hotel in that same area probably costs two to three times that if you're lucky, maybe.

Meet new people, or not

One of the defining characteristics of hostels is shared dorm rooms, usually with two to four bunkbeds, so up to eight people total. I've stayed in some rooms with no bunk beds and one where the beds were stacked three high! I've stayed in small rooms with just one other bed and a huge dorm with 32. The latter is pretty rare, thankfully, as are towering stacks of bunkbeds. I've stayed in full rooms, and occasionally I've had rooms to myself.

Regardless of how they're set up, you're in a room with a handful of fellow travelers. Do you want to meet them? I hope so. But if you don't, usually people respect others enough to leave them alone if that's what they want.

Many hostels, however, also have private rooms. These are almost like a hotel, except you'll usually share a bathroom. Prices on these rooms tend to be about halfway between a dorm room and a hotel. I don't think, in most areas, you'll be able to hit the $50 a day budget staying alone in private rooms, but if you're absolutely against sharing a room or want some privacy as a couple this is still almost always cheaper than a hotel, and usually nicer.

I don't know of any hostel that allows children under 18 to stay in dorm rooms, but many hostels have the option to rent out an entire dorm room if they don't have private rooms. Will this be cheaper than a hotel? Depends on the area, but it's not uncommon to see families in hostels, so it's worth checking the prices.

Private rooms in hostels are also a sneaky gateway to staying in dorm rooms. Once you get used to sharing your space, via the common rooms and perhaps the bathroom, you might get comfortable with the type of people you meet in hostels, which are often going to be people just like you.

Perhaps you can bond over this great book you read called *Budget Travel For Dummies.* Just an example.

REMEMBER

Just like hotels, there are good hostels and bad hostels. There are expensive hostels, and there are cheap hostels. Check the reviews before you book.

The Benefits of Hostels and Hostel Life

The benefits of hostels go beyond the initial cost savings, though that is obviously significant. Prices vary, of course, but hotels are usually around $100, often more, occasionally less. Hostels are around $25, rarely go above $50, and often are even less. So, all else being equal, you could save over $1,000 on a two-week trip not staying in a hotel.

That's only the start of the benefits. Most hostels have full kitchens, so you can buy groceries and make your own food. If you're as skilled in the kitchen as I am you can store bread and peanut butter (okay, Nutella) for sandwiches.

You also have the option to meet like-minded travelers, either to make new friends or have a temporary travel buddy with whom you can check out the area and share some adventures.

TIP

While there are lots of ways to save money on travel, one of the biggest is staying in hostels over hotels.

Drastically lower your per-day expense

No matter how you look at it, staying in hostels is significantly cheaper than staying in hotels. In any area where you can find a cheap hotel, a nearby hostel is going to be cheaper. Over the length of any trip, this could save you hundreds, if not thousands, of dollars.

Of course, sometimes this isn't possible. There are more hotels than hostels, and in some areas there just aren't any hostels available. There's also any number of legitimate reasons why you might not want to stay in a hostel. I say legitimate because "ew, no" or "I've never stayed in a hostel" aren't good reasons. I used to feel that way because that was the received wisdom I had gotten about hostels, and I was wrong. Staying in hostels is a gamechanger for budget travel.

If you're traveling with someone else, that does reduce the average cost. A $100 a night hotel is $50 per person. Still double what you'd pay for 2 beds at a $25 a night hostel, but certainly better than four times the difference if you're traveling alone.

Convenient kitchens and refrigerators

After air travel and accommodation, food is usually the next biggest travel cost. You've gotta eat, something my growing waistline can attest. There are often lots of inexpensive food options, but rarely can you beat the cost of groceries. Being able to cook up a bunch of pasta or rice to eat over the course of a few days is about as inexpensive a meal as you can have. Add in some veggies and whatever protein you prefer, and you've got some fairly healthy meals for just a few dollars.

The two issues are: Where do you cook, and where do you keep the food? Many hotels have refrigerators, and some have kitchens, but these aren't as common as those without. In some areas they can be even more expensive. The majority of hostels have a kitchen, and if they do, they likely have a big fridge for you to store your food.

It's also a great way to meet friends. I was staying in a small hostel in Nice and ended up getting to know a guy who, like me, kept extending his stay. He worked as crew on yachts and was in-between gigs. This meant he was broke. I am legendarily lazy when it comes to cooking. We worked out a fantastic deal where I paid for the groceries and he did the cooking. This played to his strengths as a cook my strengths of not being a cook. We often had leftovers, which let us both make even more friends.

Even if you're not lucky enough to find someone to cook for you, it's easy enough to store sandwich fixings, fruit, really anything you'd have at home that you can find a local version of to eat. Keep an eye out for house rules on food though. They'll want you to label your food, or it gets thrown out (makes sense). Also, like cooking fish in an office microwave, it's best to avoid stinky foods.

Location (location, location)

If you're visiting a city for the first time, it can be magical to wake up and step right out into the thick of it. One of the things I try to avoid is long daily commutes to wherever I'm visiting. Hostels can often help with this. Since they can be profitable at lower prices in smaller buildings, it's easier for a small hostel to take over a residential space in the heart of a city.

Are there also hotels in the best parts of a city? Of course! But they're often even more expensive. A budget hotel is almost certainly on the outskirts of a city, or in a less desirable area.

I've mentioned before, but it's important to include "time" as part of your overall budget. If you save a few dollars, but you lose hours a day getting to and from where you're staying, is that worth it? If it's the difference between being able to travel and not, then absolutely. If it's just the cost of one less big meal on your trip, but hours more each day exploring somewhere cool, then maybe. Staying in a hostel that's right where you want to explore is fantastic. I've stayed in a hostel in the heart of Istanbul, minutes' walk from the Hagia Sofia mosque, another right on the Sumida River in Tokyo, another just a short walk from multiple train and Underground stations in London, another with a view of sunsets over the Indian Ocean in Perth, and many more. These same locations would have cost me a fortune if they were hotels.

Easy-to-get local advice for what to see and do

All hostels are staffed either by locals, or people who have been living in that city for a while. At the very least, they're going to know what the best things to do are, and what should be avoided. Many might be able to give you an entire itinerary of cool things and great eats.

Sometimes, you can get advice like this at a hotel. What you can't get as easily at a hotel is advice from your fellow travelers. While you're cooking dinner, hanging out in the common areas, or just in your room, the other people at your hostel are either looking to do similar things as you, or have already done them. Maybe they know that something's closed even though the website says otherwise. Maybe they know something cool to do that's not on any list. Maybe, and this is always great, they want to join you.

Brilliant for solo travelers

As I've mentioned throughout this chapter, hostels are amazing for solo travelers. This is because most people staying at a hostel are also solo travelers. If you want someone to explore with, share your adventure with, split the cost of a cab, or even just to make a new friend, you're in a room with several other people who are just as nervous and awkward as you are.

Hostels know this. The best hostels run group events every night or close to it. Walking tours of the city, cooking lessons, and of course, the infamous bar crawl. I made boba tea from scratch in one hostel (Taiwan, obviously), participated in trivia/game nights, and have done numerous bar/pub crawls. Even if you're not a heavy drinker, these can be a great way to meet people and see parts of the city you might not otherwise see.

If you're open to the idea of meeting new people, you're going to meet new people. Is every one of those people going to be your new bestie? Probably not. Will you talk to them all after you all leave? Probably not. However, every once and a while you'll meet someone and make a connection. Maybe you're social media friends. Maybe you send each other memes late at night. Maybe you talk so much the distance between your respective homes means nothing. Maybe you end up traveling together once you leave the hostel, and again the next year, and the year after and the year after — travel buddies (and maybe more) for life!

Hostels for Dummies

If you've never stayed in a hostel, or it's been a while since you have, there are some unspoken (and sometimes loudly spoken) rules. These are generally the same guidelines that help roommates get along in any situation.

A hostel may have their own house rules, too, which they'll tell you when you check in. Some don't care if you have food in the room, while others strictly forbid it. Some have very specific lights-out hours, but others don't care. Keep an eye out for group activity boards if they're not specifically mentioned at check-in. Kitchens will have food-specific rules posted somewhere too.

The following sections walk you through the basics you should know before staying in a hostel for the first time.

Basic hostel etiquette

In this section, I go over some basic "rules" about staying in a hostel. Even if you've stayed in hostels before, these are worth keeping in mind. Many are the same rules that you'd have in any shared space. If you've never had roommates, or it has been a while, read on.

» Be as quiet as possible. No talking on the phone, listening to videos or music without headphones, and so on. I hate that this has to be the first rule, but I've seen offenders of all ages and cultures do this one.

» Related to the above, put your phone on vibrate or silent.

» No sleeping bags. You'll get your own bedding. They don't want you bringing bedbugs.

» Avoid plastic bags. The rustling of a plastic bag at 5 a.m. might as well be an air horn. They are surprisingly loud.

» Don't hog the bathroom.

» Keep your bunk area tidy. I don't normally see people spreading out their stuff everywhere, but it can happen and is ideally avoided.

» Store food in the kitchen unless explicitly told it's okay in the rooms. Depending on the food and area, this could lead to smells or, worse, bugs.

» It's other people's space just as much as it is yours.

Details to consider (private rooms, single-sex dorms, no kids, and so on)

While the average hostel consists of dorm rooms and shared bathrooms, many have other options worth considering. One of the most notable are private rooms. These are single-bed rooms, usually without a bathroom. They're almost always cheaper than a hotel room. I've even stayed in a few hostels that have private rooms with a bathroom and shower, so basically a hotel room within a hostel. These were cheaper than a "real" hotel, though not by much.

Then there's the room size. The more beds in a room, the cheaper it is to stay. If you're counting every penny, go for the biggest room possible. In some hostels this could be ten beds or more. For a few additional dollars a night, a smaller room with two to four beds might make for a quieter stay. I've had great stays in big rooms and small, so I wouldn't say one is better than another.

Many hostels have women-only dorms. These are usually, and inexplicably, more expensive than their like-sized co-ed counterparts. They're worth considering if you don't like the idea of sharing a space with the opposite sex. I will say one thing, though. In my experience co-ed dorms are cleaner than single-sex dorms. For whatever reason, most people tend to be tidier around the opposite sex.

As mentioned earlier, most hostels won't allow anyone under 18 in dorm rooms. If you're traveling with someone under 18, many hostels will let you book out an entire room or direct you toward one of their private rooms. Will these be cheaper than a hotel? Probably, but I've stayed in a few hostels that were a little more, I'll say, rowdy than most parents would like for their younglings. A wild hostel is going to be a wild hostel even if you have your own room. Proceed accordingly.

Since most hostels have bunk beds, it's best to request which you want ahead of time. You might not get the type you prefer, but asking before you arrive is your best chance. Personally, I prefer the bottom bunk as it's just easier, but I know many people who prefer the privacy of a top bunk.

Handy must-haves to have on hand

There are a few things that are either important, or vital, to have on hand for your hostel stay.

The first is a towel. Some hostels have towels to rent, but not all. I bring a full-sized camping pack towel with me. These microfiber towels dry you off quickly, and then dry out themselves almost as fast. They fold and roll down to the size of a paperback book. It's best to be a frood who really knows where his towel is, at least according to the Hitchhiker's Guide.

I also pack either flip-flops or water shoes. These come in handy on the beach and when showering in a shared bathroom. Most hostels clean their bathrooms daily, but hey, it can't hurt not to be barefoot.

A small lock for your locker is a good idea. Nearly every hostel has lockers or other in-room storage for your luggage. Some have locks you can rent, but you're better off bringing your own. I use the same lock to lock the zippers on my bag, just removing it from my bag and putting it on the locker.

If you're a light sleeper, earplugs are handy. I've only needed them a few times, and I wake up easily. Some hostels will offer these for free when you check in, but since they're so small and inexpensive, packing a few pairs is a good idea. Earplugs are good even if you have noise canceling headphones (more on these in Chapter 7). While they can be amazing on a plane, most noise-canceling headphones aren't great for the human voice and snore frequencies. So don't count on them to block out those noises in a hostel. Earplugs are also soft and squishy, so they're easier to sleep on.

If you think you might need it, an eye mask to block light can help. The amount of room light varies a lot hostel to hostel. I've been in some where each room has lots of windows, a few with tiny windows, and a couple with no windows (those are weird and thankfully rare). A growing number of hostels have curtains for each bed, so the light in the room is less of an issue. This feature is more common in Asia, but it's thankfully becoming more wide-spread. The extra privacy is great.

Lastly, most newer hostels will have USB or other power at each bed, but not all. I've stayed in some hostels where twelve-plus beds had to share two outlets. That was frustrating, to say the least. I recommend a good charger and a long cable or two. I will talk more about these in Chapter 7 as well.

Hostel examples around the world

This part is difficult. On one hand, I want to give you some concrete examples of amazing hostels where I've stayed. On the other hand, you're reading this in the future. Hello, future! I hope the future is cool and there's lots of ice cream.

So I've picked a few example hostels — some special standouts — that are not only places I'd go back to in a heartbeat but are also still in business several years (and one pandemic) after I first stayed there. Hopefully they're still in business when you read this. Even if they aren't, the internet being what it is, you should be able to find some photos and info about them to give you an idea what makes them special.

>> **Star Hostel Taipei Main Station:** This is the hostel that always comes to my mind when someone's face puckers at the idea of staying in a hostel. It's immaculately clean, with a big kitchen and one of the coolest features I've ever seen: a wood-framed house inside the multi-story common area. The curtained bunks offer comfort and privacy. There are even private rooms available. Best of all, the staff is some of the friendliest I've ever encountered.

>> **Chapter Two Tokyo:** This small hostel is my favorite place to stay in Tokyo. The owners are fantastically friendly and keep everything spotless. Some of the bunks have windows that look out over the river at the Skytree. It's also walking distance to two important subway lines.

>> **Generator:** These are a chain of high-end hostels mostly in Europe. They feature incredible designs, looking more like a boutique hotel. Each has local flair, and all are gorgeous. The Dublin location, for example, has exposed brick and green glass bottle chandeliers to celebrate the adjacent Jameson Distillery. The London location has part of a double decker bus in the lounge. All typically have great locations, too, near metro stops or the city center. However, they tend to be much more expensive than typical hostels, and most are enormous. Hundreds of guests doesn't mean you can't meet people. I met one of my best friends at Generator London, but these all feel very big and very corporate.

>> **Mantaray Island Resort:** This certainly stretches the definition of "hostel" but if that definition is "multi-person bunk room" with shared bathrooms, then it still fits. This particular "hostel" is an oceanside resort on one of the tiny

Yasawa islands in the Fijian archipelago with beachside hammocks, warm, azure blue waters — it's perfect. Prices vary depending on the season, but typically a bed in the bunk room is under $30, a little more than hostels on the Viti Levu mainland. However, you also have to pay $60 a day for food. Since the food is excellent, that's not terrible. While $90 a day is certainly more than my standard budget, it's for a literal Pacific Island paradise. Compare that to the hundreds per day you'd spend in a typical hotel in this region and I'll call that a huge budget win. The staff was also absolutely delightful. I wish I was there right now.

>> **Gilligan's Backpacker Hotel & Resort:** I wasn't sure if I wanted to include this hostel on the list. It is . . . an experience. Famous (infamous?) among those backpacking up the east coast in Australia, Gilligan's is more a nightclub with a hostel attached than a hostel with a nightclub. It's huge, loud, and almost always totally bonkers. I met some great people here, had some great times, but it's absolutely not a place I'd recommend to my parents. However, if you're backpacking in Australia, by the time you get up to Cairns, Gilligan's isn't anything you haven't experienced already.

There are a bunch of others I want to mention because I had such a great experience at them. That might have been the people who were there at the time, my state of mind when I was there, or just the atmosphere created by the owners and staff. To name just two, Nomads Queenstown is one of several incredible hostels in that amazing New Zealand town. The family that owns Hostel Miran in Mostar, Bosnia, and Herzegovina, are wonderfully welcoming and run a great day tour of the area.

Other Inexpensive Lodgings

There are other inexpensive options beyond hostels, of course, though they tend to be less consistent and more region specific. What might be a great option in one place won't be in another. This makes it a bit harder to give advice.

Then there's your personal level of comfort. I've met people scared to stay in dorm rooms, and I've met others who will sleep on a stranger's couch without hesitation. I can't speak to that, so it's up to you. Personally, I think a dorm, with multiple strangers, will be safer than staying with a singular stranger in their home, but your mileage may vary, as they say.

There are a lot of good people out there, and only a handful of crazies. Odds are you'll be fine, but it never hurts to be safe.

Couchsurfing

There are apps and websites that let you find people who will offer a couch, or even a spare bed, for little or no money exchanged. Some people just like meeting travelers and helping out people on tight budgets.

I have never done this, at least, not with total strangers (more on my version a little later). I have met several people who have tried this with strangers, both in Europe and Australia, two places where this is fairly popular. Their results were . . . mostly good. They usually got meals and either a comfy couch or an entire bedroom for themselves. I believe no money was asked for or accepted.

In one case, the host was, as my friend said, "a bit creepy." Nothing bad happened, but it was clear he had an agenda for opening his house to strangers. If you look like me, that might be less of a potential issue. If you don't, it's a risk. How big a risk? Hard to say. I'm sure most of you reading this who know exactly what I'm talking about already have your own internal calculation for this kind of risk, and there's nothing worthwhile I could add.

Couchsurfing is potentially an even cheaper way to travel, but like anything, there are pros and cons. With a variety of apps available, and the reviews of potential hosts they all have, it's probably the next level of budget beyond hostels that is just waiting for more people to explore. I'll stick with my method which you'll read about at the end of the chapter.

Why Airbnb isn't as cheap as it seems

When Airbnb and similar home-stay apps exploded into the mainstream, it seemed like a traveler's dream. What could be better than staying at a local's place, either alone or with them, for far less than what some corporate hotel charged. Yeah, those were the good old days.

Those days are long gone. Is it still possible to find great places to stay for cheap? Maybe? Sometimes? Rarely? With their incredible popularity, Airbnb and their ilk are big, big business. There are entire companies whose sole purpose is to find and manage Airbnb rentals. Prices have also gone through the roof, pun intended. Per-night rates are often reasonable, and then when you're ready to check out a bunch of additional fees get tacked on so you're suddenly paying more than if you'd stayed at a hotel.

Prices aside, there's also the issue of misleading posts. Multiple times I've reserved a room or apartment, only to get an entirely different apartment in the same building. Instead of skyline views, I got the security lights of Bob's Junk and Dump.

Another time I reserved an apartment for a friend and I in Las Vegas for a trade show. Airbnb took my deposit months before the event, and everything seemed fine. I had messaged the host and didn't hear back, which in hindsight was a red flag. Airbnb sent us the check-in info that day and everything still seemed fine . . . until we showed up. The door code didn't work because, incredibly, the host had literally sold the apartment months earlier and never bothered to tell Airbnb. We were lucky because we could get a hotel nearby, though it cost way more, and we did get our money back. Can you imagine that happening to you on your vacation in an area you don't know?

Another occasion I had to walk 30 minutes in the rain to get the key for an Airbnb in Gold Coast, Australia, only to get to the lock box (in the basement of a random car park no less) and find no key. I contacted the host, who responded 30 minutes later calling me a liar. They told me to send them pictures of the empty lock box, as if that proved anything. An hour and a half later they admitted they'd given the key to a guy to fix something and forgot. I got the key 30 minutes later, with visions of the Las Vegas debacle vividly in my mind.

While I'm extremely hesitant to stay in Airbnb's, there have been the occasional gems. I stayed in a penthouse apartment of a highrise in Hong Kong with 360-degree views of the city for less than any hotel in the area. A different spot in Gold Cost offered sunrise views over the ocean, and thanks to being the off season, it was super cheap.

It's a big world and I certainly can't say you'll never find a deal on a place to stay. If you're traveling with friends or family, it's often a great way to find a place large enough for everyone, bringing the total cost of the trip way down. They can be more private than a hostel, and if you're careful, cheaper than a hotel. I would just approach these apps with caution. They're often far more luxury than budget, though there are deals to be had.

The best? Meeting people and staying with them!

My favorite travel hack: Make friends and sleep on their couch! Not only have I done this all over, but even better, many of them have come and stayed on my couch! That's perhaps the benefit of living "Hollywood Adjacent" (random travel tip: the neighborhood of Hollywood is gross and the least interesting part of Los Angeles).

How this plays out varies a bit. My friend I met at Generator London was moving to Italy the following week. I stayed with her there for a few days after she moved in. I met a wonderful couple on Fraser Island in Australia. I drove them around L.A. when they visited, and later stayed in their spare room after they got home to England. I'm lucky enough to have made friends who live all over, and those that can have lent me a couch for a few nights.

The difficult part is, perhaps surprisingly, making friends. Sorry to get serious and a little deep, but making friends as an adult is hard! Depending on your age, this either reads as obvious or ridiculous. The fact is, for most people once you get out of college making new friends gets much, much harder. Everyone has less time, you're rarely forced to be in the same place, and people just have *lives*. Sure, there are adult sports leagues, religious organizations, local pubs, and other community activities, but even then it's still a lot harder to connect than when you were the same size in the same place and doing the same thing, such as complaining about the same teacher day in and day out.

Before I started traveling extensively, I'd met all my close friends in college or through work. Now, I'd say it's about 50/50 them and new friends I made while traveling. Some of the most important people in my life now I'd never have met if it weren't for travel, not least because they live all over the world.

I hate to sound like a broken record, but this really does speak to the incredible possibilities that open up when you stay in hostels. It's like you're back in school, minus the homework and curfews. You all have shared interests (travel, the city you're visiting), you're in close proximity, and for endless reasons you've ended up in that place at that time.

TIP

Remember, most people staying in hostels are traveling by themselves. Most people are also pretty shy around strangers. Most people *also* love meeting new people. You could start a lifelong friendship just by sticking out your hand and saying "Hi, I'm Geoff."

Okay, maybe not those exact words. Unless your name is actually Geoff (or one of those "Jeff" weirdos) in which case, rock on.

Chapter 6

Taking the "Lug" Out of Luggage

O ne of the easiest ways to reduce stress and make your trip easier is to pack well. And by well, I mean as little as possible. The trick is not only knowing what to pack, which I discuss in Chapter 7, but also having the right luggage. Not something you dread dragging around, but a dependable companion for easier and more efficient travel. Something you'll love so much you'll sing its virtues to anyone who will listen (okay, maybe that's just me).

That first trip where you can skip baggage claim, effortlessly navigate a metro system, and cross a cobblestoned city with ease, you'll endlessly thank your pre-trip luggage-selecting and lightly packing self.

What You Can't Leave Behind (but Should)

The worst thing to think while packing is "well, I might need it." Stop. You won't. Whether it's a third parka or your antique teapot, you won't need it. Maybe you'll get invited to a black-tie dinner at the governor's palace, but chances are you won't. It's easy to start worrying about the endless possibilities that could happen during your adventure, and then what will happen if you don't have the right clothes, shoes, or gear. Those things are almost certainly not going to happen, and if they do, you can buy what you need where you're going. Surprise dinner at a fancy restaurant? Time to treat yourself to a new shirt. New friends want to take you clubbing? Time to find a cool local dress.

It's completely understandable to worry about what might happen, but those "what ifs" aren't *likely* to happen. The most likely things are likely for a reason. The tiny chance something unexpected happens, you can deal with that in the moment. This is way better than lugging around lots of stuff you won't need.

TIP

Only pack what you can easily carry. If you can't lift it over your head, you've packed too much.

Why traveling light is the best gift you can give yourself

Picture yourself in an old city in Europe. Tiny streets of stone, narrow alleyways, and you, dragging your massive bag over yet another unforgiving curb. Or picture yourself in Japan. You're trying to get from Tokyo to Osaka. The Shinkansen is crowded. The luggage rack is full, and your bag doesn't fit on the overhead shelf. You're holding up a line of decreasingly patient Japanese commuters as you try to figure out what to do with your Kei car-sized suitcase.

These are just a few of the endless possibilities that could be avoided if you pack less. I know, because I used to pack way too much. Some would argue I still do, even though I only have one backpack. Maybe it's just me, but I still cringe thinking about the hassle I caused trying to fit my enormous luggage onto a crowded night train in China or squeezing into an airline seat with a backpack overflowing with things I'd never use on the flight.

After that China trip I vowed to pack as little as possible, and it was a game changer. My next trip I scaled down to a carry-on-sized roller bag for a three-week trip across Sweden, Norway, and the UK. Having managed that, my next trip was the start of what I call my "extended travels" — three months in Australia, New Zealand, Singapore, and Thailand, all with a single travel backpack. (I'll discuss these awesome bags later in the chapter in the section, "Backpack versus Luggage.") I went from overpacking and enduring the endless struggle of cumbersome luggage to being able to travel indefinitely with one easily carriable backpack.

REMEMBER

Having luggage you can easily carry and maneuver yourself will save you time, hassle, and embarrassment everywhere in the world.

Move fast, don't break things

I was sitting in a train station in Valencia, Spain. I'd arrived early and was enjoying a lunch of tapas and the best Coca-Cola in the world (I have no explanation for why it is, it just is). I'd been keeping an eye on the departure board for my train, a high-speed AVE to Madrid. Once there I'd have about an hour to find the bus that would take me to Lisbon.

With about 20 minutes to departure, I finally asked a station agent why my specific train wasn't on the big board. She looked at me, horrified on my behalf, telling me that I was at the wrong station. I was at València Nord. The high-speed trains left from the nearby Valencia-Joaquín Sorolla, which if you don't zoom in on the map and don't understand that a city could have two nearly adjacent stations both called "Valencia" for short, you sure could be sitting like an idiot waiting for a train that will never, ever arrive. Even better, the last shuttle between the two stations before my train's departure had just left. Google Maps listed the distance as 10 minutes, from the corners of the stations closest to each other. I was not at that corner, and I needed to go beyond the other corner to get to my actual train. If I missed this train, I'd miss the bus that would get me to Lisbon. So I hoofed it.

Now, I want you to imagine having to navigate a busy station, then out onto the street, up and down multiple curbs, weaving around meandering pedestrians, all while wrangling a heavy, bulky piece of luggage that's fighting you back out of spite because it knows you should have more closely read your ticket. Nightmare fuel, I know. Don't get me wrong, this also isn't easy with a backpack.

More than anything, I'd advise avoiding such a situation alto-gether. But having everything contained and secured on your per-son, with your hands free to use Google Maps on your phone while you half run, half jog your way to your soon-departing train, is all way easier.

I did make it to my train, by the way, far sweatier than I'd started. I hadn't even taken my seat before the train left for Madrid.

Save on luggage fees

An easy way to save money on flights is by not paying for addi-tional services. Nearly all airlines charge for checked luggage now. You can avoid these fees by having frequent flier status with the airline or by never checking your luggage.

Airlines aren't the only ones with luggage rules. Some train ser-vices might require you to reserve a space in the luggage rack. As annoying as that might be, I also can't remember the last time I saw open space for luggage on a UK train. In many places there's a maximum weight and size limit for luggage. Then there's the question of whether it will fit in a small taxi. Will it fit in a tuk-tuk? Actually, it probably will — those things can carry anything.

Travel easier on buses, trains, cars, and more

One more bag-related story: A few years ago I hatched the "bril-liant" idea of trying to get to San Sebastian, in northern Spain, from Newcastle, in northern England, entirely by train. This was partly because I thought it would be funny and partly because there were no convenient flights. Also, my editor at CNET thought it'd make for a good story, so off I went.

The result was a fairly relaxing 14-hour journey punctuated by moments of sheer panic. For instance, the Eurostar was delayed outside of Paris, meaning I had less than an hour to get from Gare du Nord in the north of the city, to Gare Montparnasse in the south. This *seems* straightforward enough, since Line 4 connects the two. The reality is somewhat different. I needed to get from the arrival platform, down several flights of escalators and stairs, just barely make it on the rubber-wheeled subway, wait impa-tiently while it made seemingly infinite stops, then out onto a crowded platform. Then up more escalators, race along apparently kilometers of moving walkways, up more escalators and stairs to the station proper, through this crowded station, all the way down to the last platform (because of course), to finally board and take my seat, sweaty and relieved, moments before the train departed for Hendaye on the Spanish border.

If I'd been slowed at any point in that, either by the stairs, escalators, or needing to finagle a roller bag through a crowd, I would have missed that exact subway train and then I'd have missed the only TGV that would have gotten me to Hendaye in time for the bus that got me across the border to San Sebastian.

You know, in hindsight, why do I do these things to myself? In this case, it made for a great story. It also solidified my love of a good backpack. Being easily mobile is a game changer, not only for self-induced calamities like the above adventure, but also the potential/inevitable time-crunch dash to get to a bus, train, or plane.

Don't underestimate the myriad ways having all your belongings well-secured to your frame will make your travel easier.

TIP

Shocking game changer: laundry

Nearly every hostel and hotel has a laundry facility. Those that don't, there's almost always one nearby. This is the easiest way to pack less. Travel with five to seven days of clothes, and if the trip is longer, carve out a few hours some morning or evening to do laundry. It will only cost the equivalent a few dollars. This is the key to all long-term travel, and why I can go for months with just one backpack. Literally no one will care if you wear the same thing twice on a vacation.

What's the cutoff for bringing something to wear each day versus doing laundry? There are a few variables. First is how much you can easily pack in your bag, which is hopefully carry-on sized. Unless you're bringing specialized gear for your adventure (scuba masks, ski boots, and so on), a typical carry-on bag can easily carry a week's worth of clothes and a change of shoes. If you're heading somewhere colder, you might only have room for a few days plus extra thermal layers.

Generally, though, there's no reason to ever bring more than a week's worth of clothes. I talk more about what to pack, and what not to pack, in Chapter 7.

REMEMBER

Don't Waste Money on Luggage

Many years ago I was on a flight that, due to some issue, had departed without luggage. So everyone had "lost" luggage. The airline promised they'd deliver the missing luggage, but for whatever reason they needed us to file a claim after we arrived at the airport.

Picture this: an entire plane full of tired and irritated passengers waiting at the lost luggage counter. There we watched, with increasing irritation, while one passenger lost their entire mind, full-on screaming at the airline employee. Were they upset about the lost luggage? Nope, this person wasn't even on our flight. This person was having an Olympic-class public freakout because the airline had . . . *scratched* their luggage. You read that right. There was a barely visible, six-inch scratch on their black designer hardshell. I'm a pretty calm person, but I wanted to toss this person onto the baggage carousel.

A few things here:

WARNING

>> First of all, your luggage is going to get tossed around. Its entire purpose is to protect your actual belongings.

Do not, under any circumstances, spend so much on luggage that you'll be upset if something happens to it. Something happening to it is its job.

>> Second, the only people more annoyed with complaints about a scratch on your luggage, other than airline employees, are the people behind you in line whose luggage is actually lost.

Now if the airline has run your luggage over with a 777 or chummed it through the 9-foot blades of a GEnx turbofan like a Cuisinart, okay sure, that's worth a complaint.

REMEMBER

The point of luggage is to hold and protect your stuff. In that role it's going to take damage. In a perfect world it wouldn't, but we don't live in that world.

Expensive luggage is a waste of money

Against my better judgment, I let a colleague talk me into reviewing large, wheeled luggage. They didn't let me say what I wanted to, which was "don't buy these." Their perspective, and they were right, was that people were going to buy these so we might as well find the best one. Okay, that's fair.

I got in massive suitcases that cost hundreds of dollars. I've lived in countries for weeks for what some of these bags cost. Was the most expensive one nice? Sure. Was it worth nearly $1,400? Absolutely not. Was it three-and-a-half times better than the $400 one? Still no.

The better wheeled luggage had sturdier handles, better internal organization, and smoother wheels. Those attributes didn't have much to do with price, however. Some of the cheaper options outperformed more expensive options. The real kicker, to me anyway, was that even the cheapest large wheeled luggage cost more than double the backpack that had been my reliable companion across dozens of countries for years.

WARNING

Spending outrageous amounts on luggage, literally just the bag you need to hold some stuff, is a waste. Get something decent, sure, but there are countless great options that don't cost the equivalent of a week's worth of travel. Also, large, wheeled luggage is too easy to overpack and too difficult to manage while you're on your trip.

Most of the world isn't smooth concrete

I traveled a bunch with a dear friend who resisted packing light. I had one backpack for three months; she had two roller bags for two weeks. The endless issues navigating trains was frustrating enough, but the real pain was trying to get from train stations and airports to where we were staying. Inevitably there was cracked concrete, unavoidable potholes, and of course the bane of all wheel luggage: cobblestones. One bag repeatedly vomited its contents onto crowded streets. It's easy enough to test out a suitcase in a store, or even at home, and think it works great. The world, however, is not a flat, smooth surface. You'll need to haul that baggage up and down hills. Worse, there are stairs everywhere. Not every hotel has an elevator, and in many parts of the world, ramps are rare. So you're going to need to awkwardly lift and lug something designed to roll, not be carried.

If you're only ever going from the airport to a taxi to a hotel, then it doesn't matter what your luggage can do. But if you're reading this, I'm guessing there's far more walking in your adventures, and that's when all wheeled luggage starts to become more hindrance than help.

Smaller luggage lets you focus on what you really need

Every luggage and backpack company wants to sell you a larger bag than you need because they're more expensive. It also plays into the inevitable pre-travel "what if" scenarios all of us ponder that leads to overpacking. If you force yourself to get a smaller bag than you think you need, it then forces you to figure out what's truly important. You can't overpack.

Now that's easier said than done. If you've always traveled with huge luggage, it's going to be quite a challenge to figure out what to pack into something the size of a carry-on. It's not hard though. I've got detailed lists in Chapter 7.

REMEMBER

You can't pack for every possible scenario, so don't. Pack for what the weather's expected to be, and if something changes you can always buy something there. It might even be cheaper than something similar at home.

If you can't easily carry it, it's too much

I keep coming back to this point because it's key: You don't need to bring an entire armoire on vacation. An airline's luggage weight limits shouldn't matter to you at all. You shouldn't get anywhere close to them. Even if you have heavy camera gear like me, it's nearly impossible to max out a weight limit with carry-on-sized luggage. Many airlines don't even weigh carry-ons.

The main exception is going on an adventure that requires heavy gear. Ski boots, scuba tanks, a saddle, sure, I can see how your luggage might weigh a bit more. Walking around a city for two weeks though? You only need a carry-on.

Backpack versus Luggage

There are endless styles of luggage, but we can sort them into two broad categories:

>> Backpacks
>> Luggage (aka suitcases, aka rollers, aka roller bags)

There are even crossovers between those two categories, "hybrids" if you will, but we'll cut the line down the middle between items designed to mostly sit on your back, and those designed to mostly get push/pulled on wheels.

Within those categories are sub-varieties that make massive differences during travel. I've reviewed all kinds of backpacks and luggage for *The New York Times'* Wirecutter and *USA Today's* Reviewed. I've also traveled extensively with many different types of both. Which is to say, I've done a lot of research on this topic. What follows is a distillation of that down into some reasonably concise sections.

No matter what kind you get, the smaller the better. You should aim to have something carry-on sized that's easy to maneuver.

TIP

My subjective opinion: Backpacks are best

I am a huge proponent of backpacks. Unless you physically can't carry a backpack, I'd start your luggage search here first. I'm sure the first image you have of someone traveling with a backpack is of a towering monstrosity that's bigger than they are, weighs more than they do, causing them to waddle their way through packed rooms, taking out unsuspecting civilians with their heavily encumbered mass. It doesn't have to be like that, and if you pack well enough, it won't be.

The beauty of backpacks is the ease at which you can navigate any terrain. Stairs, ramps, escalators, subway stations, city streets, just about anywhere you go, it will be easier with a well-fitting and well-packed backpack than it will be with wheeled luggage. You'll take up less space, you'll have both hands free, and as long as you're careful, you can weave your way through crowds without anyone giving you a second glance.

TIP

The brilliance of "travel" backpacks

It took me a long time, but I finally found the perfect travel companion (see Figure 6-1). They're a specific subsection of the "travel backpack" category that are brilliant during every stage of adventure.

FIGURE 6-1: The author (right), and his favorite travel backpack. Fuzzy friend and beloved sibling Booker, alas, does not have a passport.

Travel backpacks, at least the good ones, have a few key features that make them better than other options:

>> **Unlike traditional big backpacks, their entire front opens clamshell, like a suitcase.** One big zipper opens the entire face, so you have access to the entire interior at once. Most of the backpacks you'll find online, especially those not specifically for travel, only open from the top. These are fine for hiking but are endlessly annoying to travel with since to get anything out, you have to take *everything* out.

>> **Travel backpacks are often smaller.** Avoid 70- to 80-liter backpacks. They're too big and you don't need the space.

Or more specifically, if you have that space you're going to use it. It's a trap! Start with something smaller.

A good travel backpack usually has carry-on dimensions. For most people, sticking to carry-on size is ideal. There are some instances where bigger is okay, which I'll talk about later. For most brands their 40-liter size is roughly the same dimensions as a small roller bag. You'll easily be able to fit a week's worth of clothes, toiletries, and more.

>> **Travel backpacks have the ability to store their straps behind a cover.** Visually this gives them the appearance of a duffle bag, hiding the padded shoulder and all-important waist straps behind a zippered panel. So if you need to check your bag or make it more manageable in situations where the straps get in the way (the luggage storage under a bus for example), it's easy to do. Sometimes this cover doubles as a rain cover, other times a separate rain cover is stored elsewhere on the pack.

>> **Like most good backpacks, a good travel backpack will be highly adjustable and with padded straps so it's comfortable to wear.** Part of the reason travel backpacks are better than, say, a roller bag with built-in straps, is the internal frame of the backpack is designed to distribute the pack's load so it's easier to carry. Being highly adjustable to fit your specific torso is ideal for comfort.

>> **My favorite travel backpacks have one other brilliant feature: detachable daypacks.** These small, 15-or-so liter daypacks are enough to fit a camera, battery, laptop, or snacks, sneakers, and so on. These daypacks are what you'll put under the seat in front of you on a plane or have with you during the day's adventure while the main pack stays at your hostel. When you're ready to move on to your next destination, the daypack mounts to the main pack so they and you move as one.

Figure 6-2 shows the Osprey Farpoint 55 from Figure 6-1, split into its two constituent backpacks. A colleague once referred to the main pack (left) as the Command Module and the daypack as the Lunar Excursion Module (LEM). As a huge nerd, this is what I call them now. In Chapter 7, I show you how much you can fit inside.

FIGURE 6-2: The roughly 40L main pack (left) and 15L daypack of my Osprey Farpoint 55. These mount together, as seen in Figure 6-1.

I talk more about this in Chapter 7, but the short version of how I pack is as follows: The daypack gets my camera gear, laptop, headphones, battery, and a few other small odds and ends including medication. Basically, anything I don't want to risk losing for any length of time, as this pack never leaves my person. The main pack gets five or six pairs of underwear, socks, t-shirts, and unless I'm headed somewhere cold, two pairs of shorts and one pair of jeans. This bag also has some less important camera gear, toiletries, rain gear, and an extra pair of shoes or hiking boots, and depending on the location, a prescription dive mask. There are a few other key items I talk more about in the next chapter, but that gives you the general idea.

TIP

The weight of a backpack should rest on your hips, *not* your shoulders. This is why many people hate backpacks, they're simply wearing them wrong and ruining their shoulders.

Reasonable reasons to get wheeled luggage instead

I talked my dad into traveling with just a backpack. This is after spending decades of travel struggling with luggage. His suitcase for his first trip to Europe in the '60s didn't even have wheels! Sounds horrifying. His first trip with a travel backpack, a "hand-me-up" gift from me, was when he was 74. Admittedly, he's in better shape than I am. Pack light, and a backpack is a lot easier to manage than it seems.

I want to be clear, though, that my dislike of big, wheeled luggage doesn't extend to people who physically can't carry a backpack. If that's you, ignore my yapping. I want everyone to travel more, and if the only way you can do it is with wheeled luggage, go for it. I still think small and light is the way to go, and there are infinite wheeled carry-ons to choose from. Just don't spend too much.

Also, if you know your trip is going to be airport-taxi-hotel then taxi-airport-home, whatever luggage you have is probably fine. Just keep in mind that future, less-planned, adventures might lend themselves to more maneuverable luggage.

Hybrids

As I mentioned earlier, there are endless variations in size, style, and function with both suitcases and backpacks. I want to specifically address a niche I'll call "hybrids." These have wheels like a roller bag but also straps like a backpack. The straps typically stow away behind a zipped compartment, so unless you're wearing it, it looks just like any other piece of traditional luggage.

I'm not a big fan. I've tested several and traveled with two. For shorter trips where you know you're only going to be carrying the bag for short distances, they're okay. My issue is that by trying to be the best of both worlds, they end up being a fairly mediocre version of either. Because of the flat sides and rectangular ergonomics, they're not as comfortable as a backpack designed to be a backpack. There's also the extra weight of the wheels and handle. The space taken up by the straps isn't a lot, but it's space that could have otherwise been used for whatever you're bringing.

I get the desire, perhaps more common among travelers, to get specialized items that combine multiple tasks. All-in-one gear seems like a great idea from the comfort of your couch, but in practice small and simple versions of each thing are likely cheaper and work better than the one that's marketed as travel friendly. Hybrid luggage can work if you know you're never going to walk long distances with it on your shoulders. To me that's fairly limiting, but to each their own.

To Carry On, or Not to Carry On

One of the biggest debates among frequent travelers is whether or not it's okay to check luggage. Many would say no, it's never okay. That side of the argument has a lot of compelling reasons. The most common is the cost, which is often steep, and the possibility of your luggage getting lost. Both reasons are perfectly valid. Many airlines charge $50 or more to check your luggage. If you need to change planes between your departure and arrival, there's a chance your luggage won't make the transfer. This is even more likely if the layover is short and at a big airport.

Personally, I'm less strict about this. Yes, generally speaking, it's better to keep your luggage with you at all times. I regularly check my bag, though. This is pretty controversial, I admit. To be clear, there are some specific reasons checking luggage not only works for me, but in over a decade of extensive travel, across hundreds of flights and hundreds of thousands of miles all over the world, I've never had a problem. In the 20-plus years I've been traveling on my own, I've only had my luggage lost once, and only for a few hours. I wrote about that earlier in the chapter. Lost luggage just isn't as common as some make it out to be.

Over the past decade the amount of lost luggage has decreased dramatically. And while it has increased a little since the pandemic, the average is less than one bag lost per 100 passengers (0.76 per 100 based on the most recent, as of this writing, SITA study). You're even less likely to have an issue if you don't have a layover and if you're not transferring between different airlines.

It's also quite rare that luggage is ever truly "lost." It just didn't make it on your plane for whatever reason. The airline knows where it is and will likely just put it on the next flight to your destination. Usually, they'll deliver it to your hotel/hostel/home when it arrives. Ideal? No, but in the rare case you get separated from your bag, it's likely just a temporary issue.

Another reason for my neutral attitude on checking luggage is that the specific "carry-on" size varies per region and often per airline. What's small enough in one area might be too big in another. Because I travel so much, and regularly with non-US airlines, I'd have to go with the smallest possible bag to be able to always carry it on with me. That's quite limiting.

While I generally pack light, I'm a photographer and make videos on YouTube. That means I have to carry multiple bulky and heavy items, namely a large camera and three huge lenses, plus at least two action cameras, all their varies batteries, chargers, grips, and so on. While the rest of what's in my backpack could fit into something quite manageable, I also have all this stuff. My daypack is nearly the same weight as the main pack and can't fit anything in it that would take some space out of the larger pack. Which is to say, if I didn't have all that camera gear, I'd easily be able have even smaller luggage and never worry about checking a bag.

I've been able to make it work, however. For years I've traveled with 55- and 65-liter packs. These consist of 40 to 50L main packs, which are sometimes but not always carry-on sized and a 15L daypack. I've brought a main pack as a carry-on, but that specific pack was technically too big by a few inches. It had got soft sides, so unless someone physically measured it, there was no way to tell from a distance. I could though. I'm not a big fan of sneaking like this but to each their own.

Lastly, because I fly so much, I have some frequent flyer status with a variety of airlines, so I can usually check my luggage for free. I know that's not going to be the case with everyone, which is why I say that for most people, you should aim to just have carry-on-sized luggage or a backpack. Or to put it another way, I'm not pro checked bag, but I'm not strongly against it either.

With careful packing and the right-sized bag you can have the option not to check your luggage, and that's ideal. You should be able to fit everything you need for any length of trip in a carry-on bag. How is that possible? The next chapter is about exactly that.

IN THIS CHAPTER

» **Packing one week of clothes that can last indefinitely**

» **Filling in the gaps with local shopping**

» **Worthy (and unworthy) travel tech**

» **Following my packing list**

Chapter **7**

Packing Light, Packing Perfection

By the standards of the micro-packing "one bag" crowd, I pack *way* too much. I typically bring five to six days of clothes, doing laundry on the seventh day. Some people bring half that or less. I met one woman, a flight attendant, who could travel indefinitely on a bag smaller than my daypack.

There is no better gift you can give yourself than packing light. Fortunately, it's really easy to pack light and still have everything you'll actually need on any adventure. But what does "packing light" even mean? Can serial over-packers really scale back? That's what this chapter is all about.

FIND ONLINE

Check out some links to my reviews and recommended items, along with other helpful resources, at www.dummies.com/go/ budgettravelfd.

What to Pack for Unlimited Travel

My longest trip so far was just shy of four months. It was one of several trips that year, and I could have kept going were it not for some work-related reasons that required me to tap home base. I packed basically the same things for that trip that I have for shorter, multi-week trips. Once you crack the code for traveling light, packing is easy. I once started packing for a multi-month trip the morning I was due to leave.

I advise starting a packing list. You can use the same notes app I talk about in Chapter 3. You can add things as you remember them, but more importantly, you can remove things as you realize you won't need them. This latter part is key, and the hardest part. Believe it or not, I still struggle with bringing things I won't need. I'll be fine, nearly ready to go with a partially packed bag that's nowhere near full. Then, about 24 hours before my flight, the anxiety will hit. It's a struggle at that point not to load up my bag with useless things.

TIP

This is another reason it's great to have a smaller bag. You physically can't fit extraneous stuff.

Don't try to bring everything

You can't, no matter how big your luggage, bring everything. The first step in embracing traveling light is accepting this fact. You can't bring it all, so don't even try. What do you truly need? Strip away everything that's not crucial, and what remains? Some underwear and socks, a few shirts or blouses, a pair of pants or two, and a toothbrush. That's your starting kit. Obviously if you have any medications or if you're going someplace cold/wet/ sundrenched that requires specific attire, pack that, too.

This core kit will easily fit in any carry-on-sized baggage with room to spare. You'll be able to travel indefinitely with just the above. The next tier of items is best thought of as luxury items, not for their cost, but for their mass. Packing light is the key, so anything outside of your core kit is a bonus. This can be a fancy dress or pants for a night out or some shoes instead of comfortable sneakers. Rain gear can be a nice addition, though most places with regular rain will have umbrellas to buy or borrow.

In this category you can also include any special conditioners, moisturizers, and so on. Technically, I include sunscreen in this category, but my dermatologist would be exceedingly annoyed with me. I call it a non-optional option. Pretty much every hotel and hostel will have shampoo and body wash available. A better choice, unless you're particularly particular, is just buy what you need when you get there. It will likely be cheaper, and there's zero chance of it bursting due to the difference in pressure on the plane. It will be easier to get through airport security as well, or it will let you avoid checking a bag due to large containers of liquids.

Two caveats: If you're partial to a specific product, you might not be able to find it. You'll have to make do with a local equivalent. No judgment if you don't want to do that. I'm that way with my sunscreen. Second, while most locations offer inexpensive options for shampoo, moisturizer, and the like, not everywhere will. If you're headed to an island or remote location, things will almost always be more expensive than home. Best to bring at least some of what you need in resealable travel bottles.

Either of these options is likely cheaper per ounce than getting travel-sized items from a store at home. Small refillable bottles are handy, though on longer trips you might still run out. Something to keep in mind as you visit grocery stores on your trip: How much are the basics, and what can I get? I once bought orange-flavored toothpaste in Japan because I ran out of my own and I was curious. It was, let's say, different.

If you're only staying in hotels, you won't need a towel. In a hostel you probably will. I recommend a full-sized microfiber "pack" towel. These are soft, dry you fast, dry themselves fast, and can roll up into something the size of a big paperback book. A great purchase.

That's basically it. This will cover you for nearly everything on nearly every adventure. And if you're saying "but what about . . ." the next section in this chapter has you covered.

TIP

No one needs a different change of clothes for every day of a trip. That mentality inevitably and inexorably leads to overpacking.

If you "think" you might need it, you won't

It's easy, in the days/weeks/months leading up to a trip, to let your mind wander about all the endless possibilities of what could happen. Maybe you'll get asked to join a band onstage, so you'll need your velour suit. Maybe you'll be asked to guest star on local TV, so you'll definitely need a shirt your mom won't be upset you wore. Maybe it will snow in the Maldives or rain in Dubai, the possibilities are endless.

Except, they're not. Is anything possible? Yes. Is everything likely? No. Your trip is almost certainly going to go exactly as you expect. On the off chance it doesn't, you'll be able to buy what you need when the need arises. That can be one of the great joys of travel, as I'll discuss later in the chapter.

The big trick, as you're panic packing your 13th pair of jeans in case something happens to the other 29, is to embrace the fact that the most likely things to happen, are the most likely things to happen. The rest is infinite, and can't be planned for, so it's best to just deal with them in the unlikely event they do happen (which they won't).

TIP

Pack for the most likely weather and most likely activities. Everything else is just added, unnecessary weight and space.

Seriously, just do laundry

I talk about this in Chapter 6, but it really is the key to packing light. Carve out a few hours about a week into your trip to do laundry. Nearly every hotel and hostel will have facilities to do so either on site or nearby. Inevitably on every trip there's going to be a few hours where you'll just want to relax for a bit, and this is a great opportunity for that. Catch up on social media, watch some shows you missed, check email/Slack/Teams (or even better, don't), and do a load of laundry. You'll have the rest of the day free plus the gift of small, light luggage to get around for your entire trip. I think the most I ever paid for a washer and dryer was $10 total. I've also paid that to have the hostel wash, dry, and fold it for me. Either way it was a few dollars well spent.

You don't even need to bring laundry detergent, as any place you're staying is used to catering to travelers, so they'll have single serving packets of detergent to use or buy.

Wise readers will be asking, at this point, what do you wear when you're doing laundry? A great question. I bring one extra t-shirt to wear just on this day. It can also double as a nightshirt. I'll wear that with swim trunks for that effortless style for which I'm so famous. Many women I've met in hostels will do their laundry in their pajamas, but if that doesn't appeal to you, one extra comfortable "laundry day" outfit (with pockets!), should still fit easily in your luggage.

Another option is to wash your clothes in a sink. Personally, I'd rather pay a few dollars for a machine to do this for me, but if you really go down the light packing rabbit hole and only have a couple of changes of clothes, this becomes a more valid option. However, this isn't very feasible if you're staying in a hostel with shared sinks. Plus, there's the issue of drying what you've washed. This is fine in, say, the dry Mojave Desert, less so in the insane humidity of Singapore.

TIP

A few hours every week to do laundry is an easy price to pay for lighter, more maneuverable luggage every day on your trip.

Packing less than one week's worth of clothes

Here's a specific packing list that will cover just about every destination. There are obviously endless options to modify this list. If you can bring even less, that's fantastic! I've met plenty of people who pack even less than I do. The idea here is to give you an idea of one way to do it, since the majority of people *way* overpack.

>> **Six pairs of underwear:** Since you'll likely be walking a lot, whatever bra and underwear you find most comfortable is ideal. I'm a fan of the Ex Officio brand as they offer some underwear that's comfortable in a variety of climates, roll up small, and resist odors. Those features are great, but any brand you like is likely fine.

>> **Six pairs of socks:** Make your life easier and just get six pairs of the same socks. Life's too short to sort socks on vacation.

» **Six shirts/blouses/dresses:** I used to travel with special "travel" shirts, but honestly, what you wear at home is probably fine. Generally, I travel with three to four t-shirts and two dressier shirts. The latter were part of the same weekly rotation, not something I "saved" for a special occasion. You can't pack for unforeseen special occasions. Having a shirt/blouse or two that can double for such a thing isn't a bad idea. Really, though, the specifics here depend on your style and the climate where you're headed. I'm jealous of people who wear dresses, as they're great for warmer climates and can roll up to a size barely larger than a t-shirt. The key is having all your tops match whatever shorts/pants/skirts you bring and only having six or fewer tops.

» **One to two pairs of shorts/pants/skirts/jeans:** I don't know anyone who washes jeans more than once a week, and for most people even that's a lot. If you have the space and think you'll need more, that's fine. Being able to match all your tops with all your bottoms is going to make your life way easier. If you wear jeans at home, they're brilliant for travel — rugged, match with a variety of tops, and not too heavy or too light. They're not ideal for hiking hot or humid areas and that kind of thing, but for a lot of locations they're as ideal as they are at home. If your chosen shorts/shirts are lightweight and roll-up small, an extra pair or two is probably fine. These extra items should be the first to toss if you need space in your bag while packing.

» **Swimsuit/PJs:** If neither of those will work for laundry day, include something light and simple for when you're washing everything else. Rinse off or shower with your swimsuit and it's ready to go for the next poolside or beach adventure. As far as pajamas go, remember you'll have roommates in your hostel. Choose accordingly.

» **Warm top:** For the plane or cool nights, having an extra layer is brilliant. This barely counts as something you need to pack, since you'll be wearing it on the flight. At various times I've traveled with zipped hoodies, but I love a good Smartwool medium-weight pullover. They're warm and they breathe, a great combination for just about all weather above "cold" and below "warm." If I'm traveling someplace where it's warm during the day but cold at night/early morning, I'll bring a pullover and a hoodie and wear the former under the latter. It's all about layers! If hoodies aren't your thing, a stylish, but lightweight, jacket is another option.

>> **Optional:** A pack towel will be great in hostels and at the beach.

>> **Optional #2:** An extra pair of shoes. Personally, I travel with a comfortable pair of walking shoes. Adding in hiking boots if you're so inclined, or water shoes, sandals, and so on, can come in handy, depending where you're going. The latter two are great for showering in hostels, too. Dressier shoes are fine if you can fit them and you know you'll be going out.

>> **Optional #3:** Rain gear. I like a thin rain shell that can smoosh down to something burrito sized. Alternatively, a collapsible umbrella can also work. This is optional because you should be able to get an idea about the weather before you leave. You can always buy a cheap disposable poncho if the weather changes after you arrive.

You'll modify this to your own style (I hope!), but it should give you an idea where to start. Don't start adding too much, though, as that's a slippery slope. Avoid packing things you'll only wear once unless you have a lot of extra space in your, hopefully, carry-on-sized bag. Certain historic, and especially religious, locations have a dress code, usually long pants, perhaps long sleeves. If you know you'll be visiting such a place, check online for what you'll need. Sometimes such places will have something you can borrow, but not always.

Figure 7-1 shows the travel backpack I'm wearing in Chapter 6, and it holds everything needed for weeks, months, or really, as long as I want. Everything to the left of the big pack fits inside it, everything on the right fits in the smaller daypack. (Not shown are packing cubes for the shirts and underwear.)

For an exact list of my kit, check out www.dummies.com/go/ budgettravelfd.

FIND ONLINE

If you're not going the travel backpack route, consider some other way to securely carry your belongings while you're exploring. Putting your wallet in your back pocket or loosely carrying a purse over one shoulder is a sure way to get pickpocketed in a crowded area. If traditional backpacks aren't your thing, there are lightweight and crushable daypacks as well as crossbody bags/slings that are easily packable in your main luggage.

FIGURE 7-1: Here's how I pack everything I need for a travel adventure.

TIP

I'm a big fan of packing cubes (see Figure 7-2). These rectangular zippered pouches allow you to organize and compress your clothing. Underwear in one cube, shirts in another, and so on. It makes it easy to find what you're looking for, and it helps you compress everything down so you have more space. Think of them like little removable drawers for your backpack/luggage. They're a real game changer when it comes to efficient packing and way better than just having everything loose in your bag. There are also "compression sacks" that smoosh things down even further, but honestly you shouldn't be packing so much that you'd need those.

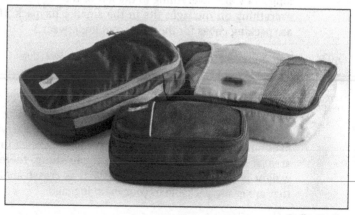

FIGURE 7-2: Three sizes and brands of packing cubes.

No one will care if you wore the same thing twice in the same two-week trip. Even if someone notices, they're going to be too busy being jealous about your epic adventure.

Packing for different climates

The above list will get you by for most spring, summer, and fall locations just about everywhere in the world. I know this, because it's basically my exact kit I've traveled with for years across dozens of countries all over the world.

However, it doesn't work as well on the climate fringes. If you're traveling to cold or rainy locations, you'll obviously need to pack more. Hats, jackets, maybe even boots and snow pants, all take up significantly more space than short shorts and tube tops (which always find a space in *my* bag).

Since these items are also expensive, it's unreasonable to think you'll buy them when you arrive. Though it is worth keeping in mind that many ski resorts will rent all kinds of gear. That's worth checking ahead of time.

For me, the most difficult packing I experience is trying to do multiple climates or situations on each trip. I brought a second bag (I know, the horror), on a trip where I needed to attend a trade show for a week. I hated every second of hauling that second bag, but I couldn't rock up to a professional event in a t-shirt and jeans. On another trip I started in the Australian winter, went to always hot Bali and Qatar, then to a brisk European autumn, before arriving in Iceland at the beginning of winter. I felt like an absolute fool hauling a heavy jacket through the oppressive 110-degree heat in the Middle East, but being just barely comfortable watching the aroura above Thingvellir National Park in western Iceland made it totally worth it.

Which is to say, don't overpack by bringing things you "might" need. That rule doesn't include, however, things you absolutely will need because of your specific adventure.

Shopping Locally

The benefits of packing light vastly outweigh the slim chance you'll be on an adventure and find yourself needing something you didn't bring. A slim chance is not no chance, however. This might be because an opportunity for something unexpected came up and you need something specific, or it could also be something simple like a forgotten toothbrush.

Regardless, it's almost always easy to find a local replacement. Nearly everything you buy at home can be found away from home. Sometimes it's exactly the same, maybe with a different logo or packaging. Other times it's basically the same thing, just formulated for local preferences.

TIP

Even if you bring two 50-pound bags packed full of everything you can imagine, you'll inevitably still forget something. Fortunately, you can almost always find what you need where you're headed.

The joy of buying something you need while traveling

I'm not big on souvenirs, but I have a few items that I use all the time that count as souvenirs because I got them while traveling. My favorite is nothing more than a simple black belt. While rushing through Istanbul airport, I accidentally left my belt at security. By the time I noticed I was well past the point where I could go back and get it. So I spent five days in Hong Kong for work, unable and occasionally forgetting to go look for a belt. Then I arrived in Taiwan, and on my first day I set out on a mission to find a belt. In reality, it was just an excuse to go explore. But I ended up finding a shop that sold nothing but belts! The shopkeeper was delighted to help me find the right belt for me, and I was delighted to have solved this inconsequential problem by exploring a vibrant city. Now every time I look at my belt I think of this story and the great time I had looking for something as simple as a belt.

I have several items like this, including a heavy jacket I needed because Scotland in the summer is colder than Los Angeles in the winter. I also have some water shoes that saved my feet from an unexpectedly rocky Italian beach.

Imagine having items you use every day reminding you of a specific adventure. Little delightful moments of fond memory, prompted by just putting on a sweatshirt or hat. Sure, ideally you won't need to buy anything on a trip, but you shouldn't fear forgetting something at home. You can always find a local version that might be just as good made even better because it has a story attached.

It's yet another reason to pack light: space in your bag for something to bring home.

Most of the world has the same things you can find at home

Walk through any store anywhere in the world and you're likely to see many of the same brands, logos, and products. Sometimes they might have a local name, but the packaging looks familiar because it's actually the same thing you have at home with different branding. Sure, there are local products that never get exported or low-cost items that never make it to your local shelves, but for a wide range of products you'll be able to find them just about anywhere.

I'm always amazed how many forget that people live their everyday lives in "exotic" travel locations. They brush their teeth, comb their hair, put on their togas one wrap at a time. What's special to you is their normal life. So you don't need to bring everything from your closets and cabinets. If you truly need something, you can find something similar when you arrive.

However, "similar" is doing a bit of heavy lifting in that last sentence. Can you find shampoo? Almost certainly. Can you find the exact shampoo you need for your hair? Maybe not, especially if that area doesn't have a big population with your hair type or the product is from a smaller, more boutique brand. The same is true for cosmetics. Local options might not be ideal, of course, but hopefully for the sake of adventure, and the limited time, they're okay.

Tech Must-Haves to Bring on Every Trip

Despite traveling with an entire backpack full of electronics, I'm the first person to say that most people don't need most of it. I bring a laptop and a bunch of camera gear for work and making videos on YouTube.

That said, there are a handful of items I wouldn't travel without and I highly recommend. I've tested countless travel tech for a variety of outlets, including the New York Time's Wirecutter, the Wall Street Journal, CNET, Forbes, and more. This is my bread and butter, so to speak.

A few key items can be a huge help for any adventure, and thankfully they don't cost a lot.

USB-battery packs (aka power banks)

These have gotten popular enough that I bet you have one already. If not, they're small, portable battery packs that can recharge your phone and other USB-powered gear. Depending on the capacity you can get a few full charges of your phone before you need to recharge the battery itself.

This is first on my list because they're invaluable while traveling. You'll probably be using your phone all day, checking Google Maps, taking photos/videos, and if you're like me, listening to music. All that can wear down your battery fast. Topping up your phone's charge while you pause for lunch or a coffee can let you finish the day without stopping.

Most modern devices recharge via USB as well, so if you have a battery large enough, you can also recharge your GoPro, tablet, wireless headphones, and more. Many modern laptops can recharge via USB as well, extending the amount of time you can sit at a table outside a restaurant writing a book called *Budget Travel For Dummies*, for example.

There's also the safety aspect. Need to call the hostel for directions? Running late and want to make sure you can still check in? Need directions because you got lost after dinner? Miss the last train to your hotel and need a taxi/Uber? Don't let your phone die when you're out in the unknown.

My favorite size is 10,000 mAh, which is roughly the size of a smartphone. It can charge most phones two to three times but isn't so bulky as to be a nuisance. There are higher capacity options, but they get physically larger. There are smaller options too, but I'd recommend getting one that can at least charge your phone to full once (around 5000 mAh).

Plug adapters

International travel often brings you to a place that has different outlets than those at home. You shouldn't rely on finding random USB outlets to charge your phone and other electronics. Nearly all modern chargers can work everywhere in the world, as long as you can plug them in.

So how do you plug it in? One of the most common, and widely advertised, are all-in-one travel adapter cubes that have multiple plug types on each side. They supposedly let you plug into any outlet in the world. I've tested a bunch and own several and to be honest, I don't like any of them. They're surprisingly bulky and less useful than they seem. Almost all are extremely poorly made and often fall out of the wall outlet once you plug in your charger.

Instead, I swear by simple plug adapters (see Figure 7-3). These tiny converters are barely larger than your charger's metal outlet prongs. They slide over them, letting your charger fit the power outlet. They take up next to no space, they're cheap, and you can get one for every charger you want to bring. Even if you plan on visiting multiple countries with different outlet types, several of these are still smaller than one of the all-in-one cubes. Best of all, no moving parts so they're basically indestructible.

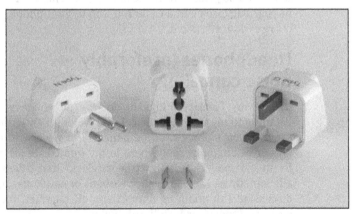

Geoffrey Morrison

FIGURE 7-3: I've used the same plug adapters from Ceptics for years.

TIP

Oh, and if your curious if your charger will work, check the fine print. Somewhere on the charger it will say something like "Input: 100-240, 50/60Hz." This covers nearly every mains power in the world. The United States, for instance, is 110-120 volts at 60 hertz, the UK is 220 V at 50 Hz as are India and Zimbabwe. Japan is 100 V at 50 *and* 60 Hz, depending on where you are. While a device's physical plugs may be different, the internal circuitry of nearly all modern power adapters ("wall warts") are designed to work everywhere. Just search for "Mains electricity by country" or the countries you're visiting and "outlet type" to find out which style of plug you'll need.

Cables and a good charger

Related to the above, it's worth investing in a good charger and some long cables. The charger that came with your phone is probably quite poor. One that fast-charges multiple devices can be a huge help when you're stuck in a hotel or hostel with limited outlets.

A well-made cable, six to ten feet in length, is massively helpful as well. You'd be surprised how poor the outlet placement is in many hotels. Many hostels have outlets at each bed, but not all. If you want your phone near your bed, you'll want a cable that can reach. It also gives you the flexibility of having your battery bank in your backpack and a cable running to your phone, letting you charge while you use it.

Headphones (preferably noise canceling)

One of my favorite things to do is explore a new city while listening to my favorite music. I also wouldn't fly without noise-canceling headphones. To be honest, I'm never without a good pair of headphones somewhere in my immediate vicinity. I prefer in-ear models, usually "true wireless" that have no wires at all. Sometimes these are called earbuds or earphones, but for this discussion I'm going to clump them all together, including big over-ear models, as just "headphones."

So the question is, what makes a headphone "good"? In terms of sound, that varies a lot and could fill an entire book. If you love how your headphones sound, that's enough. If you think they're "fine," it's worth considering a better pair. If they came with your phone, they're probably not great.

Noise canceling is wildly misunderstood. The best noise canceling can significantly reduce low-frequency droning sounds, like jet engine noise, car engine noise, and so on. They do very little to reduce voices, babies crying, or anything high frequency. You might get some reduction if the headphones fit your ears really well, but no noise-canceling headphone can create "silence." There's also good noise canceling and bad. Most headphones that claim to have noise canceling actually reduce very little noise. This can be the difference between "I guess these are working" on a mediocre pair and "Wow!" on a great pair.

I review lots of headphones for the Wall Street Journal and Sound-Stage Solo. In the past I reviewed lots more for Wirecutter and Forbes. Here's a bit of a secret: You don't need to spend a lot to get great headphones. That's not to say all headphones sound the same. They're all massively different, but there are some excellent headphones for under $100 that have above-average noise canceling. Most are water resistant, too. There are some great, expensive models, but also some great inexpensive models. The best inexpensive models might outperform some expensive models. If it all sounds confusing, it is.

I can't recommend specific models or brands since any such list would be instantly obsolete. I'll just recommend giving some reviews a look — mine if you want, or any of the big sites like Wirecutter, CNET, and so on. Good noise-canceling headphones can make long flights far more tolerable, and loving the sound of your headphones can make your music really come alive.

Memory cards (if you have a camera)

One thing you don't want to buy on the road is a memory card for your camera. Memory cards, like the SD and microSD cards found in most cameras, are astonishingly overpriced in just about every store within miles of a tourist destination. Yet online, they're usually very inexpensive.

I've purchased some huge SD cards for my cameras, plus a smaller backup or two, from name brands, and none cost a lot. These same cards at a store that caters to travelers would likely cost three to five times more. It is definitely best to buy an extra before you leave. You'll almost certainly use it eventually.

Even with huge memory cards that can store a whole trip, I still back up my videos and photos to the cloud and a portable hard drive. That's probably overkill for most people, but those are a portion of my income, so it's better safe than sorry. This was one of the reasons why, when I had my gear stolen in Italy (see Chapter 2 for that story), it wasn't as heart breaking as it could have been. I'd backed up nearly the entire trip to that point to the cloud. The memory cards were gone, but the photos and videos themselves were safe. Check out Chapter 8 for more about cloud storage.

Travel laptop or tablet

For years I travelled with tiny, 10-inch laptops my Wirecutter colleagues called "craptops." They were well under $500, incredibly slow, but they had great battery life, were very light, and so cheap that if anything happened to them I wouldn't freak out. I used these to travel for months at a time writing articles, editing photos, and even running Wirecutter's A/V section as editor for years, all with a laptop the size of a tablet. I still would be travelling with one of these if it weren't for the decision to start making videos for YouTube. You can't edit videos on a laptop that has the processing power of a donut.

For the most part, I don't recommend anyone buy a laptop specifically for travel. If you need to replace your current computer anyway, and you want to use it regularly for travel, something travel friendly is worth considering.

What makes a laptop travel friendly? For me it's size, weight, and battery life over all else. I also want the ability to charge via USB-C, so I don't have to bring a separate power supply. I can just use the charger and cable I bring to charge my phone and cameras. Unfortunately, thin, light laptops with decent batteries are also often quite expensive. That's why I started traveling with the tiny and cheap "craptops."

 Somewhere in between those price extremes are Microsoft's Surface Go series. I've had three generations of these, and they're great, if a bit pricey. They're smaller than a typical laptop, more capable than a "craptop," and unlike a tablet, they run Windows and all Windows software. Price-wise they can be similar to the cost of a traditional laptop but are much smaller. They can't do video editing or elaborate gaming, but for web, email, video calls, spreadsheets, photo editing, and so on, they're fine.

Kindle or other e-Reader

File this under "optional." If you're not a heavy reader, don't spend money on an e-reader for an upcoming trip. If you are, and you don't already have one, an e-reader like a Kindle has certain advantages over an analog (aka paper) book or reading on your phone/tablet.

For example, the best e-reader options have a built-in backlight, so you can read without the lights on. This is ideal if you don't want to disturb your travel partner or roommates. They have long battery life, so you don't need to worry running down your phone battery. Lastly, they're much, much easier to read in direct sunlight compared to any phone or tablet. This is because they use a different technology for their screens compared to phones and tablets.

Some models are water resistant, fairly rugged, and all of them typically last a long time. As in, you won't need to replace them every few years like a phone.

Saving money on camera gear

I'll talk more about this in the next section, but most people don't need a camera for travel. Your phone's camera, if you use it well, can take some incredible photos. The quality of the camera is often secondary to the skills of the photographer. Those skills can be learned by anyone who wants to.

One exception are action cameras from companies like GoPro, Insta360, and others. Small, waterproof cameras are unobtrusive, and let you take lots of photos and videos you can't or wouldn't want to take with your phone. Scuba diving the Great Barrier Reef? Learning to surf in South Africa? Skydiving in Las Vegas? You *could* take your phone on adventures like these, ideally within special protective cases, but personally I'd be far too anxious to enjoy myself. Most action cameras are quite rugged and designed to take a beating.

If you've decided to dive into the lovely hobby of photography, it can get expensive. Not necessarily to start, as entry-level cameras aren't too bad. It's once you start learning what's good, what kind of photos you want to take, and all of a sudden you're looking at full-frame cameras and eye-wateringly expensive prime lenses. Ask me how I know.

What you can do, however, is buy used. If you don't have a camera store near you that deals with used gear, there are a number of online options that buy used gear, inspect it, then resell it at price based on the condition. I've bought and sold some lenses through KEH, and there's also MPB, LensRentals, and others. While you might be able to find even cheaper options on a direct auction site like eBay, that's riskier since you don't really know what you're going to get.

That said, if you're not interested in photography as a hobby, you probably don't need a "real" camera for travel. More on this in the next section.

Gadgets and Gear to Avoid

Now that we've got the cool stuff out of the way, let's talk about stuff to avoid. There's a huge, and highly profitable, industry aimed at creating products for the unsuspecting traveler. If you follow any travel accounts on Instagram, Facebook, TikTok, or anywhere else, you're almost certainly inundated with ads for flashy and seemingly cool travel gear. Save your money. Almost all of it is over marketed, under designed, and could be replaced by something simpler for a fraction of the cost.

Ask yourself, "Would I use this at home?" If the answer is no, it's probably not worth it.

Pretty much any "travel gadget" (especially advertised on social media)

It's easy to get sucked into the slick advertisements for travel gadgets. They're designed disturbingly well to poke the traveler's brain into thinking "I need this cool thing!" Even knowing this, I still click on them sometimes. Sometimes it's just to see what they're about. Other times I'm suckered into the gear's concept. However, no matter how good the ad looks, or how cool the gadget seems, you almost certainly don't need it.

What do you need when you're traveling? Basically, just what you'd bring wandering around your hometown. Special clothes and special gear will not only identify you as a tourist, though that often can't be helped, it's also money you could have spent on something else. That something else could be dinner at a nice restaurant, more travel, or most usefully, something you'd also wear or use at home.

I'll also include in this "travel-sized" items like sunscreen, shampoo, etc. Unless you have special products you can't live without (fair, I know I do), the basics are often available everywhere. Or, instead of buying overpriced travel-sized versions of things you already have, just get small, airport-friendly (3.4oz/100ml), water-tight (that's key) bottles, stored in a watertight bag. Fill these with your favorite products. For longer trips, I just bring the full-sized version in a water-tight bag since I know I'm going to use it all. You'll need to check your luggage if you do this though.

TIP

My general rule for products of all kinds: the bigger the marketing budget, the worse the product. As in, the more ads you see, the less you should be interested. It's not always true, but it's a good starting mindset.

"Travel SIMs" (probably)

These are still fairly common and are almost always best avoided. They're 3rd party SIM cards that promise "cheap" data while you're traveling. Is the data actually cheaper than your home plan? Maybe. It's almost certainly more expensive than getting a local SIM card or one of the many eSIM options available for certain phones.

The convenience of these is definitely alluring — being able to get your data situation sorted out before you leave (or at the airport) — but that convenience comes at a cost.

Not all of these are bad, but most aren't great and should be viewed with caution. There's more to it, which I dive into in Chapter 8.

Special "travel clothes"

I have a confession: I've fallen for this. I used to have special travel pants that you could zip off the bottom of the legs and convert them to shorts. They had lots of pockets. I looked like such a dork. I still look like a dork, but slightly less so without those pants.

If you want to buy something to look cool on your trip, I'm all for it. If you think you *need* to buy something for your trip, that's a different story. Pack and dress for the climate and expected weather where you're headed. That's really all you need to do. Also keep in mind that looking "cool" or distinctly stylish means you're likely going to stand out as a tourist. Not a judgment, just something to keep in mind.

If you fully embrace the "one bag" mentality of packing super light, the exception to the above is certain travel-friendly clothing that's easy to wash, dry, and pack. Companies like Columbia, Patagonia, Ex-Officio, and others offer clothing like this. I've tried some, and even travel with some, but if you're doing laundry once a week, these can be excessive.

REMEMBER

Look at it this way, if someone was travelling to where you live, would they need special travel-specific clothing? No matter where you're going for travel there's someone who lives there who doesn't need laser-cut, carbon-infused, hydrophobic, 20-pocket, $150 shorts to walk around.

Bulky laptops

I know, it seems like just a few pages ago I was recommending laptops. I was, but I was recommending specific laptops. I've seen countless people lug huge and heavy laptops while they're ostensibly on vacation. Big "desktop replacement" laptops are quite popular for their screen size and performance, but when it comes to travel, they're horrible. Reducing the amount you pack encompasses tech too, and these are often just a weighty anchor for something that most people will use sparingly.

Then there's the broader question: Do you even need to bring a laptop? If you plan on working during your trip, sure. If not, if it's just a what-if situation, it's far better to leave it at home. Save yourself the space and weight. If you don't have a tablet, your phone will almost certainly cover you for the various internet-related things you might need on your trip. Even checking email and Slack, while more cumbersome than something with a big screen and a keyboard, can be done in a pinch. There are a variety of inexpensive tablets that can work to watch shows and movies on the plane and give you a larger screen size for the inevitable "I know you're on vacation but . . ." emails.

If you plan on traveling regularly, and I hope you do, consider size and weight a priority for your next laptop purchase, as I talked about in the last section.

Money belts

So many people swear by these. Money belts are special, I don't know how else to describe them . . . money underwear? I suppose they can help keep your money safe from a basic pickpocket, but if someone's going to actually mug you, they're almost certainly going to check for a money belt. Then you're in a worse situation.

Use your best judgment here. On one hand if they make you feel safer, that's great. On the other, if you know about them, criminals know about them. You're not "hiding" your money, only making it temporarily less accessible. Maybe that's enough though. There are a lot of variables.

I just advise against carrying a lot of cash. If you're carrying enough to justify needing one of these, you might be making your trip unnecessarily stressful. That can vary depending on location, of course, but for many destinations credit cards are better if you have that option. For more on this, check Chapter 2.

Anything that attaches to an airplane seat

This is a contentious and controversial issue. There are a variety of products that attach to the seat in front of you. These range from head hammocks to help you sleep, to tablet/phone holders, to devices that prevent the person in front of you from reclining.

I'm going to take a hard stand here and advise against all of these. It is unconscionably rude to do anything to the person's seat in front of you during a flight. It may not seem like you're doing much, but I can promise (and tell you from experience), every tap, bounce, and bump is extremely noticeable to the stranger in front of you. This includes interacting with the seatback entertainment screen. Be gentle!

Whether or not you should recline your seat is a debate for another time by people with far more patience than me.

As a general rule, don't touch the seat in front of you unless you have to, and then only gently.

Portable solar panels and solar-charging batteries

There are lots of USB battery banks available with built-in solar panels. While I appreciate the concept, the reality is far different. The problem is solar panels produce very little energy per square inch. This means the panels on the side of a portable battery, even a big one, will take ages to recharge that battery. In some cases, it could literally take days in strong sunlight. You're better off getting a battery with a larger capacity, and one that can charge quickly, than thinking you can spend an afternoon in a park and recharge all your gear.

Related, there are also collapsible panels designed to charge your phone. These fold open, revealing several small panels that work together like one larger panel. An attached USB cable connects to charge a device. While these theoretically create more power than the small ones built into a single battery pack, they're not much better. For the ones that could easily fit in a backpack, they put out ten watts or less. That's less than a mediocre USB charger, and far less than the better chargers. And that's *if* you have strong, direct sunlight.

If your trip includes time off the grid, or you just like the idea of being able to charge your gear without plugging in, don't count on these. They're a novelty at worst, and a slow alternative to a power outlet at best.

Sleeping bags

If you know you're going to camp, then sure. Otherwise, skip the sleeping bag. Hostels rarely, if ever, want you using them (for fear of what creepy crawlies your bags might bring). The majority of hotels clean their sheets between guests. Rentals and other home-stays should offer clean linens. A sleeping bag will rarely help in those situations anyway since you're inside and not strapped to the side of a glacier in Wrangell-St. Elias.

Sleeping bag liners, on the other hand, might be the solution if you can't stomach the idea of sleeping somewhere that's not your bed. These are thin sleeping bag-shaped "sheets" essentially, that can add some warmth to a sleeping bag or work on their own if you're inside or somewhere warm. Again, hostels won't like these, and I don't think they're necessary, but I've met some people who just can't sleep on sheets they didn't wash themselves.

You probably don't need a camera

This is probably unexpected advice from someone who admittedly travels with an entire backpack full of camera gear, well, "unexpected" if you haven't seen my multiple references to the idea elsewhere in this book.

Don't get me wrong, I would love for more people to get into photography as a hobby. There are certainly types of photos that are only possible with a real camera. I also loving taking and sharing great photos, and I don't want to deny someone else those same feelings. There's also a great sense of accomplishment getting decent (good even?) at something challenging.

Like I've mentioned before, photography is an expensive hobby. Like nearly all hobbies, it has a learning curve. Are you willing to learn what aperture priority is and why you'd want to use it? Do you know why you'd want a 50mm prime lens over a 100-300mm zoom? Is f/2 or f/8 better for this scene? If you don't know what these terms mean, and aren't interested in finding out, there are better ways to spend your money than on a camera you won't use more than a few times.

On the other hand, if you do want to learn, awesome! Welcome to the club! I hope your credit card has a high limit, there's a used camera store near you, or both.

What would be far less expensive, and a good entry into photography in its own right, is learning how to take better pictures with your phone. Most modern phones have excellent cameras and can take some fantastic photos. I've shared photos on social media where people ask what kind of camera I used, and it was just my phone. Learning the basics of framing and exposure, understanding the camera app's various features and modes, will all go a long way toward improving your photo-taking skills. If you find yourself getting into it, awesome! Getting an entry-level interchangeable lens camera can teach you the next steps. Before long, you'll be lugging around a backpack full of expensive gear just like the dummy writing this.

TIP

The two most world-changing tricks for every phone camera are these: 1) Keep the lens clean. Every time you take the phone out to take a picture, make sure there are no smudges or fingerprints on the lens. 2) Tap your subject. When you've got a photo lined up, tap the screen on your subject. This will automatically adjust the focus and exposure so the subject looks its best. Usually, not much will change. In certain situations, a lot will change. If you're trying to take a photo of someone in front of a window, for example, it can be the difference between seeing the person at all or having them be an unrecognizable shadow.

Packing for Dummies

From ascots to zip-off pants, this is the ultimate budget travel packing list. It includes no ascots or zip-off pants, but it does include all the important items for any length of adventure. Start with the core items, as they're what you'll need pretty much everywhere. Then add in only what you need for what's most likely to happen during your trip, for example the actual forecasted weather or the expected weather for the season.

Lastly, there are some optional items. "Nice haves," if you will, that aren't necessary but can be handy on many trips if you have the space and budget.

Core items

By "core items" I mean the basics necessary for living somewhere out of reach of your wardrobe. Definitely bring less if you want to go even lighter, but be wary about adding more.

Five to six tops: Shirts, blouses, and so on. Add one that you'll wear on transit days.

Five to six pairs of underwear: Bras, boxers, whatever you normally wear. Again, add one for what you'll be wearing on transit days.

Five to six pairs of socks: Something comfortable, and ideally all the same style to make organization easier. Add one pair for transit days.

Around two bottoms: Jeans if you wear them, shorts, skirts, leggings etc. If you wear dresses, you can count these as either tops, bottoms, or both depending on your style. Stick with around six total outfits for space, though. I recommend wearing long pants for flights, which can be one of these two or a third pair.

Sleepwear: Whatever you normally wear, though make sure it's reasonably presentable since in a hostel you'll be sharing a room. These can optionally also be worn on laundry day.

Toiletries: Toothbrush, toothpaste, sunscreen (a must!), any medications, and your preferred period products, as you might not be able to find a specific brand or type everywhere. If you have hair and skin care you prefer, get some small, reusable travel bottles. Don't bring the entire container as it will take up too much space. Don't worry about bringing too little, you can always buy the same or similar product during your trip. Condoms are a good idea, too. Better to have and not need than need and not have, right? Just make sure they're stored safely away from anything sharp.

Outer layer: For most locations this means a hoodie, zip-up, pullover, light jacket, and so on. You don't need to "pack" this. Instead, wear it on the plane. For colder adventures, see below.

Chargers and adapters: A good multi-outlet charger is a great purchase, letting you charge multiple devices quickly from one charger. Plug adapters let you plug in anywhere.

Pack Towel: A "microfiber" towel that folds down small but can dry you quickly. It dries out quickly itself. You can also use it on beach days.

Flip-flops/sandals/water shoes: Something to wear at the beach and in the shower at hostels.

Laundry bag: Ideally something that collapses into something small. Can also be used as an extra tote for day excursions.

Climate/trip-specific items

Headed somewhere warm, cold, wet, or dry? Many typical tourist locations have fairly simple packing requirements, but sometimes specialized items are needed.

Bathing suit: Most countries that have beaches don't have specific rules for attire (beyond covering your bits and bobs). However, a few countries are stricter, especially for women. Worth checking before you leave.

Heavy jacket: Instead of the light jacket. Generally, you'll want to carry this on the plane so you don't have to make room for it in your bag. However, if it's really big, that might be a challenge. Most airlines won't count it as a separate item, though that's worth checking ahead of time.

Merino wool socks: I love big comfy socks when the temperature calls for them. I'm partial to Smartwool, but there are other, similar options. They can be a little expensive, but they're very rugged and great at keeping your feet warm on cold days.

Hat: As someone follicly challenged since high school, I'm the first to put on a warm hat and rarely travel without one. For the same reason, I wear some kind of hat when it's bright and sunny. That's in addition to sunscreen. Skin cancer is no joke, and literally everyone can get it (though some of us are more susceptible). Which is to say, a weather- or seasonally appropriate hat is good addition for most adventures.

Hiking boots: Personally, I've never found hiking boots to be particularly comfortable when exploring a city of paved streets and cobble stones. If you're going offroad as well as on, bringing a pair of hiking boots is certainly warranted.

Optional items

Once you've got the basics covered, plus anything needed for your specific location for the time you're visiting, the following are potentially very useful if you still have room.

Packing cubes: Zippered pouches to hold and compress clothing and other items. Can make packing and organization easier.

Decent sunglasses: If you're from more northern latitudes (northern parts of the US, Europe, and so on) and you're headed somewhere further south (southern parts of the US, most of Australia, anywhere along the Equator), get some polarized sunglasses. They don't have to be expensive (unless they're prescription), but your eyes will thank you.

Rain gear: I travel with a waterproof jacket that fits in a small pouch. A small umbrella wouldn't be much larger. You could also just wing it, and if a storm does head your way, it's fairly easy to find disposable ponchos or cheap umbrellas in most locations.

An e-reader: A Kindle or something similar will be far easier to read in the sun than your phone. Also they're a great way to refer to *Budget Travel For Dummies* during your travel!

Longer cables: A six-foot cable or two can really help if the outlet and charger is in an unfortunate place. I like braided cables as they seem like they hold up a little better. There are options that cost about the same as non-braided. Don't expect any cable to last more than a few trips, however, so don't overspend. Expensive cables aren't worth it.

Action camera: I don't think most people need to spend money on a camera. Most phones will do a great job with photos and videos. An action camera like a GoPro can take some epic videos and photos, though, and they're waterproof.

Selfie stick: If you can't reach far enough to get a good photo of yourself and your surroundings, get a selfie stick. They're inexpensive and make getting a great photo a lot easier. Just be extra aware of your surroundings when you're using it.

Chapter **8**

Getting Online While on the Road

From vital tools like Maps and Translate, to restaurant reviews and booking sites, to posting photos and videos to social media, having internet access while you're traveling is one of the simplest ways to make your adventure easier. Being able to use your phone exactly as you do at home can be the difference between a stress-free trip and one mired in issues.

There are multiple ways to get cheap data abroad, which I discuss in this chapter. Just as important is making sure your accounts are secured and you're able to back up all your travel photos and videos. Leaving with the right apps pre-installed is key as well. So this chapter provides all you need to know to get the most out of your phone while traveling.

FIND ONLINE

You can find links to all the web addresses from this chapter, as well as other helpful resources, at www.dummies.com/go/budgettravelfd.

You Don't Need to Do without Data

Most mobile phone providers such as AT&T, Verizon, and others, make roaming data outrageously expensive. Upwards of $5 to $10 a day for a pittance of megabytes can seriously eat into your budget. Their pricing is all the more offensive when you find out how much cheaper it can be.

For instance, I pay $70 a month and my phone has high-speed data in nearly every country on Earth. I land, my phone connects, and I have unlimited data. Well, sort of unlimited, as I'll explain. The way I do it is just one option. You won't even have to change your current service provider if you don't want to.

So if you want to be able to use your phone while traveling and avoid costly fees, check out the various easy, inexpensive options featured in this section to get roaming data while you're out roaming.

Why you should make sure you have data/internet abroad

I can totally understand the desire to disconnect and enjoy travel without the constant nagging of notifications, email, Slack, and so on. However, having data while you travel can make the entire process infinitely easier. If something goes wrong, it can be an absolute lifesaver. It also lets you adjust plans as you go, giving you the flexibility of a true expert traveler.

I was on a tiny island in the Fiji archipelago when a menacing hurricane increased in intensity overnight. We had to evacuate immediately. Because I had internet on my phone, I was able to book one of the last available rooms in a hotel on the mainland while the rest of my fellow travelers fought over the only two public computers on the island. Or another time, when a cleaning woman came to my door in France confused as to why I was still in the room, I was able to use Google Translate to explain that I'd rebooked the room for two more nights. My French teacher would have been so "proud." Then there are the countless times I needed to message or call a friend to meet up, find a restaurant, navigate to a hostel, and more. I also use the internet to post to social media and work, but those are secondary to the infinitely more important uses of having working data while you travel.

Most fees for international roaming are absurdly high. Fortunately, there are easy, cheap alternatives.

How to get inexpensive international data anywhere

There are three (ok, technically four) main ways to get cheap, or even free, data while you're travelling.

Finding free Wi-Fi

The first option is the least convenient but also the cheapest. Free Wi-Fi is widely available. Hotels, hostels, even most rentals/ homestays will have internet available. Restaurants and museums often have public Wi-Fi too. You can download maps and Google Translate language packs when you have data, and then leave your phone in airplane mode during the day. This method is fine, but you can do better. It's super easy to get cheap data so that your phone works just like it does at home. The only reason to just use Wi-Fi is if you really want to disconnect and actively *don't* want your phone to work, or the idea of even spending about $20 for your entire trip is beyond your budget.

Replacing your phone's SIM card

The second option for cheap/free international data is one I did for years: replacing your phone's SIM card. A SIM (Subscriber Identity Module) card (see Figure 8-1) is a tiny, removable chip that identifies your phone to the cell towers and their associated telecommunication companies. It's about the size of a microSD card like what cameras use. Nearly every phone has one, or a slot to install one. Some phones have two. Most modern phones have a small hatch on the side or top. Older phones had the SIM mounted inside. If you change your phone's SIM card with one from a different company, that company's cell towers will recognize your phone as one of their own, letting you use their network as if you'd bought your phone from that company. Or to put it another way, if you bought your phone from AT&T and put in a Vodafone SIM card, Vodafone will recognize the phone as being from Vodafone. Once you return home, you put your original SIM card back in the phone and once again AT&T will recognize it as an AT&T phone.

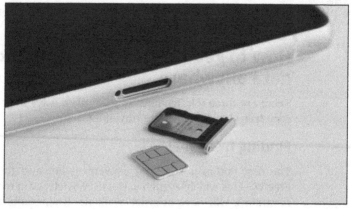

Geoffrey Morrison

FIGURE 8-1: A SIM card (foreground) is a tiny device roughly the size of a fingernail that identifies your phone as yours.

This process is easy. My dad is 81, and he's done it on his own several times. Generally, the process is after you arrive in a new country, go to a local telecom "phone" store (like Verizon, Orange, Three, Optus, and so on). You look or ask for a "temporary" or "prepaid" SIM. The names might change, but every store I've ever visited knew what I was looking for when I described it. Many had entire walls of cheap SIMs for sale. Most last for a few weeks, some for a few months. I don't think I ever paid more than $20 for a month's worth of data. In most places it was way less. I think my record was 6 gigabytes for two weeks for $6.

After you purchase the new SIM, most stores will help you install it. Generally, that process is just turning off your phone, opening the SIM slot (either via a special tool for that process which they'll usually have, or the end of a paperclip). Remove the old SIM and *keep it someplace safe that you can close securely.* Don't lose your original SIM or you'll need to get a new one when you get home. Put the temporary SIM in the holder and restart your phone. With most phones it will automatically connect to the new network and start working immediately. Some phones require some settings adjustment, which the store will probably help you sort out. You could also, before you leave home, check out the process for your specific phone in case there are extra steps required. The whole process will just take a few minutes.

With the new SIM, your phone will work pretty much just like you bought it in the country you're in. High-speed data, a local phone number, and so on. However, this does mean your home number will go to voicemail until you return home and put your original SIM back in. You might not get text messages to your original number either.

These prepaid, temporary SIM cards should not be confused with "travel" SIMs you buy in advance. A local SIM card is one directly sold by a local, and ideally major, telecom company. These are the cheapest and fastest options. "Travel SIM" are sold by a third party and almost always offer slower data for more money per gigabyte. They "piggyback" on a local network and might only have 4G on a 5G network, or worse.

Before you leave, check what the biggest telecom providers are in the country you're visiting, and check where the closest store is to where you're staying. If you want to save money, don't get a SIM at an airport or train station. They'll be more expensive and often there are limited options. Check the next section "Unlocking your phone and other potential issues" to make sure your phone is compatible.

eSIMs

Similar to replacing the physical SIM card, many modern phones have an eSIM, a.k.a. an embedded-SIM, that can be changed with software. This feature is available on recent iPhones and higher-end Android phones.

The method to change your eSIM varies slightly per phone, but generally you buy the eSIM via a website or app, and it will come with instructions for how to activate it on your phone. This process can be as simple as scanning a QR code with your phone's camera while you're on Wi-Fi. Some phones let you have two accounts active at the same time, namely your original eSIM and your new travel eSIM. You can easily research and buy an eSIM before you leave so you'll have it ready to go when you arrive. It might work right when you land, or you'll just need to use the airport or hostel/hotel's Wi-Fi to get it started.

If you're not very tech savvy, the local SIM option might be better as there will be someone at the store that can help you with any issues activating your new SIM card. While eSIM prices can be cheaper than a local SIM, they might be data only, as in no phone number. Not a huge deal to me, but that's worth keeping in mind.

Like changing a physical SIM, your phone has to be compatible, which I'll discuss in the "Unlocking your phone and other potential issues" section.

Switching service providers

The third international data method is the one I've used for several years now. It's switching to a service provider that's friendly to travelers. This option won't be possible for everyone, nor can I say if the providers I like will still be offering these great plans I'm going to describe, but they have for years and hopefully they still will when you read this.

The two best options for frequent travelers based in the US are T-Mobile and Google Fi. Both offer free international roaming. Google Fi has the fastest speed available on the foreign network, so in most places that means 4 or 5G. So your phone basically works the same as it does at home. It's called "unlimited" but if you use too much data, they will cap it. They're just opaque what that amount is. I hit that cap once, and I was using a lot of data, so for most people it's probably fine. T-Mobile's international roaming is a little more expensive, and caps data at 5 gigabytes per month, but as long as you're not streaming music or videos all the time that should be fine for most people.

Unfortunately, these two providers are only available to Americans at the moment, though that might have changed by the time you read this.

For some areas this whole process is a lot easier. For example, if you're European, or you're using a European SIM, you can travel across most of Europe using the same SIM.

Generally, don't buy SIM cards at the airport or train station. They'll be much more expensive.

TIP

Unlocking your phone and other potential issues

Replacing your SIM or switching to a new provider should work for most people, but there are some important caveats. The biggest is your phone has to be "unlocked," which just means your current provider allows you to use the phone on a network other than theirs. In the US, if you either paid for your phone outright, or it is paid off, your provider is required to unlock it if you ask.

If you're paying it off monthly, or you got it "free" for signing up for a multi-year contract, you might have more trouble. Depending on your provider, you might need to pay it off, pay a fee, wait a certain length of time, and so on. Search for your provider plus "phone unlock" to find out.

If you can't unlock your current phone, you could use an older phone instead. Most older phones can still run map and translate apps. Some have the ability to create a "hotspot," broadcasting their data connection via Wi-Fi, which you can connect to from your new phone. This drains the battery quickly, however, and some providers don't allow hotspot data.

Most phones have the ability to work on any modern network, but some older US phones were "CDMA only" and won't work in most other countries. It's unlikely you have one of these, but if it's more than around five years old it's worth checking if your model will work in the country where you're headed.

While most countries allow anyone to buy a local and temporary SIM, you might need your passport to do so. Make sure to bring it (though you should keep it on you at all times anyway). Some countries require a local address. Your hotel/hostel might be OK, but it might not. You can check this online before you leave. Check multiple sources as websites often have old info about this.

If you're outside the US, you might be in better shape as telecoms in many countries don't lock their phones.

If you travel a lot, it's worth saving up and buying your phone outright so you don't have to worry about being locked to a network.

TIP

It's absolutely worth spending some time before you leave to figure out which of the above methods is best for you. Don't leave it to the last minute and *definitely* don't just assume you can just use your phone abroad. That's a great way to incur massive roaming charges that could cost you hundreds of dollars or more.

Password managers and locking down your accounts

There's always a risk that someone will get ahold of your phone, tablet, or computer. It's not likely, presuming you take basic precautions, but it's worth taking some time to lock down your various accounts so it's hard, or nearly impossible, for someone to access your private data.

The easiest way is to enable what's called two-factor authorization (2FA). This means that to be able to log into your account you need your password *and* something else, usually a text message or email. This is not perfect, but better than nothing. However, if you're not using your home SIM, getting text messages might be impossible. That might make things difficult, or at least annoying, but the added security for important things like bank accounts might be worth it.

I also strongly recommend a password manager. This is an app on your phone and a plugin for your computer's web browser. It creates elaborate and essentially hack-proof passwords for your various accounts. The only password you need to remember is the main one for the manager, it then fills out the password field of various websites and apps. It simultaneously makes each account harder to access and prevents you from reusing passwords (you know you do). It also means you can make one, more secure, main password, since it's the only one you'll need to remember.

TIP

The password manager I use locks itself as soon as you move away from the screen, so even if someone grabbed my phone while I was looking at the app, there's minimal chance they can get access to anything.

There's a lot to password managers, more than I can get into here, but I wanted to mention it to help you add some digital security to your accounts before you travel. They're absolutely worth it. I recommend checking reviews to see what's the best option when you read this. I'm partial to my colleagues' work at Wirecutter, but there are a number of great websites that review these apps.

Making Sure You Can Back Up to the Cloud

When I got my camera stolen in Italy (more on this in Chapter 10), I wasn't as devastated as I could have been. I didn't lose all the photos of Sicily, Portugal, and Scotland from the trip leading up to that point. This is because I regularly backed up all my photos to the cloud.

Setting up an automatic cloud backup is worth every one of the handful of minutes it takes. Not only can it save you storage space on your phone or camera, but it also keeps your memories secure in a place that's not on your person.

TIP

There are a variety of inexpensive or free cloud backup options. For a few dollars a month you can get enough to back up your phone multiple times over.

What's a cloud backup?

The easiest way to understand "the cloud" is that it's a hard drive that's owned by someone else. They keep it in some building you never see, make sure it's well taken care of, and is always accessible to you.

Examples of this are Google Drive, Microsoft One Drive, Apple iCloud, Amazon Drive, Dropbox, and so on. Some of these come pre-installed on most phones, and if you haven't set it up you should do so now.

Most options have 5 to 15 gigabytes for free, with 1 or more terabytes available for just a few dollars a month. It's absolutely worth it. Start with the free option and see how quickly, if at all, you fill it. For our purposes you'll mostly want to back up your trip's photos and videos as you go, but you can also store other important files to make them accessible to you anywhere.

Saving all your photos and videos on the go

Generally, the auto-backup of a cloud storage app only works on Wi-Fi. That's fine, as otherwise you'll be using a *lot* of mobile data. Just make sure when you make it back to your accommodations that your phone connects to the Wi-Fi and starts its backup of your day's adventures. It might take a moment, but if it's taking too long you can also manually start the upload. Usually if you set one photo or video to upload, it will start the rest shortly after.

If you have a separate camera, it will require the extra step of downloading the photos/videos to your phone or computer, and then sending them up to the cloud. Some cameras, like most recent GoPro models, will connect to some Wi-Fi networks and automatically upload their files after you set it up in the app and connect it to power.

Don't assume that any of this works. Seriously. Regularly I've thought a device was uploading, and it would either stop, or just not start at all.

Stashing a copy of your passport and other info

Once you've secured your phone and accounts, you can store important info in the cloud. I keep a picture of my passport as a backup. You could take pictures of tickets and other important documents. Will this get you out of every potential issue? No, but it could help. Imagine losing all your identification. Being able to log onto a computer and print out a copy of your passport with the number and your photo could help expedite assistance. A photo of something isn't a legal document, but it could be one step in proving you are who you say you are.

Is storing documents like this 100 percent safe? No, but nothing is. Chances are if someone has gotten access to your cloud backup account, they probably have access to your email and other accounts, too. In other words, they have everything anyway. So, there's a risk/reward calculation to be made. Does it make you feel safer to have a cloud-based backup of your IDs, or not to have that saved somewhere online? If you make your accounts as secure as possible, as mentioned earlier in the chapter, they should be as safe as anything is online.

Memorize your passport number. At the very least it will make filling out immigration forms slightly less annoying.

REMEMBER

Downloading Movies, Maps, and Other Cool Apps

While many new apps require an internet connection, many others will work just as well, or close to it, offline. Even if you use one of the methods I mentioned earlier to get data while you're traveling, there are going to be times when you just don't have a connection. That can be anything from being on the plane, to hiking, to being on many metro systems. Downloading some things either before you go, or when you're on Wi-Fi, can make everything go more smoothly.

What are you going to listen to?

One of my favorite pastimes is walking around a new city listening to music. In the age of the iPod this was pretty easy. Since most of us now, myself included, use streaming apps instead of MP3s, there's a new level of difficulty while traveling. Even if you have cheap international data, it might not be enough to handle streaming music every day. That can eat through even generous data plans. There are also times when you might not have data at all, like on airplanes, ferries, and many other situations. Then what are you going to listen to?

The easiest solution is to download songs to your device. The major streaming apps support this, letting you store a certain number of songs for a certain number of days before you need to connect to the internet. There are two main issues with this. First, it takes up space on your phone. That space might be needed to store photos and videos of your trip. The other issue is that you have a limited number of songs. That might not be a huge deal, as in many cases that limit can be quite high. You can also download new tracks when you get to the Wi-Fi at your hotel or hostel. Personally, I love finding new music and almost always listen on random. Maybe you're the type of person who listens to the same ten songs all day long. To each their own. You certainly won't need to worry about storage space.

Another option is an inexpensive portable media player, aka an iPod. Apple discontinued the actual iPod years ago, but you could use an old phone or one of a myriad cheap options that now fill this space. The benefit is not filling the storage of your phone and not wearing down its battery listening to tunes. A portable media player isn't really necessary for most people, but if you're a music weirdo like me, it's actually quite handy.

Download maps to use later

You should absolutely do this even if you're headed somewhere you've visited before. Having a usable map even if you don't have service can get you out of a lot of potential jams. The exact method to download a map tends to change as companies update their apps and sometimes varies depending where you are and what version of Android or iOS you have. Here's the way the two main map apps work as of this writing. If this doesn't work, a quick Google search should get you started.

>> **Google Maps:** Search for the city or area you're visiting. Make sure you're specific, but not too specific. Cover the area you'll likely venture during your visit. "Sao Paolo" is good, "Brazil" is too general. Once the area appears, swipe upwards on the info bar that covers the bottom half of the screen. In the upper right of this new screen, look for the three vertical dots. Tap, then tap on "Download offline map." You'll now be able to use the map just as if you had internet.

>> **Apple Maps:** In the Maps app, select your profile, and on this new page select Offline Maps. Then press Download New Map. Enter where you're visiting, and then zoom in or out as necessary. The bigger the area the bigger the file, but unless you're severely limited on storage space it should be okay. This downloaded map will either just work if you're in the area, or you can check it and any other maps you've downloaded in the Offline Maps section of your profile.

You should be able to view the downloaded maps on the Apple Watch, just like normal, but only if your phone is nearby. The maps don't "save" to the watch's internal storage.

Shows and movies to watch on the plane

In-flight entertainment has gotten a lot better in the last few years. Most long-haul aircraft have a variety of reasonably recent shows and movies to watch, all via seatback touchscreens. Will you find enough to keep you entertained for a 17-hour flight from Perth to London? I wouldn't count on it.

Many streaming apps like Netflix have the option to download shows and movies for offline viewing. This doesn't always work as well as advertised. Most services limit which titles you can watch offline. Sometimes you'll download everything, and it will seem to be good to go, only to find out on the plane it didn't actually work. This has happened to me on numerous occasions.

REMEMBER

Downloading shows/movies in apps primarily only works with phones and tablets. A few might work on laptops via the same company's software, but this functionality comes and goes on the whims of the companies, so I wouldn't count on it.

Must-have apps

It's a bit of challenge to recommend digital apps in an analog book, but I'm going to do it anyway! All of these apps, some of which I've mentioned in other chapters, have been around for a while. So hopefully they'll be around by the time you read this.

Download any apps you might use before you leave home. Airport Wi-Fi can be finnicky, and it's better to have everything set up before you arrive somewhere without cell service.

Google Translate

I already talked about this app in Chapter 3, but it's worth including here, too. The ability to "talk" to anyone you meet is invaluable. Being able to read menus and signs is an added bonus.

Google or Apple Maps

I'm partial to Google Maps, but Apple's version has come a long way. I know a lot of Apple fans who still use Google Maps. Just saying.

Rome2Rio

I've mentioned this app and website throughout the book as it's one of my favorites. Basically, enter any two places and it will give you all the available options to travel between them. Bus and train routes, ferries, taxis, everything. It will show you some prices for airfare as well.

While it has become more heavily monetized in recent years, offering booking and services in the app, the overall usefulness is unabated. This app/site is one of the ways I'm able to travel without a plan. No matter where I end up, I know I'll be able to find my way back out again . . . probably on a bus. There's always a bus.

Polarsteps

This is a fun app that tracks your journey and overlays it on a satellite map of the world (see Figure 8-2). You can share your location, more or less real time, with friends and family, or just keep it private and enjoy a graphical representation of your adventure.

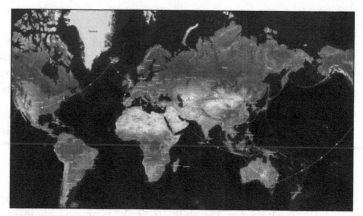

FIGURE 8-2: A recent adventure as shown and tracked by Polarsteps.

WhatsApp

For the most part, your phone's built-in text messenger isn't going to work abroad. WhatsApp works separately from your phone's text messages, so it will work anywhere as long as you have an internet connection. It's also an easy way to keep in touch with people you meet abroad.

Make sure you set it up at home, though, as you'll need to initially set it up with your phone number. Swapping out to a travel SIM shouldn't affect anything, but it might ask if you want to change your number, which you don't. Changing numbers makes it a "new" account, and you'll lose your contacts and messages. Also, don't accidentally delete the app because if you need to re-verify your account you'll need your home SIM and access to text messages or voice mail to do it.

It's worth getting your parents/siblings/kids/friends on, too, so you can keep in touch with them while you're traveling. If they haven't used it before, make sure they understand how it works and to look for the new notification.

Google Photos/Apple iCloud/ other cloud backup

The path of least resistance here is whatever's already on your phone. Make sure it's set up to auto-upload when you're on Wi-Fi and you're good to go. Well, "good to go" in theory. Definitely worth checking that the upload starts when you're on Wi-Fi.

Apple Pay/Google Pay

I talk about contactless payment and why it's awesome, in Chapter 2. I highly recommend setting this up before you leave. Not only is it very convenient, it's also safer than cash or using your physical credit card.

A booking app

As I mention in Chapter 4, there isn't much difference between the various booking apps. You might be able to get a deal through one that's not available on another, but that one might not offer one that is available on a third. The most important thing is getting one that you're comfortable using, has features you want, and you can navigate quickly. This will come in handy when you need to find a nearby hotel because your Airbnb vanished and you're standing on the sidewalk in the rain.

Options include Booking, Orbitz, Kayak, Hostelworld, and so on.

Your airline's app

Though not required, it can make things a little easier having your airline's app installed. You'll get push notifications about flight delays, a secure place for your ticket, smoother online check-in compared to their website, and so on. Some airlines even let you track your baggage.

Uber

It pains me to recommend Uber as I'm not a fan of their business practices. However, it's the most widely available rideshare app, found in 70 countries. If you need a ride and can't find (or don't want to use) a taxi, this is a convenient option. Alternatively, see if there's a local taxi app.

Apps to (probably) avoid

A bad app isn't likely to derail your adventure. At least, I hope not. If you're using some random app that promises huge discounts but has no reviews online, that's a big red flag. What's more likely is a bad app will be frustrating to use and won't do what it promises. I'm all for finding and trying new things, but if you've found a new app with few or no reviews, I'd caution against using it for any key aspects of your trip.

There's an additional category of apps that aren't bad *per se*, but they have better or free alternatives.

TripAdvisor

I can absolutely understand why this app and website got popular. The idea is great, with people posting their own reviews of places and stays. It has morphed into something significantly less useful. First, far more people are likely to post a bad review than a good review. That's true of any public ratings system, to be fair. Also, the people posting often have zero experience with the cuisines they're rating. Why would you take the advice of a traveler from your country about food in a different country? This isn't a "bad" app, but I'd take their recommendations with a grain of salt.

Most paid apps

This pains me to say, because I want people who create things to get paid for them. However, the vast majority of travel apps that cost money have free options that are just as good, if not better. There are exceptions, of course, but keep in mind nearly all apps have ways of making money without asking for a contribution from you. It's just worth considering what that app truly offers over an app that doesn't cost you anything.

That said, if you find an app you love from an independent developer and there's an option to give them money, it's a great gesture.

Chapter **9**

Living Locally on the Cheap

One of the greatest joys while traveling is getting fully absorbed in the local culture. Well, as fully absorbed as possible anyway. Often this feeling can come about just from the adding up of little, everyday things, like how you get from place to place, what you eat, and where you shop.

Often, as an added bonus, experiencing a place in this way is also a great way to save money. For instance, you can avoid the over-priced places that typically cater to tourists, you can get around without wasting money on taxis or rideshares, and more. In this chapter, I show you how.

FIND ONLINE

Head to www.dummies.com/go/budgettravelfd for links to help-ful money-saving resources mentioned in this chapter.

Eating Like a Local

There's a common desire among travelers to "eat like the locals." Usually this is followed by questions about restaurants. The real-ity is a bit different. Most people cook and eat at home. It's way cheaper. A lot of people eat at restaurants you can find near your house. McDonald's, KFC, Subway, Pizza Hut, Burger King, Starbucks, are popular all over the world. Will you feel "like a local" if you eat at a place you know from home? Probably not, but there are some surprising things about eating at places you think you know from home.

Don't get me wrong, there are often excellent local eateries unknown to the average traveler. These can be absolutely amazing experiences. You might find one where you're the only foreigner, which can be epic. You also might find a place where the food is great, but all the customers are tourists. It can be a mixed bag.

Wanting to immerse yourself in the local culture is a laudable goal and can sometimes be as simple as asking people you meet where they'd eat on a random Tuesday or where they'd go to celebrate something. Make sure you're clear about the price range, though. They might send you, the "rich" traveler, to some five-star restaurant they've always wanted to try but could never afford.

Thinking of grocery stores as an adventure

One of my favorite, and free, activities in any new location is checking out the grocery store or market. If you've never tried this, I can understand it sounds weird. Aren't grocery stores just . . . grocery stores? Well, yes and no. While the types of items are usually similar — veggies, cereals, and so on — the specifics can be quite different.

For instance, there could be fruits and vegetables common to the area that you've never seen before. Not all produce travels well, and even more has limited international appeal. So, you might see all sorts of interesting things. The infamous durian, from Southeast Asia comes to mind. It looks like a spiky football, smells like death, yet it's loved by many. Or the dragon fruit, which looks like a flaming, Technicolor hand grenade. Could you find these at home? Maybe, but there's a good chance they'll be fresher and tastier in areas closer to where they're grown.

Then there are the many local brands that aren't popular outside of certain areas. Everyone thinks whisky is the national drink of Scotland, but it's actually IrnBru. It's an orange-colored soft drink that tastes vaguely like cotton candy. One of my favorite activities in Japan was what I called "iced tea roulette." Every corner market has a wall of refrigerators that in the US would be full of sodas, water, and in some places, beer. In Japan, it's nearly all, top to bottom, tea. I am no tea expert, nor can I read Japanese. Instead of inspecting each label with Google Translate (see Chapter 3), I'd pick one at random. Some were great! Most were . . . fine. Some were, let's say, not to my tastes. The point and the fun was trying something that was familiar, yet different.

Restaurants eat your budget, but go anyway

One of my favorite *expensive* activities is trying new restaurants. It's not just about the food. Okay, often it is just about the food. But sitting outside, watching the city move around you, can be a remarkable and relaxing break in a day of exploring. Unfortunately, it's often quite expensive.

Throughout this book I've tried to recommend spending money on experiences, not "things." If something creates a memorable moment, it's probably worth splurging on. Restaurants can be that. I'll never forget having sushi at 6 a.m. at the Tsukiji fish market in Tokyo, some of the fish just moments from the boat. Or dinner at Restaurant Maison Des Tanneurs, which is in a building that's over 450 years old overlooking one of the canals of the river Ill in Strasbourg. Or a legendarily good cheese plate with varieties I've never heard of in Taormina, Italy at a restaurant with tables on the many, many stairs in that town. Or tapas overlooking the 230-year-old Puente Nuevo bridge in Ronda, Spain. I have so many stories that revolve around food, sometimes I annoy myself with them. Which is to say, eating at restaurants is worth budgeting for.

REMEMBER

Eating at restaurants is great fun and definitely worth spending money on, but it's also a great way to burn through your budget so plan accordingly. Buying groceries and making meals at your hostel can help you keep regular food costs down so you can splurge on a restaurant or two during your trip.

Checking out familiar chains in unfamiliar places

Let me describe for you an epic burger I once ate. It had a fluffy, butter-dipped, golden bun with a flawless dome shape, a wide, perfectly cooked slice of smoked bacon, an almost impossibly circular sunny-side up egg, smooth melted cheddar cheese, a savory beef patty, finished with a layer of a rich, delicious sauce. It was called the Gold Moon and it was incredible. One of the best burgers I've ever had, a fast-food burger no less, and I live in the land of In-N-Out. Where did I get this masterpiece of culinary alchemy? McDonald's. Specifically, McDonald's in Japan during Tsukimi, the mid-Autumn "moon-viewing" festival.

Chain restaurants often tweak their menus or flavors to suit local tastes. KFC has a shrimp doughnut in Thailand, for instance. I'm not, however, recommending you regularly eat at restaurants you could find at home. A huge part of travel is trying new things, and that often means the local cuisine. But if you're in a hurry, want something easy and or cheap, or you just want a taste of home, there's nothing wrong with checking out something that seems familiar, but might offer something that's a little different.

Avoid eating in tourist spots

It's a pretty safe rule that the worst, and most expensive, restaurants are going to be within walking distance of tourist destinations. If you want to enjoy a meal with a view of the Champs-Élysées, Grand Canal, or Copacabana beach, go for it. Just know that you're paying for that view specifically and often quite a lot. The food might be okay, but in my experience it often isn't. You could get the same quality food for a lot less somewhere else or spend the same amount and get something epic elsewhere.

TIP

My advice, if you don't have your heart set on a specific view or location, walk a few blocks in any direction and see what you can find. A place filled with locals might be a great spot.

One of the best meals I've ever had was exploring Ljubljana with my dad. We found a random restaurant a few blocks from the city center. It was all locals when we arrived, and we stayed for hours, eating and drinking. Then some musicians came, and the restaurant became so packed they started to run out of food! It was magical and a night I'll never forget.

The fridge at the hostel or hotel can save you money

Buying groceries and eating them over several days is one of the easiest ways to save money. Having access to a kitchen, something almost a given if you stay in a hostel, lets you save even more. This is one of the main reasons I recommend hostels so strongly (and extensively in Chapter 5).

Just about everywhere in the world you'll be able to find a market or grocery store where you can stock up on inexpensive but filling meals — pasta or other noodles, bread and cheese or meat, whatever you're comfortable making. You should be able to find some resealable containers too if you just want to cook a batch and have leftovers.

There are hotels with in-room or guest-accessible kitchens, but they're not nearly as common. Slightly more common is a fridge and a microwave, which aren't quite as good as a real kitchen but can certainly do in a pinch. Pre-packaged noodles and microwave dinners are quite common.

The glorious wonder that is "street food"

Whether it's a vendor with a pushcart or a semi-permanent stall at a market, the highly portable and often delicious "street food" can be some of the best ways to experience local food and eat cheaply. Even better, you can enjoy it while you're on the go. Some of my favorite food experiences were inexpensive mini-meals made right in front of me in a tiny, portable kitchen. The night markets in Taipei come first to mind, but there are places like this all over the world. I tried frog's legs in Kuala Lumpur, snails in Madrid, and uniquely seasoned sticks of various meats pretty much everywhere. For the equivalent of a few dollars or less you can experiment with things that maybe you don't want to risk the full cost of a meal on. One of my favorite meals, which I've mentioned before, was at a market in Singapore. It was simply two steamed pork buns ("Cha siu bao" if I remember correctly) and I believe a steamed "ma lai go" cake. I'm not sure because I just pointed at the pictures on the menu. Both were perfection. I think the meal cost less than $3 US.

The question often asked, especially by those less culinarily adventurous is, "is it safe?" I've got peculiar health issues that make me more susceptible to food issues than most, and I still make an effort to try whatever I can. In many cases, the food is being prepared right in front of you, so you can get a sense of that proprietor's food safety precautions. In most places these vendors set up in the same place often, and they don't want to poison their regular customers. Is it possible you'll get food poisoning? Sure, but that's true of literally anywhere. The worst food poisoning I ever got, which laid me out for several days in ways I'll mercifully spare you by not describing here, I got at a well-known chain restaurant in Las Vegas. I was with a group of ten people, most got the same thing I did, and I was the only one who got sick. Luck of the draw, I guess.

So personally, I don't see much risk . . . in most places. If there's a crowd of locals and a line to order, that place is almost certainly safe. If there's no one around, it smells weird, and the guy wipes his nose before reaching into a bucket of lukewarm chicken — maybe not. If your innards are of the more delicate variety but you still want to try new things (yes!), it never hurts to keep some loperamide (or other anti-you-know-what) pills in your backpack.

Exploring Efficiently . . . or Not

Time is your most valuable resource. On one hand, I advise planning less and slowing down so you're not feeling stressed and rushed. Spending time in a place is better than constantly rushing to the next place.

Depending on where you're going and how many things you want to see, having an efficient plan to navigate the city can be worth it. It can save you time lost and wandering.

However, let me make a case for lost and wandering as a goal. Personally, I love it. If you want to get really absorbed in a place, just *being* in that place is a huge part of it. Rushing from tourist spot to tourist spot is certainly one way to travel, but walking around a city just exploring is just so much fun. I've had countless incredible days where I've had one destination in mind but taken circuitous routes to get there — a long and winding road where you can find shops and food and sights and sounds that you'd miss if all you see of a location is the highlights and the inside of public transit.

TIP

Having a day just to explore, especially if it's the first day in a place, can ease your way into a trip. It also means you're less likely to miss a must-see location because you're jetlagged. Plus, it gives you a greater understanding of how that place works.

Loosely planning your route

In Chapter 3 I talk about how great it is to keep your planning to a minimum. Being flexible is key to minimizing stress. There is one aspect you can plan, however, and that's the route you take to explore. I'm a vocal proponent of having no plan when you explore a place, but if you only have a few days, sketching out an efficient route can save you time and money.

If you know, for instance, there are certain things at the top of your must-see list, checking the local metro map to plot out your general direction can help minimize time lost being lost.

However, I've had some of my greatest travel days just being lost. There's a fine line to be walked here (pun intended). My general rule here is to have a plan, but to be willing to change or ditch that plan the moment you find something interesting.

Taking advantage of "free" walking tours

Many touristy cities, as well as many hostels, will have some kind of walking tour. These might be a few hours or all day and will lead you through a new city hitting all sorts of cool spots. Some of these will be free, while others will have a fee. I did one in Prague that included lunch and two free drinks for less than the price of a meal.

I highly recommend walking tours. First of all, you're often getting shown around by a local. One of my closest friends did this for years in Tijuana, Mexico and let me tell you he knew all the best food in that city (and there's a *lot* of great food in that city). The best tour guides are knowledgeable and funny, and you'll almost always come away with a far better understanding of the area than you started with.

Best of all, it's easy to meet new people! Here you are, spending a few hours with some other tourists who all selected the exact tour you did. By the end you'll have a shared experience and a solid understanding of who in that group are likely to be your kind of people. Easy enough to transition from walking tour to dinner to pub crawl to travel buddies to lifelong friends.

Just keep in mind that even with "free" walking tours you should expect to tip your guide, in cash, at the end of the tour. How much varies depending on the area and, of course, how much you can afford. I tend to be a big tipper to help offset people who aren't, but to each their own. You can always ask an employee at the hostel, hotel, or wherever you heard of the tour, to find out what's an appropriate tip.

Checking for free days or discounts at museums and monuments

Many large museums will have free days. Many will also offer discounts for active-duty military personnel, seniors, students, and more.

Many cities offer special passes for tourists that offer admission to various attractions all for one potentially discounted price. These can be hit or miss. Some can save you money, reducing the price you'd pay buying each ticket individually. However, it's important to read the fine print closely. Does it work every day and for every attraction you want to visit? Will it only work for a day, meaning you'll need to cram everything into a few hours?

Related, many cities offer coupon books that can offer discounts on tickets as well. Many of these will be available in hotel and hostel lobbies. Again, these might be great, but others might just be a sneaky way for local businesses to advertise. For example, a restaurant offering a coupon for a free drink with a meal. Is that really a bargain or is that restaurant overpriced and underwhelming and that's *why* they need to advertise?

One of my favorite versions of these, and an absolute bargain for travelers in many parts of the United States, is the America the Beautiful pass available through the National Park Service. At the time of this writing, it's $80 a year. However, that gets you into every US National Park and a variety of other locations. Since these parks can be around $30 per vehicle or $15 to $20 per person, having a pass for $80 more than pays for itself after a few visits. Each pass can get everyone in a vehicle or up to three other people if you walk in.

Allowing yourself to get a little lost

In my days as an extensive planner, I more or less accidentally had an unexpectedly amazing day getting lost. I was looking for a specific famous location in Venice (okay, I was looking for the square in front of the "library" where Indy and Elsa emerge in *Indiana Jones and the Last Crusade*). This was before free roaming data (see Chapter 8) or extensive Wi-Fi, so while I had a general idea where I was looking, I didn't have an exact route. Eventually, as the tourists thinned out, I realized I'd wandered away from the typically traveled areas and more towards where the locals live (yes, amazingly enough there are still locals in Venice). I think it was a combination of not truly being able to get "lost" since it's a small archipelago and the desire to actually see more than what's on the postcards that I kept going. I found quiet alleyways, sleepy canals, locals going about their lives, and absolutely none of the crowds found elsewhere.

Since I've ditched the extensive planning, I've done this kind of thing on purpose all over the world.

REMEMBER

If you've got data on your phone or if you've downloaded maps for offline use (see Chapter 8 for more on both topics), then it's hard to get truly "lost."

Knowing how to get from anywhere to anywhere

One of the ways you can feel more comfortable in a place is learning how easy it usually is to get around. Remember, you're visiting, but people live there. They need to get around too, and in many places a car is either a luxury or just unnecessary.

Before you arrive, it's worth getting an understanding of what the local public transport is like. Places as different as Spain and China both have extensive high-speed rail networks. The east coast of Australia has several bus companies that run multiple journeys per day to get you to all the tourist spots. Even if you're only planning on visiting one city, knowing ahead of time that it's just an hour or two to visit a nearby city can open your options.

Then there are rail pass options like Eurail, JR Pass, KR Pass, and others. For a fee, these let you ride the national or regional train network basically as much as you want for a set amount of time. These passes were once incredible bargains for the budget traveler, but far less so now. They typically only cover intercity transport, have heavy restrictions, and must be used on consecutive days. It's possible that your plans would match one of these passes being a good deal, but make sure you calculate how many journeys you'd need to make the cost worthwhile. I've considered these multiple times and never found them to be cost-effective. However, it's worth running that math for yourself.

There are some apps that make longer journeys easier, which I talk about in Chapter 8. In addition, local bus and train lines might have their own apps, with more up-to-date schedules.

Car rental dos and don'ts

My basic rule for renting a car is don't. There is nothing less budget than car rental, and that's true everywhere. However, for some adventures it can't be avoided. On other adventures, it's necessary. I live in Los Angeles when I'm not traveling, and my number-one piece of advice for visiting Los Angeles is to rent a car. In terms of square miles, it's one of the largest cities in the world. While we do have a growing public transportation system, including a subway (shocking, I know), it won't get you everywhere. It's just brutal to get around without a car. Well, given the traffic, it can be brutal to get around with a car, too.

TIP

My biggest tip is to check the prices at different locations. Renting from an airport, often the most convenient, is also often the most expensive. Many cities, even mid-sized towns, have a rental agency downtown in addition to the airport. While you'll need to get to that location, it's entirely possible the cost of getting a taxi or Uber will be more than offset by a cheaper per-day rental.

Many credit cards offer some amount of car insurance, but you should read the fine print. Will your regular car insurance cover you abroad? It might not.

Most people like big cars, but in many countries the roads just aren't designed for the size of vehicles driven by most Americans. Save money and get a smaller car. Since you've packed light (you read Chapter 6, right?), you should be able to fit in a small car with ease. This is still true if you're renting a car in America. I'm all for the Great American Road trip. I've certainly done a several, but unless your dream is specifically driving a Mustang on Route 66, you'll be fine driving a small car. I did a 30-state, 10,000-mile road trip in a Mazda Miata, basically the smallest car you can buy in the US. It's absolutely doable.

You can also rent campervans and RVs in some countries, but these are very expensive even if you include the fact you can sleep in them.

Sleep in your car?

Whether you're driving your own, or renting, sleeping in your car is often a temping alternative to hotels or hostels. After all, many modern cars are easily big enough for adults to sleep in the back, just by folding down the rear seats. Converting an inexpensive van to be a comfortable place to sleep is a popular trend as well, one I've done myself. Regardless of the vehicle, the question becomes where do you park that's safe and cheap, or ideally free?

Unfortunately, multiple US states have passed laws against sleeping in your vehicle, including the parking lots of previously RV and car-camping friendly companies. The politics behind this are beyond the purview of this book, but suffice it to say these laws are impacting far more people than those just looking for a cheap place to stay while adventuring. These restrictions can cover everything from parking lots to highway rest stops to residential areas. If you're planning a road trip and want to sleep in your car, check the laws for each state you're passing through. The laws vary throughout the world, too, with some places having no problem with it, others restricting it to certain areas, and others forbidding it.

TIP

In the US at least, one option to consider is truck stops. Big chain truck stops like Love's, Flying J, and Pilot offer showers and usually a place to park overnight (sometimes for a small fee). These are generally clean and safe, though you'll likely have to listen to idling diesel engines all night. Walmart and some other large retailers are also notably RV friendly, but it's at the mercy of local laws. You'll also need permission from the store manager.

Generally, you're better off "car camping," which is just the fancy way of describing driving to a campsite and setting up a tent.

Campsites are extremely common in the US and in many places around the world. Some might just be flat spaces with no running water while others are big chain companies with most locations offering everything from hot showers to swimming pools. Many US National Parks have campgrounds, as do many state parks, though these are often very popular and sell out months in advance.

Electric scooters

Many cities, at least those that haven't outright banned them, have a variety of electric scooters for short-term rental. Companies include Lime, Bolt, Neuron, and many others. They're often outside popular places, at intersections, and near transit centers. These, quite often, have a bad reputation. When they first started to become popular, they were *everywhere*. Like battery-powered wheeled locusts descending upon an unsuspecting public. Since then, the total amount has often decreased, but poor behavior by those riding the scooters has maintained the negativity in the minds of many locals.

They're really fun though. The wind in your hair (I assume), the rush of speeds slightly faster than running, and all joking aside, being a great way to see a city that's faster than walking but more involving than a subway, bus, or taxi. I've rented these in Australia and all over Europe, and I had a blast. I limited my low-speed, eco-friendly Hells Angels cosplay to places with bike lanes. Cars aren't particularly impact friendly, and I see how little the average driver pays attention when I'm driving my small car. A scooter is even harder to see.

REMEMBER

A few things to keep in mind. One, read up on local laws. Are you allowed to ride on the sidewalk or are you restricted to streets? Do you need a helmet? Where can you park them? All have apps that restrict where you can leave the scooter when you're done, and you don't want to be 10 minutes into a ride and realize you're nowhere near a drop-off location. They can also be quite expensive. A short ride might cost you more than a taxi over a similar distance. That varies a lot per location, but it's something to keep in mind.

Bicycles

One of my favorite travel days ever was renting a bike with a friend and exploring Oslo. I haven't mentioned Norway much in this book despite its beauty because it is the opposite of budget. A medium pizza and two Cokes cost me over $50 and that was over ten years ago. However, on this amazing day my friend and I got explore all over this gorgeous city for relatively little money.

Many countries, especially in northern and western Europe, are particularly bike friendly. The locals in many countries quite famously prefer bikes over cars. That raises a whole new set of potential issues if, like me, your bicycling experience dropped to zero once you got your driver's license. Trying to merge into the flow of seasoned expert riders can be an intimidating challenge in itself.

The benefits are multi-fold. Bikes offer a faster way to explore than walking in a way that's typically cheaper than buses or rental scooters. You get to see and experience a city in a far more organic way than metros or from the inside of a vehicle.

As with anything, read up on local laws. If they don't require a helmet, can you still get one? You should, head injuries are no joke. Where can you park the bike? If there aren't bike lanes, what are the laws and etiquette? Can you ride on the sidewalk?

TIP

While "riding a bike" is synonymous to an intrinsic ability you can't forget, if it has been years or decades since you last rode a bike and you're planning on renting one during your trip, it might be worth trying to rent or borrow one at home to get the hang of it again.

Metro Movin'

There are few things that make me "feel like a local" more than the ability to quickly and efficiently navigate a foreign metro system. Slap down my metro card, head directly to the platform, queue or not depending on the area, and then get whisked underground at rapid speeds to my destination. It's simultaneously exciting and mundane. Millions do it every day, but how many people back home have done it here? How many tourists clog the flow of traffic standing in the wrong place or block passageways staring at wall maps.

Cities like New York, Mexico City, London, Paris, Tokyo, and dozens of others become almost unmanageable, or at least exceptionally expensive, if you don't take advantage of their public transportation. This section offers a few general tips.

Navigating local metro systems

Don't try to navigate a metro system for the first time during rush hour. You're just going to be in the way. Sometimes it can't be helped, so at the very least, try to stay out of the flow.

Ask people at your hostel or hotel if there are any local rules or customs with the metro. Some places don't care if you eat on board; others forbid it. Some places have women-only carriages. Some places want you to form an orderly queue to board; on others it's a free-for-all. Some, amazingly enough, don't have ticket readers, instead relying on the honor system. Don't get caught without a ticket, though, as the fines can be steep.

Maps can sometimes be hard to find. Instead, download the area to Google Maps (see Chapter 8). This should let you navigate underground even if there isn't phone service, which is common. There's likely also a dedicated app for that metro system, which I talk about more in the section later in this chapter, "Using the local metro app."

When in doubt, ask! Many metro systems will have people in larger stations, especially those near touristy areas, whose sole purpose is to help people navigate the system.

TIP

Just because an airport is connected to public transit, doesn't mean it's included in the price of a metro ticket. Many places charge separately for airport access. Some have special "airport express" lines that are expensive, but fast. A cheaper, slower option is often available but less publicized.

Getting a metro card

I love getting metro cards. I have a stack of them because I'm a huge travel nerd: Oyster, Pasmo, Viva, Charlie, go, and so many more (see Figure 9-1). They're like useful collectables, or dare I say it, "souvenirs," I can re-use on a return visit. That Oyster card is practically a collector's item now, but it still works!

The larger benefit to metro cards is they're often vastly cheaper on a per-ride basis than buying individual journeys. Many metro systems are designed to overcharge visitors to subsidize locals.

Save that money by getting a card like many of the locals do. It will also save you time during your visit, since you won't need to buy tickets for every journey.

FIGURE 9-1: A collection of metro cards from Japan, Australia, Portugal, and the UK.

Metro systems all over the world are moving towards "contactless" payment methods. This uses the same technology that enables paying with your phone like I discuss in Chapter 2. The idea being, you unlock your phone or use a credit card with contactless capability, then tap it to the turnstile as you pass through. Your account will be charged at a discounted rate compared to buying a single ticket.

This is technically better, I guess, but I still like the idea of getting a metro card. Maybe that's just me.

Using the local metro app

Google and Apple Maps have a pretty extensive collection of transit system layouts. In some cases they even have real-time train information. For the most part, they'll get you from where you're staying to where you want to go. They aren't, however, perfect.

Most metro systems have their own apps. These vary in quality, as you'd expect. The better ones will have route planners and even tell you when the next train is departing. You might even be able to buy tickets.

Fitting In

Many people, while traveling, are desperate not to stick out. They want to blend in as much as possible. I don't fully understand this, but that's at least partly because outside of America and the UK, I don't fit in anywhere. I am quite obviously American, descended from Brits, and no amount of local clothing is going to mask that. I'm too tall, pasty, and more recently let's say "calorie dense" to fit in most places I visit.

I can see where this mindset comes from, though. Not wanting to stand out as a tourist can certainly be safer. There are also the opportunities that might arise if you're better blended into the local society.

However, there are cultural issues here that need to be navigated carefully. By trying to fit in you could stand out even more, or worse, offend the very people you're visiting.

Spoiler: You won't fit in and that's okay

Maybe you look just like the people in the country you're visiting, maybe you don't. Maybe you speak the language, maybe you don't. Maybe you bought all new clothes at local shops, and maybe you didn't. Even if you do everything you can to fit in, you still might not. In fact, you probably won't. That's okay.

There are endless reasons to travel, but one of the big ones is to see and experience new places. That idea, by its very nature, is temporary. As in, you're a short-term visitor. If you're respectful of the people and culture and you're as friendly as possible, that's all you can reasonably do. The majority of people are going to understand that you're a visitor and judge you solely on your actions. If they negatively pre-judge you just because you're an outsider, there was no amount of masking your origins that was going to help. It might make it even worse.

A big smile, wide-eyed enthusiasm, and an overall friendly attitude can go a long way in bridging any cultural misunderstandings. A friend of mine once described my demeanor while traveling as "like a golden retriever." I'll take that compliment.

Most people appreciate people visiting their country, learning about their culture, and I'm sure that even if they're neutral on those aspects, they almost certainly don't mind you bringing money into the local economy. Sorry to be so crass, but tourism is a huge part of many countries' economies. It employs hundreds of millions of people worldwide. To be clear, though, that doesn't give anyone the right to treat someone differently. Be the best visitor you can be.

The faux faux-pas of different places and offending people

The internet is rife with articles and videos that warn "OMG Don't Do THIS When Visiting X." These bombastic headlines make it seem you'll get tarred and feathered if you miss some seemingly inconsequential local social norm.

Don't get me wrong: You should absolutely try to learn what some of the basics are. Don't stand your chopsticks in your bowl of rice, remove your shoes inside in many places, all sorts of hand and finger gestures all over, eating with a certain hand, and so on. Make an effort to conform to the local etiquette and try not to be rude, but don't get stressed about it. Remember, you're a visitor and everyone knows you're a visitor. Most people are going to forgive you, or at least politely inform you, if you've done something wrong.

Even better, teach yourself to be observant of things you take for granted at home. How do people queue for a bus or subway, or do they do that at all? Are people standing on one side of the escalator, freeing the other side for people in a hurry? Is anyone else talking on the phone on this metro (hopefully not)?

Will you offend people if you mess something up? It's certainly possible, but what's important is how you handled everything leading up to it and after. If it's clear it was an honest mistake, that you're otherwise trying to respect the locals and their society, that should count for a lot. If you apologize after, that should, too. If someone's *still* upset with you, well there was probably nothing you could have done.

Local clothes (proceed with caution)

There's a fine line between celebrating a culture and cultural appropriation. Dressing up in local clothes and costumes can be an easy way to offend many, many people. Just because there's a photographer on a busy commercial street that offers photos in the local garb doesn't mean that's okay or a good idea.

It's not always a bad idea, however. Some cultures love it when foreigners (you) celebrate their culture by wearing their iconic clothing. In some cases, they think *not* sharing their culture in this way is the offensive thing. What might be "cringey" back home is actually welcomed by the locals. Then there's the possibility that you have relatives from that region, in which case these clothes are your heritage so go for it . . . probably.

Which is all to say, tread carefully. This is a potential minefield of offense. Personally, looking how I do, I avoid this in its entirety. I'd rather be the oddball standing out in sneakers and a t-shirt than the rude, clueless American dressing up in inappropriate clothing. Use your best judgement, and if there's any question, there's no question. Just don't do it.

Ask locals

REMEMBER

When it doubt, ask the locals. Not the person trying to sell you a photo package or specific clothing, but people who work at the hostel or hotel, and so on.

While you're at it, and they're willing, you can ask about what they think are things visitors to their region miss or get wrong. It's no one's job to educate you in such matters, but if they're open to the conversation it's certainly worth having. You are a guest in their country, and far too often visitors ignorantly or accidentally disrespect a culture in a way that can be easily avoided just by talking to some people who actually live there.

Learning the language

I speak English reasonably well and French, German, and Spanish very, very poorly. How poorly? Maybe I can ask where the bathroom is, but it might come out as a mangled insult against their lineage.

I'm regularly asked about how I'm able to get by in all the countries I've visited. I wish I could speak a dozen languages, but that's just not a skill I've acquired. Which is no doubt unfortunate since there is a level of understanding that just isn't possible if you're not fluent, or at least very familiar, with the local language.

That said, not knowing the language shouldn't prevent you from traveling. What's important is knowing a few key words and phrases (thank you; toilet; how much; and so on), and above all else, patience and empathy. English is essentially the lingua franca of the world. If someone's job is to interact with tourists, they almost certainly know a few words of English. Many people learn it as a second, or third, language, just to make communication easier during their own work and travel. Speaking slowly and clearly, not shouting when people don't understand you, and doing it all with as friendly a demeanor as you can, will all go a long way. Sometimes that's enough. Sometimes a few words in their language will show that you're at least trying. Even in places like France that are stereotypically resentful to those who don't speak their language, you'll find plenty of people who are delighted and amused when you try.

TIP

If you're planning on staying in a country for a while, or visiting often, I definitely think you should try to learn the language. It will open doors to experiences and situations that wouldn't be possible otherwise. If you want something more interactive than the many language apps, many places will have classes available for people just like you.

Homestays

The popularity and availability of homestays varies a lot per region. Staying with a local family can be one of the best ways to truly immerse yourself in the culture. You'll be able to do things like practice the language in a stress-free environment, try local food that you might otherwise have missed, and often you can make new friends. It's also usually one of the cheapest ways to stay in an area.

As I talk about in Chapter 5, homestays aren't for everyone. While most people stay with strangers and have no problems, that's not to say there aren't bad apples that can ruin your trip (or worse). Generally, I'm of the "most people are good" mindset, and there are a variety of websites where people interested in homestays can look for hosts and hosts can publicize their homes.

IN THIS CHAPTER

» **Marketplace bargaining 101**

» **Finding and declining hidden fees**

» **Attempting stealth mode**

» **Knowing what to do if you get robbed**

» **Avoiding common blunders**

Chapter **10**

Sidestepping Common Blunders

Your adventure is going to go smoothly. Probably. Certain things are out of your control, but other aspects are well in your control. Being aware of common scams, tactics, and run-of-the-mill cultural differences can make everything a little easier.

This chapter covers ways to avoid some common travel blunders that should help ensure your trip goes off without a hitch.

Note: Some of the advice here might be considered, by some, as "common sense." I disagree. What's common sense to one person is surprising news to someone else. In addition, what's common sense to someone with one cultural background might seem completely foreign to someone with a different cultural background.

Shopping in a Marketplace: Hustles versus Bargaining

Exploring various markets can be a great, and potentially free, way to get a sense of a place. What kind of products are people selling? What's the food like? It might also be a great way to find some locally made goods that are infinitely better than the cheap stuff you often find in souvenir shops. Then again, it might all be the same junk found in those stores. It varies a lot per region.

It can be quite common for the prices at a market to be rather . . . flexible. This might be the practice so vendors can take advantage of tourists, or it might be the cultural norm to expect haggling. This too can vary a lot depending on where you're headed. This section covers what you should keep in mind.

Cultural differences

In certain cultures and situations, the price of the item is the price of the item. In high school and college I worked at Circuit City selling audio gear. Every new item had a price, and that price was the price. No amount of haggling was going to get that any lower. I remember some people getting very upset when I wouldn't budge on the price. I literally wasn't allowed, but that subtlety was lost on some people. Was I insulting them by not bargaining? I doubt it. I think some people just wanted a deal.

There are places, however, where it's expected that you'll at least try to haggle. If the prices are shown at all, they might be set high with the hope you won't haggle so they're able to make a huge profit.

TIP

Bargaining/haggling is common in the Middle East, parts of the Mediterranean Region, China, and many other areas. It might not be expected in a grocery store, for example, but is expected in a market. It's worth researching about the country or region you're visiting before you leave. And as always, it's best to ask a local, perhaps at the hotel or hostel, what you can expect.

This is a "pick-your-battle" situation. Not everything can be negotiated. It's unlikely you'll get a deal haggling at chain hotels, car rentals, and so on. It certainly can't hurt to ask about discounts. You never know what could result with the right attitude on your part and kindness on their part. Just don't get upset if it doesn't work.

In other situations, prices are more fluid. Shops in a market, people selling trinkets on the street, those could net some deals. Keep in mind, though, that while buying things during your travels can be fun, and it's nice to have a memento, it would worth viewing any purchase through the lens of "what experience could I get with this money?" Is that $50 tchotchke worth a full day of travel?

The hard sell (just say no)

Walk away. Not only is walking away the best way to remove yourself from a situation, but it's also a fantastic bargaining technique. You must be willing to leave whatever item you're trying to buy. More often than you might expect, seeing that you're willing to leave might compel the seller to lower their price or at least change tactics.

And then other times, they'll be willing to let you leave, content that another mark will arrive shortly.

REMEMBER

Don't ever feel pressured to buy something you don't want. That pressure is an extremely successful sales tactic. You don't need to buy it.

Bargaining is a skill and they're professionals

If you're not from a culture or family of hard bargainers, you're at a severe disadvantage. The people you're dealing with do this all day, every day. It's a skill, and they've had lots of practice. Plus, they know you're interested and have the advantage that maybe you can't find that item elsewhere. Keep in mind that far too often what seems like a cool and unique handmade local item is actually made elsewhere and sold in every shop in the city.

From a budget standpoint, it's worth approaching any purchase like this as something you do not need and something that will harm your budget. Maybe it will, maybe it won't, but if that's your starting mindset, you'll be in a far better place to negotiate.

TIP

Always be willing to walk away. Sometimes, that's the key to a lower price. Other times, it's the best way to get away from a high-pressure salesperson.

Spotting Hidden Fees and Trying to Decline Them

One way to quickly blow your daily budget is getting tricked into paying surprise or hidden fees. These come in a variety of fun flavors, some of which I talk about in Chapters 4 and 5. Common ones include baggage fees for airlines and resort fees for hotels. You might also see things like destination fees, housekeeping fees, property service charges, and in some areas a tourism fee.

Sometimes these "fees" are legitimate taxes by the local government. Tourism fees are often an example of that, where the city or state/province/district has a small local tax on hotels to support the infrastructure needed to handle lots of tourists. At least, that's the idea. Where the money actually goes is the topic for a very different book than this.

Many of the other fees are just additional ways for the hotel or rental to squeeze more money out of you without inflating the supposed price of the room or rental. It's not a scam *per se*, but it's definitely sneaky.

REMEMBER

Visitors to the US should keep in mind that tipping is not a "hidden fee" and generally should not be thought of as optional. Waitstaff in many restaurants are paid an extremely low wage, sometimes just a few dollars an hour. Their income is almost entirely tips. It's a bizarre situation, but it's what we've got. Often our restaurant food is cheaper because of this, but that's not always the case. In most situations 15 percent of the total bill is the minimum, 20 percent or more is better.

TIP

If you see an additional charge on your bill, a quick web search will help you figure out if this is a mandated fee by the local government. If not, you can try to get it taken off your bill. Don't be surprised if you can't, however, since it's a significant revenue stream for some accommodations.

Airline fees

I talk a lot about these in Chapter 4. Nearly all airlines will charge you for checked luggage. Most will charge you to select your seat or to get in an exit or bulkhead row (usually more legroom). Some airlines are even charging for window or aisle seats now.

One way around this is to be a part of the airline's frequent flyer program. Often just being a member of the program gets you some perks. In other cases, you'll need a certain status level in the program. Most airlines have their own branded credit cards. These not only get you extra points, but many give additional perks like free checked luggage.

If you don't want to go the credit card route, it will take some extra time to find airlines that don't charge extra fees and the ticket prices are the actual ticket price. I wish I could give you a list, but listing what airlines charge which fees is impossible because it constantly changes. As a general rule, though, budget airlines almost always charge the most fees. That doesn't mean you can't get a cheap ticket with them, but once you start adding in "perks" like luggage, seats, and so on, all of a sudden the price is the same as a non-budget airline that *maybe* includes those things. As I mention in Chapter 4, the same route on the same day rarely varies too much in price once you factor in these various extra charges.

"Late" checkout fees

I was staying in a small, but adorable, hostel in Nagoya, Japan. I had made a few friends and after a day exploring the city we capped off the night with Ichiran Ramen (a chain, but amazing) and some assorted beverages back at the hostel. The next morning, I took my time getting ready to leave, chatting with my new friends one last time before I continued south. On my way out, I heard an exceedingly friendly Japanese voice say, "Excuse me, late checkout." Confused, I turned to see a gentle tapping of a sign that said checkout was 10:00. It was literally 10:05. I asked if they were kidding. Most of those 5 minutes was just getting back down to the lobby from my room. Insistent, they tapped the sign again. It blew my mind that they would risk a bad review over 5 minutes. They wanted their 500 yen (about $5), and I didn't feel like arguing, so I paid it.

Most hotels and many hostels are far more relaxed when it comes to checkout time. A few minutes isn't, usually, going to get you in trouble. If you know you're going to need a late checkout, most places will accommodate you without a charge, especially if you ask ahead of time. I stayed at a great, and cheap, hotel in Bali. My flight was at midnight, and they let me store my bags and hang out by the pool all day, for free, although admittedly, they had a restaurant there, and they knew I'd want food.

"Resort" and cleaning fees

Sometimes, the price you pay at booking is not the final price of the accommodation. Many places are charging "resort" fees that are paid on your arrival. These can range from a few dollars to a lot more. Why do these exist? Hotels know that most people choose hotels based solely on price, so they advertise an attractively low price. In the fine print of the booking, they'll mention the resort fee. However, most people don't notice that fine print and get surprised with the extra cost when they arrive. Hotels are counting on this, which is why so many do it. You can try negotiating this fee, but in the end most of the power rests with the hotel since you're already there and likely don't want to find a new place to stay.

"Cleaning fees" are a similar tactic. These have been the scourge of Airbnb for years. You think you're paying one price, only to find massive nonsense cleaning fees. The good news here is you'll see these before you book. Unfortunately, you might have gotten your heart set on some cool place to stay at a "great" price, only to find out the real price is actually double or more.

WARNING

Related, there are some stories about dishonest Airbnb hosts claiming messes and damages to extract extra money from their unsuspecting guests (you!). You might be able to fight these, but it's best to take pictures of the space when you arrive, and again when you leave. That's not a guarantee you'll escape the scams of a particularly motivated and nefarious host, but it should help.

Can you decline the fees?

Maybe. How good are your haggling skills? As I mentioned, some fees aren't really fees. They're called that but they're actually taxes. If you've paid up front and agreed to the price, it's unlikely you'll be able to get any of that back. If it's something additional you're asked to pay at check-in or check-out, it's possible you just need to ask to have it taken off your bill. Your success is going to vary quite a bit. Sometimes the desk staff or clerk has no ability to change a bill.

TIP

Non-Americans visiting America: Taxes aren't included in the price. Americans visiting most other places: Taxes are included in the price.

There are different schools of thought when it comes to haggling about prices. Personally, I'm a fan of the polite route. I see how far my dopey smile and lots of "please" and "thank yous" can get me. To a more rigorous haggler, this is naive and borderline moronic. Their tactics are more direct and often confrontational. I'm not a fan, since the person you're dealing with, at least in terms of these kinds of fees, is usually not the person who sets the prices. Then you're just making their day worse for something not their fault and out of their control. I understand that there are cultural differences when it comes to this kind of thing, but personally I'd rather be as nice as possible and potentially miss out on saving a few dollars than wasting my time, the poor employee's time, and creating a scene just to save a few bucks. Just my perspective. To each their own, but I've had jobs where I've dealt with customers, and they're the worst. So now I have no interest in making someone's job harder.

Being the Least Obvious Target

No matter if you're tall or short, wide or narrow, menacing or adorable, it's worth taking some precautions to try to be the least obvious target. Imagine you're a criminal looking for a mark. If someone is moving with a purpose and their belongings are secured tightly to their person, that's not as appealing as someone with their bag draped over one shoulder, their phone loose in their hands, watching a street performer.

Then there's the "common sense" advice I'll repeat here for the sake of completion: Don't leave your backpack, purse, phone, or wallet loose on a table. Don't hang things over the back of a chair in a restaurant or café. Keep your bag in front of you on public transport. Don't let people stand close to you, though that last one is way easier said than done in some places.

Statistically speaking, it's unlikely you'll get robbed in most tourist destinations. Reduce that number even further by taking a few simple precautions.

Most places are safe . . . mostly

If you talk to enough people about travel, even me throughout this book, you're eventually going to hear a story. I got robbed on a night train. I know a guy who was held at knifepoint in Cape Town. You'll inevitably hear about someone's cousin's roommate's friend who got mugged in Lisbon or maybe it was Lima 15 years ago. These things can happen, and they do happen. Will they happen to you? Maybe, but probably not. Statistically speaking, the actual number of people robbed in most locations is quite small when you consider the sheer number of people passing through them.

There are absolutely places less safe than others. My assumption throughout this book is that many of you are fairly new to travel. Most inexperienced travelers tend to head to more touristy areas in Europe, Asia, and so on. Most places with a big tourist industry are pretty safe.

If it's your dream to head to some lesser visited locations, that's great! But it's worth researching *why* they're not commonly visited. There's only so much Google can help here, since no matter where you're headed, *somebody* probably had a bad experience there. That's one thing, but if *everyone's* saying, "don't go to X," maybe there's a reason worth considering.

It's also worth noting that while I do carry a lot of expensive gear on me, so I'm particularly cautious, I have the privilege of looking the way I do. I'm taller than the average male in the majority of countries I visit, carrying more than my fair share of mass, and generally have a (I'm told) menacing scowl most of the time (I'm actually nice, I swear!). I also tend to walk fast. These combinations of things make me a less interesting target, generally speaking, than someone without those features. If your visage is more Mickey Mouse than Batman, you might need to take more steps to stay off the radar of the lesser cretins of society.

Look like you know where you're going

You'd be amazed at the power of just looking like you know where you're going. I had a friend who once claimed he could get into any building or area anywhere just by walking with a purpose and wearing a high-visibility jacket. There are a bunch of videos on YouTube of people "sneaking" into places by carrying a ladder. This aura of invisibility is like a version of what the great bard Douglas Adams called an "SEP Field," as in, Somebody Else's Problem. It's an incredible thing how all our minds just assume that if someone looks like they're supposed to be there, walking with a purpose, most people just don't question it. The moment that interloper stops to look around, check their phone, and so on, the field is broken and everyone notices them.

REMEMBER

Is walking with a purpose going to magically prevent you from getting robbed? Of course not. However, it generally will make you a less appealing target, and that's the goal.

Don't display expensive items

I met a lovely person in a hostel in London. It was their first time traveling alone, first time outside of the country, and the first time away from their small town. Their excitement was contagious. They asked me if I wanted to explore the area and get some lunch. It's always a joy to experience something with someone who's discovering it for the first time.

We left the hostel, and they immediately made several rather cringe-worthy mistakes. Their huge phone was sticking half out of their back pocket while we walked and stood among some crowds. They wanted to find something buried in their bag, so they proceeded to empty all the items out on a bench on a busy street. Standing at a street corner they proceeded to count their cash out in front of them trying to figure out what they needed for an Underground ticket.

I wish I was making this up. I hate being the guy to be like, "Uh . . . don't do that," but for their own safety I felt obliged. London is a relatively safe city, but that doesn't mean there aren't opportunistic pickpockets.

This is *Budget Travel For Dummies*, so I would guess you don't have $3,000 watches and $10,000 earrings, but it's best to just leave all that stuff at home. Being the least interesting target is your best defense. Look like a poor traveler eating noodles and staying in hostels. Which is to say, look the part! Let the ne'er-do-wells hunt for the rich folks (of course, ideally, they don't go after anyone, but so it goes).

REMEMBER

Inevitably, we all have and use things that have value. Phones, cameras, headphones, and so on, are just part of the modern world. You shouldn't be afraid to use them, but it's always a good idea to be aware of your surroundings.

Locks and codes

It's a good idea to have small TSA-approved locks on your bags. It's not going to prevent them from getting stolen, but if a criminal is scanning a crowd looking for a target, seeing a bag that might be hard or time consuming to get into might be enough of a deterrent.

There are some bags that claim to be knife or otherwise theft resistant. I think these are overkill. If someone wants your bag enough, they're just going to take it. Maybe there's a chance that someone will walk past your bag and slice it open, but it's much more likely they'll just pull it off your shoulder and open it somewhere out of sight. Also, and I hate to say this, but if someone's willing to use a knife to get your stuff, maybe your stuff is a reasonable price not to deal with that person.

Make sure your phone has a code to unlock. I've met a few people, typically older, who find phone passwords annoying. They walk around with unlocked phones *like absolute maniacs.* I can't even imagine, and I'm guessing most of you can't either. However, if you're one of these people, add a password to your phone right now and not "1234" or "0000" either. Those are the first things people check. Most phones have a biometric lock component now, like fingerprints or face unlock. These are fine, but they still need a code backup.

A common alternative to number codes is drawing a shape, connecting the dots so to speak. These are less safe because if you look closely at your screen, you'll probably notice a smudge in the exact shape of your password pattern. This will allow a thief access to your phone with just a few tries.

TIP

Adding two-factor authorization (discussed in Chapter 8) to whatever app offers it is one more level of security in case something happens. It's well worth the time and occasional hassle. Just remember that if the 2FA requires a text message, you might not be able to get those when you're abroad. A backup email is good. Though of course if you don't have access to that it's a problem too. There's no simple answer here, but generally it's better to be more safe than less.

Don't keep everything in one place

If you're able to secure your main bag, either in a locker at a hostel, your hotel room, or some other safe place, it's worth considering leaving a few things behind. Maybe that's an extra credit card if you have one, or a few days' supply of any medications you need. I've mentioned elsewhere in the book that I'm not a big fan of carrying lots of cash, but hiding enough for a meal or two or a taxi somewhere, might save you a lot of hassle in an emergency.

I tend to be a big fan of redundancy when it comes to safety and security. Is this excessive? Perhaps, but it gives me peace of mind. There's no real right or wrong answer here. For most people their trip will go off without a hitch. So whatever level of all this you feel comfortable with, that's probably enough. Well, as long as that amount is *some* amount, since there are scumbags out there. Chances are you won't come across them, but it's worth being careful since you might.

TIP

Memorize the actual drug names, not the brand names, of any medications you take. For example, "atorvastatin" not "Lipitor." The brand name might not be international, but the drug name often is.

Be aware of your surroundings

There's a fantastic line in the classic 1998 movie *Ronin* (which, unrelated, features some of the best car chases ever put on film), where Robert DeNiro says, "I never walk into a place I don't know how to walk out of." It's a brilliant line that explains a lot about the character, and it stuck with me. Do you need that level of diligent awareness everywhere you go? Almost certainly not.

However, it's very easy to get caught up in your surroundings. The excitement of a new place, a grand adventure, the understandable desire to take pictures of everything, it's all endlessly amazing. While enjoying yourself and lining up the perfect photo, is there someone lurking nearby who isn't? Someone looking at the tourists, not what the tourists are looking at? Will you be able to spot the pickpocket before they strike? Almost certainly not. For lack of a better description, they're professionals. This is how they make money, and if they're able to keep doing it, most likely they're good enough to remain unnoticed.

I'm willing to bet most of you have your own checklist for walking at night, what you do if you see a group of people just milling around, and so on. Being cautious doesn't mean you shouldn't enjoy yourself and enjoy the moment, but a quick scan of your vicinity to see if you spot anything out of the ordinary, or more importantly, show that you're *looking* for something out of the ordinary, can be a deterrent in itself.

WARNING

If a stranger tries to hand you something, do not take it. It's absolutely a scam.

What to Do if You Get Robbed

You shouldn't spend an inordinate amount of time worrying about what might happen if you get robbed. It's almost certainly not going to happen. If you take the above-mentioned precautions and you're aware of your surroundings when you travel, you're even less likely to have a problem.

Even if you're the most careful person on Earth, it's possible it's just your day. In my case, as I talk about in Chapter 2, it was on a night train in Italy. Luckily, we had no interaction with the perpetrator. We just woke up and a bunch of stuff was gone. I remember my heart sinking as I lifted my once stuffed, now far-too-light backpack.

Oh well. It's just stuff. If you do have the bad luck of getting robbed, hopefully you'll have the "good" luck that it's just belongings getting stolen and nothing more severe.

An unfortunate possibility

The main way a foreign city is more dangerous than your hometown or closest city is the very nature of just being there, out and about. Pickpockets are going to go where the pickings are most plentiful, and typically that's touristy areas, crowded metros, and so on.

There are certainly places in the world where it's more likely you'll get robbed than others, just as there are places to visit where it's way less likely. For instance, I feel like if I dropped my wallet in

Taiwan that everyone within 20 feet would stop, all would try to pick it up to hand back to me, and then they'd all want to make sure I was doing okay. Conversely, when I reported my robbery to the police in Rome, the officer was baffled I would even report such a thing and then told me I should have kept a better eye on my stuff.

The fact is, in a world of infinite possibilities, there are infinite outcomes. You could travel all over the world for decades and never have a problem. You could go on one trip and have your wallet lifted out of your pocket. Statistically, the most frequently visited places are as safe as any big city. If you're truly concerned about it, there are also lots of countries with very little petty crime, and you can start your adventures there.

Reporting the incident to the local police

You're not going to get your stuff back. You're just not. Theoretically it's possible. The guy I knew who got mugged in Cape Town got his wallet back because a bunch of people saw it happen and tackled the thief. My camera gear is, I hope, being used by someone who bought it in a used camera store in Italy and is none the wiser.

Reporting the crime to the police does have its benefits, however. Some insurance companies require a police report to file a claim. Most insurance covers electronics at a steep discount and high deductible, so don't expect to get much from them either. It might not even be worth the hassle and hours, maybe full day, that you lose going through the process. My experience with the railroad police in Rome was so negative, and because I basically didn't get anything from my insurance, I'm not sure I would have even bothered had I known what would happen. But then I wouldn't have had this fun story. Swings and roundabouts, as the Brits say.

Canceling cards and changing passwords

The first thing you should do, once you're in a safe place to do so, is cancel your credit cards. Some banks even let you do this on their app. Many credit card companies, wanting you to use them as much as possible, will send you a new card anywhere in the world.

If your phone was stolen, most likely they won't be able to access anything on it, but there's a lot of variables. It's best not to take the chance. This is another benefit of the password managers I discussed in Chapter 8. Many will automatically change passwords to multiple websites. If you don't have one of those (you should!), you should start the long process of changing your passwords to anything you accessed on whatever was stolen, be it your phone, tablet, or computer. Start with your email, then bank accounts, then social media. If they have access to your email there's untold amount of damage they can do. Way worse than even banking access.

Contacting your insurance

This is worth doing when the incident happens. You might not need to fully go through the claim process until you get back. Putting it "on their radar" so to speak, can at least get the process moving on their end. They also might have advice that supersedes anything I've mentioned here.

If you have travel insurance there might be funds available because of your situation. Travel insurance, like other forms of insurance, doesn't typically cover electronics, but a little is better than nothing.

Finding local replacements

This, at least, is kinda fun. Whether or not you're going to get the full replacement value of what was stolen, you probably need to replace at least a few things. A phone, a camera, a tablet, whatever core items you need to complete your adventure. Don't let some jerk ruin your trip.

Fortunately, the global economy means that most things are available in most places. You'll be able to find most electronics in just about any city or town. Will it be exactly the same? Maybe not. Do you need to replace the latest iPhone with the same model while you're on vacation? Probably not. You really just need something to get you by, and ideally one with a decent camera.

Speaking of, after my gear was stolen in Italy I was lucky enough to be staying with a friend in Vienna (that's where I was headed). Her neighborhood had five used camera shops within a short walk. I was spoiled for choice. They didn't have the exact DSLR I wanted, so I got that at the local electronics store. I spent several days drooling over new-to-me lenses though. Since I needed all this gear for work, the expense of buying it all was necessary. I'd even spent enough to get some of the taxes back when I flew home.

A few years later, I ended up replacing the camera I bought in Vienna. While the replacement is better in every way, it doesn't have the story to go along with it. Sure, getting robbed was a bummer, but in the end, stuff is just stuff, and I got a story out of it.

Other Common Blunders

There are a bunch of other potential blunders I've talked about in other chapters. I want to recap a few here specifically from the perspective of how things can go badly if you get them wrong. While I'll be the first to admit you can have a great adventure not doing anything I've listed here, in my years of travel these are some key things I've found that make travel easier, and I'd rather you not learn the hard way.

Overpacking

I can't stress enough how much more annoying a trip is with big, heavy luggage. In and out of transportation, up and down stairs, over curbs, across cobblestones, even just trying to get it to fit in an overhead bin, it's *always* going to be a hassle. Travel can be stressful enough without having to constantly drag an entire walk-in closet across the Serengeti.

For more about luggage and packing, check out chapters 6 and 7.

Overplanning

The perils of overplanning come in micro and macro forms. Both come from the totally understandable mindset of wanting to see as much as possible during your expensive trip. However, trying to see too much adds significant stress and often means you can't enjoy what you're actually seeing.

In the micro, don't try to schedule dozens of things to do every day. You'll only end up feeling rushed. In the macro, don't try to see lots of cities or countries each trip, unless you definitely have enough time. A few days to see some huge city is probably not enough, and then spending a day traveling to some other city to rush through for a few days, means you'll probably not get a great sense of either.

That's not to say it can't be done. Sometimes a few days is all you need, but I've heard so many stories of people trying to do half of Europe or Asia in a week and I'm like . . . oh no.

For more on planning, check out Chapter 3.

Jetlag!

If you're headed east, you're almost certainly going to have jetlag. If you've never traveled across multiple time zones, jetlag is just your body sticking to its known sleep schedule when you're physically in an area where day is, for example, in the middle of your normal night.

If you're lucky, you might only feel the effects for a day or two. Those days, though, are going to be rough. You'll be tired at weird times, hungry at weird times, and speaking from experience here, kinda cranky.

I find going west way easier, and most of the around-the-world trips I've done I've headed west and kept going, rarely suffering from much, if any, jetlag.

There's no "cure" for jetlag, though I have a few tricks that have worked to help me minimize the effects. If you've flown a long distance east, from the US to Africa or Europe for example, you'll probably arrive in the morning or early afternoon. My advice is to try to adjust as soon as possible, but more than that, be outside. Be in the sun. It sounds weird, but trying to convince your brain that no, it's actually daytime, helps. Along the same lines, if possible you should sleep with the curtains open. Try to let the sun wake you up, at least for a few days until your jetlag has passed.

If you absolutely need a nap, make sure you set an alarm. It's going to be *very* hard to get up, especially if you sleep until it's dark (which is a bad idea). Then you'll never get to sleep at a normal time. An hour or two nap on your first day is probably okay, but you should resist doing so on the following days.

If you're headed west, you'll often arrive late afternoon or evening. Regardless, don't nap and just stay up as late as possible. If you can make it to your normal bedtime, or at least within a few hours of it, you'll probably be ready to go in the morning. Likely way earlier in the morning than you normally would wake, but that's okay — more daylight for your adventure!

I know some people have advice about having caffeine or not and eating or not, but I've never found any of those specific tricks to work. Just try to adjust as quickly as possible, try to line up your schedule with the new location as best as possible, and get on with your adventure. Stay hydrated, though.

Oh, and do *not* constantly check what time it is "back home." That's amusing at first but just ends up frustrating your attempts at getting on the new schedule.

Not incorporating rest or downtime

This ties into the jetlag conversation as well as for planning. Unless you normally walk all day long around your hometown, you're going to get pretty tired doing so around some new place. Then there's the excitement of just being in that new place, all the many activities you'll do, and more, so it's understandable you're going to get tired. If you have 50 things planned between 3:00 and 3:15 before you need to get to the next location for 50 more things, you're just going to get worn out and eventually, burned out. You don't want to be five days into your two-week trip exhausted, in a bad mood, and wanting to go home. Pace yourself!

The first few days of your trip should be light, so you can ease into the new time zone and deal with the jetlag. Days with lots of walking and adventuring should have some downtime during the day or the next day to recharge. Being in a new place is an adventure in itself. You're there, you're doing it! You don't have to cram every day with endless things to do. The whole thing is going to be fun. You can spare a few hours to sit someplace pretty and chill. The rest of the trip will be better for it.

WARNING

If you're not from a hot and dry climate, don't underestimate how quickly you can get dehydrated with heat and low humidity. In more desert regions, drink (and bring with you) more water than you think you need.

IN THIS CHAPTER

» **Knowing how and when to extend your stay**

» **Avoiding travel burnout**

» **Moving on to a different city, country, or continent**

» **Dealing calmly with emergencies**

» **Keeping friends and family in the loop**

Chapter **11**
Time to Head Out — Or Is It?

S ometimes you just don't want to leave. I get that. I really get that, quite a lot. There have been countless times where I've found the perfect place, with perfect people, at just the right time — a magical confluence of events that's the ultimate of what travel can be. As you take a moment to enjoy this perfection you think: "I wish I could stay here longer." Well, why don't you?

This is the biggest reason I'm such a proponent of planning less and staying flexible. It's to allow for the possibility of these perfect moments in time. The moments you remember for the rest of your life. The times you wish lasted forever. They can never last forever, but maybe you can make them last for a little longer.

That's what I'm going to talk about in this chapter: changing plans based on the moment. Figuring out when it's right to stay and when it's right to move on. Most importantly, what are the logistics of changing plans?

Staying Flexible

Being able to adjust your trip based on the needs of the moment can be the difference between a good trip and a bad one or a decent one and a legendary one.

The reasons why you want to change your plans can range from something tangible, like a typhoon baring down on your tropical island, or intangible, like you are or aren't enjoying the location, the hostel, or the people you've met. Having as little a financial penalty, ideally no penalty, to change your plans is ideal. You shouldn't be forced to endure a mediocre situation just because you planned for something and the reality was different.

Following the weather (or not)

The weather is probably the biggest unknown for any trip, especially if your destination is a national park (see Figure 11-1), a beach, or is otherwise outdoor-oriented. Sure, if you're headed to Los Angeles, you can probably assume it's going to be sunny or that India will be raining in June. In some parts of the world, weather can be a huge, widespread event, but in others, it's hyper local. The good news is, weather changes. The bad news is, weather changes.

Geoffrey Morrison

FIGURE 11-1: National parks, like Yosemite in the US, can be incredible — if the weather cooperates.

I can absolutely understand the increasing horror and anxiety as your trip approaches and the weather keeps getting worse and worse. There's no way to guarantee the weather during your trip, but there are ways to roll with it. Depending where you're headed, perhaps the weather is different just a few hours away. A short bus or train ride away from your destination may not be exactly what you planned, but perhaps discovering a new adventure with decent weather is better than trying to make your original plan work while you're wet and miserable.

REMEMBER

Also keep in mind that just because the weather forecast says one thing, doesn't mean it's going to be that one thing all day. There are lots of places that have "rain every day" but it's for about 15 minutes and then it's perfect.

Or, just bring rain gear and embrace the deluge. The best day I've ever had in Paris was walking around during periodic downpours. It would start raining and everyone would rush inside. Then the sun would start to come out and I'd have a short time to myself on the glistening, empty streets. The people would return until the rain started again, and then I'd have the place to myself again. It was glorious.

For longer trips, you can even follow the weather as it changes. You could work your way north to follow the cherry blossoms as they bloom in Japan. You could work your way north along Australia's east coast as the summer turns to autumn, staying with the warmth.

If you're lucky, you won't have to worry about the weather at all. Staying flexible if the skies take a turn is ideal.

Being able to change locations for any reason

You should feel comfortable bailing on a place for any reason. If you end up not liking the vibe, not liking the crowds, even if it just wasn't what you expected, leave! You've spent a lot of money to be there, sure, but what are you really spending money on? You're spending money on the experience. If the experience is bad, don't fall for the sunk cost fallacy (throwing good money after bad). Find your own adventure. Find something different. Maybe it's a different area, or a different city, or hey, why not a different country? Once you're exploring the world, you'll start to realize how small it is.

Remember, just because "everyone" loves some place doesn't mean you have to. Maybe that city/country/region just isn't your vibe. Maybe you thought it would be, and it turns out it wasn't. That's totally valid. You tried it, that's the important thing. Now find an adventure you prefer.

WARNING

Resist, however, the temptation to go home. I've certainly met people who get quite homesick, even during short trips. If this is your first time away from home and family, it's a natural feeling. My advice is to push through it. Chances are you'll end up enjoying yourself and you'll be glad you didn't quit.

Going Slow (No, Slower)

One of the most common complaints I hear from infrequent travelers is how tired they are when they get home. That they always felt like they were running a marathon. That they "need a vacation from their vacation." This is the main consequence of planning too much. If you've always got something to do, or you're trying to see too much in limited time, you're going to end up exhausted.

I can absolutely understand this. If you've got the American-typical two weeks of vacation, it's logical to try to cram as much as possible into that limited time. It feels wasteful not to try to fit everything possible into every minute. But it's not wasteful to do less. The adventure is the thing, and it can be far more rewarding and satisfying spending more days in fewer places than just a few hours in lots of places. One of your most memorable travel moments could be just relaxing in some park, or sitting beside a river, just being in the moment in someplace that's not home. If you're an inveterate planner, plan time to do nothing.

If your travel goal is to check off that you've been to certain places, then okay. Fit in as much as you want. But if your goal is to actually experience a place, be in a place, then it's far better to take your time and slow down. For example, the fairytale-esque Strasbourg, France (shown in Figure 11-2) is certainly a worthy spot to experiment with a more leisurely travel pace.

FIGURE 11-2: Give yourself time to just enjoy being in a place as magical as this one.

Avoiding burnout

I'm sure there are some people who would thrive hitting eight cities in seven days, but I don't think that's most people. I think the potentially toxic "once in a lifetime" mentality makes people think this one trip is the only time they'll have to see that part of the world. As such, they feel they have to do *all the things*. I hope that one of the biggest takeaways you get from this book is that travel can be affordable enough that you can do it on a regular basis. This should help alleviate the pressure to do everything all in one trip.

Being able to take your time, largely by not scheduling too much or at least scheduling in days where there's not much planned, not only gives you the flexibility to enjoy what you are seeing but also have the time to check out things you didn't know when you were planning from home.

There's no hard-and-fast rule of what constitutes "slow." Personally, I try to spend at least three days in any location. Sometimes it's way more. I could spend a week or several just in Tokyo or London and always find something to do. There's nothing wrong with spending more days, too. I know a few frequent travelers that aim for five days. If you want to spend your entire trip in one place, that's great, too.

Broadly speaking, if you have more than one long transit day in a week, it's probably too much. Each transit day is generally a wasted day. It's a day you could have been exploring, not cramped on a bus/train/plane. I *like* being cramped on a bus/train/plane and even I try to keep those days to a minimum.

That's not to say you can't have multiple long travel days in a week but keep the "about one day per week" as a sort of reference point. It gives you three days in each place, which still might only scratch the surface, but you'll at least get to see a fair amount.

Keep in mind I'm not saying you have to spend three days in a town with three houses and no stoplights (though that can be fun!), but if you're exploring big famous cities, it's going to take some time. These are guidelines, not rules. The idea is to not feel rushed, or at least, keep the days that you feel rushed to a minimum. Otherwise, your vacation might start to feel like work.

Enjoying yourself instead of checking things off a list

I love lists. I love making them and I love checking things off them. I enjoy seeing famous landmarks, buildings, and scenic vistas. They're famous for a reason! But it can be a trap. Overly focusing on famous places and things can cause you to miss the epicness of everything else.

Everyone knows about the Mona Lisa, but the rest of the Louve is one of the best of the art museums in the world. The Walk of Fame in Hollywood is boring, crowded, and gross, but a short drive away are some fantastic buildings, views, and hikes. Look, I don't want to yuck anyone's yums. If the reason you're traveling is to see some specific thing and take some specific photo, then go for it and don't let anyone tell you otherwise. However, if all you want to do is see those famous spots, I hope you also built in time to just explore where you are.

This is where a good walking tour, or something similar, can be a big help. They'll often hit all the landmarks, but also a lot of the smaller, lesser-known ones, too. Plus, once you've seen the checklist items, you'll have more time to explore and find cool things not on any list.

Remembering it's all an adventure!

Seriously, it's all an adventure. The flight, the bus, the metro, the hostel, walking around, sitting around, grocery shopping, everything. If the museum you wanted to visit is closed, that's okay! If it's raining, that's okay! You're travelling. You're on an adventure.

REMEMBER

Do your best to forget about the money and the stress and just try to enjoy being on a different part of this tiny ball of rock and water.

When It's Time to Move On

Eventually, it's time to move on. Maybe you've explored every street and alley, so you want to see some mountains (like those in Figure 11-3). Maybe you've seen enough mountains and want to explore some streets and alleys. When do you know the time is right? That's entirely up to you. As I mentioned earlier, being comfortable changing plans on the go is key, and part of that is having the right tools to do so.

Geoffrey Morrison

FIGURE 11-3: The road to Sólheimajökull glacier, Iceland.

Ideally, you haven't booked everything in advance. That way, you won't have cancellation feels to worry about. Even if there are fees, it's worth weighing that cost versus the excitement of a new place. Generally, I'd say leaving a place you're no longer enjoying is worth a pretty high price.

Being comfortable changing plans is the first part of this. The second (and third) is booking new places to stay and figuring out how to get there.

Finding new accommodations

This is why it's important to have data for your phone and a booking app you like. While you're sitting having lunch or a snack, you can check hostels and hotels in another location.

You might be surprised to learn how easy it is to find accommodations at the "last minute." I've booked hotels and hostels the morning of the day I was going to arrive. In fact, I often book my next stop just a day or two before I leave my current spot.

Rarely, if ever, have I had difficulty finding the next place to stay. Sure, if you're in some busy area in the high season, it might be a lot harder. It's possible your first choice won't have space, but in most popular areas, there are lots of hotels and hostels.

REMEMBER

Ideally you won't be traveling in the high season anyway, since shoulder seasons are cheaper and not as busy. Then you'll have even greater choices.

Transport options

There's always a bus. Okay, not *always*, but buses are how most of the world gets from one place to another. After that, there's trains. These are usually faster, but also more expensive. In many parts of the world, the cheapest option over longer distances is actually a plane. Many areas around the world have extensive low-cost air connections.

Renting a car can be brutal on the budget, but in some places it's the only way to explore.

In some places there are also ferries, which are super slow. Some are even overnight. Personally, I enjoy a good slow ferry. I traveled with a friend who got seasick. She did not like ferries, slow or otherwise. Some passenger ferries have restaurants and bars, some don't. Some are mostly cargo, with a few cabins and a lounge for people. Many include cars, if you want your road trip to lose the road (check your rental agreement and insurance though). If you're not used to this kind of travel, it can be a unique experience.

In the US, Europe, Australia, Japan, and a few other places, there are a wonderful anachronism called "night trains." Usually these will have some kind of bed, sometimes in a shared cabin. You'll rattle your way across the countryside to arrive at your destination sometime the next day. I've done these all over the world, and generally I love them. Again, they're the kind of unusual experience I seek out. They require a bit of a price calculation, though. On one hand, you're not paying for accommodation that night. You'll also, generally, board and disembark right in a city's center. However, they can often be quite expensive. Worth it for the experience? If you've never done it, and it sounds cool, yes. If the destination is more important than the journey to you, then no.

TIP

I'll once again recommend the Rome2Rio website and app. It will give you just about every option to get from one place to another, usually with prices.

Heading to a different city or even a different country

The world can seem like a big place, especially if you haven't traveled much. The modern world, though, is very, very small. You can get on a plane, take a nap, and be on a different part of the globe. Every major city on Earth is at most a day's journey from every other major city. Most are even closer than that. Once you get the hang of it, heading to a different city/country/continent is easy and everything just seems a lot closer together.

In many parts of the world, different countries are close enough that you can drive or take the train there in just a few hours. On several occasions I've traveled to another country for a day, on a whim. In certain places this is a lot easier than others. In Europe you could quite easily visit three or more countries in a day. You shouldn't move that fast, but you could if you wanted.

Why would you do this? Well, why not? Even if that other nearby country wasn't on your initial travel list, it's *right there*. If you don't need a special visa to visit, and you have the time, why not go? Politics aside, borders are just lines on a map. Don't be intimidated.

Or, you can think even bigger. If you're ready to move on and you've found a cheap flight to someplace even farther away, why not? Infrequent travelers might find this to be madness, but really, what's the big deal? It's just another flight. Once you've got the hang of booking things as you go and you've taken care of figuring out how to get *back* (or if continuing the long way around is cheaper), then there really isn't any reason not to follow cheap flights, a new interest, or as I've done on several occasions, taken someone up on their offer for a stay on their couch!

Following friends

One of the biggest mistakes and regrets I had when I first started my extended travels was sticking to a plan and not changing it based on the circumstances. Specifically, I've mentioned before about the great people I met in Melbourne. I was having the best time I'd had in years, yet I felt I needed to continue on based on reservations I'd made. They all stayed. I was happy to see them on social media still having a great time but sad I was no longer a part of it. What other epic memories would I have had if I'd stayed?

I don't dwell on this too much, as I met more amazing people later. But eventually I realized the only person that cared about my plans was me. I could just . . . stop and stay in a wonderful location with wonderful people (as I did in Northern Ireland in Figure 11-4).

REMEMBER

You should always feel like this is an option. If the cost is prohibitive or if you've run out of time, that's totally different. That's just life. But if you have the time and the price to change your tickets or reservations isn't a lot, it's likely a small price to pay to stay where the vibes are right.

What to Do if There's a Problem

As I've said before, things will almost certainly go great. Crazy things don't happen all the time. If they did, they wouldn't be crazy. They'd be normal. Be prepared, of course, but don't stress about the unlikely chance some random horrible thing will happen. In all probability, it won't.

Geoffrey Morrison

FIGURE 11-4: Exploring Giant's Causeway in Northern Ireland with friends.

There aren't many situations that will require you to radically change your plans or cut your adventure short, but in that rare situation where something does go pear shaped, having prepared a bit will make the situation way more manageable.

Local emergency numbers

FIND ONLINE

Many countries around the world have a three-digit number that will connect you to emergency services. In the US, it's 911. Other common numbers are 112 (Europe and parts of Asia), 000, and 999 (UK). Some countries, like Brazil and Canada, both 911 and 112 will both work. Others might have different numbers for police, fire, and ambulance. For instance, in China and Japan it's 110 for police, and 119 for fire/ambulance. It's worth learning what the local number is before you need it. You can find a link with a listing of local emergency numbers at www.dummies.com/go/budgettravelfd.

Interestingly, most mobile phones will be able to call a local emergency number even if the screen is locked, or there's no working SIM card. I wouldn't count on this; I still recommend a working phone like I discuss in Chapter 8. However, in a serious emergency and you don't have any other means, it's worth trying.

If you're traveling with friends or family, share this info with them, too.

Other phone numbers

I can tell you my phone number from when I was a kid. I can tell you my phone number now. I think those are the only two numbers I have memorized. I bet most of you are in the same boat.

Sure, ideally you'll memorize other important numbers, like your spouse/friend/travel buddy, or someone at home who can help you out. That'd be great, but is anyone going to do that? I don't. Having a card in your wallet or bag that has a few key numbers on it is a good idea. This could include an emergency contact, your doctor, maybe your credit card companies. Just don't write any passwords on it.

Letting Your Family/Friends Know Where You Are

Most of your people back home aren't going to understand what you're doing. Most people think of a "vacation" as a set event with a specific place that ends at a certain time. When you deviate from that, people will be alarmed. That's on them, but you can at least keep them informed so they know where you are.

The easiest way to do this is via a messaging app. This is one of the reasons I recommend WhatsApp since it's easy to use and works anywhere there's Wi-Fi. This could just be a simple "Hey, I'm headed to Uruguay for the weekend" message, but you can also share your live location within a chat message.

You can also share your live location with Google Maps. Apple Maps allows you to send a location but won't follow you. Instead, the Find My app has this option, though keep in mind the other person will need an iPhone or iPad as well.

An additional option is an app like PolarSteps. This has roughly real-time GPS tracking overlayed on satellite maps. It tracks your adventure and at the end of your trip you have a cool line that shows everywhere you went. You can make this public, though I don't love the idea of strangers knowing where I am while I'm traveling. Instead, you can just share the link with those who you're comfortable with knowing where you are. You can add photos, too, if you're not a fan of the bigger social media apps.

There's also good old-fashioned email. I forward my flight info to a few key people, just so they have it.

REMEMBER

Whatever option you use, just make sure it works and your loved ones understand how to use it before you leave.

IN THIS CHAPTER

» Organizing your life so you can be away from home

» Making changes to your flights

» Knowing when you need a visa

» Transforming into a "digital nomad"

» Working from home from anywhere

Chapter **12**

Settling In for an Extended Stay

To me, the idea of budget travel goes beyond the desire to spend as little as possible on a specific trip. To me it's about having the "tips and tricks" in your arsenal to make travel affordable enough to do on a regular basis.

What's the logical end point of that idea? Is it being able to afford a trip every year without being rich? I hope so. Is it being able to visit "expensive" locations despite being on a budget? Absolutely! Is it traveling for months or years on end? Oh . . . now there's an interesting idea.

Sticking Around When You Can't Tear Yourself Away

When everything aligns — the perfect place, the perfect people, the perfect moment — life is good. It's important to hold onto those moments.

What if, after those few days, you still didn't want to leave? What if you just . . . didn't? What if you stayed or kept going? There's a lot of adventure to be had out there: new friends to meet (see Figure 12-1), new food to try, new vistas to see.

Photo by Geoffrey Morrison/CNET Media Inc.

FIGURE 12-1: If you met these two kangaroos (beacharoos?) in Lucky Bay, Australia, would you want to leave?

There's a pervasive mindset, especially in America but common elsewhere, too, that there's life and there's vacation, and travel is only something you do during the latter. But what if it wasn't? What if you could afford to do this more? A lot more.

This is not easy, nor is it possible for everyone. But I firmly believe that extended travel is possible for a lot more people than currently do it. If your job is sometimes remote or occasionally or regularly "work from home," it's theoretically possible to do that from anywhere.

I just want to plant the seed in your head that maybe, just maybe, you can travel more than the corporate world's "generous" two weeks they don't really want you to take.

Even if you're in a field that can work remotely, getting from "vacation" to "digital nomad" is not, typically, an overnight thing. It takes a lot of planning and convincing. Everything is set up to prevent you from doing what you're trying to do.

In the meantime, adding a few extra days to your vacation isn't the worst thing.

Staying for an extra day, week, or month

Breaking out of the "two weeks" mindset is exceptionally hard for most Americans. I know retirees that still think in these terms. They don't have a job to return to. They're retired! They have a reasonable budget, and yet they go on two-week "vacations." To each, their own, I guess.

It's worth looking at what's typical in other countries. Sure, there are some that have even bleaker restrictions on time off than the US, but not many. Far more typical is three to four weeks, and in some cases, even more than that! In fact, many people are shocked at how few vacation days Americans get.

It's hard, if not impossible, to fight this from within. You can't just go to your boss and say, "I want four weeks' vacation this year." Or maybe you can. If so, awesome! I was lucky, early in my career, to have a fantastic boss that would let me take as much time off as I wanted as long as I got my work done on time and traveled somewhere. Sadly, such understanding bosses are rare.

TIP

There is a separate path, however. Instead of taking time off, you just permanently, or semi-permanently, "work from home" where home is wherever you want it to be. This is commonly referred to as being a "digital nomad."

The first step in becoming a digital nomad, aka someone who works remotely from anywhere, is to break free from the mindset that travel is a thing only done for a few days a year. Once the possibility of extended travel becomes something that's maybe, *just maybe*, attainable, you're on the right track.

Can you just not go home?

The hardest part of transitioning from "work from home" to "work from anywhere" is convincing your boss. I've had mixed success with this. When I first decided to travel more or less full-time, I had two main freelance jobs where I had responsibilities ranging from regularly writing articles and reviews to leading a team of four other people. After I decided to become a digital nomad, I sat each of my bosses down and had a serious discussion of what I was planning on doing and why it shouldn't affect my work in any way. To prove that, I revealed that I'd spent half the previous month working from a beach in Hawaii. Both of them enthusiastically supported my decision, and to my knowledge, neither regretted it. I hope you have such understanding bosses in your life.

Five years later, after I had been doing my job from all over the world, a new boss came in and couldn't fathom how I was doing *any* work since I wasn't in an office. Despite my repeated explanations and years of proof about my work ethic, he fired me. Over email. (I'm not bitter at all.)

What that taught me was there are going to be some people who just don't understand. I'd hoped that in the post-COVID era, a time that proved that *many* people could actually work just fine from home, there would be a greater acceptance of working remotely. That turns out not to be the case. In many companies, if anything, the opposite is true.

Which is to say, becoming a digital nomad is an uphill battle. Wanting to stay traveling is not the "normal" thing. Bosses, even friends and family, are likely going to resist the idea that you can be on the road for more than the prescribed and mandated two weeks a year. Having been lucky enough to be doing it for years, I can attest that struggle is worth it. It's not going to work for everyone, unfortunately. But if you think you might be able to do it, it's worth trying. (Unfortunately, the monasteries in Meteora, Greece, shown in Figure 12-2, are unavailable for working remotely.)

Photo by Geoffrey Morrison/CNET Media Inc.

FIGURE 12-2: The monasteries in Meteora, Greece.

What to do about mail, bills, and more

The trickiest part of organizing your life for extended travels is dealing with the endless paperwork that comes with being an adult in the modern world. Even if you sign up for "paperless billing" there's always going to be something that arrives in the mail that you'll need to access.

For longer trips, but not permanent roaming, you can hold US mail for up to 30 days. You can have someone pick up the mail for you at that point, but that requires extra steps you'll need to do before you leave. Canada Post and UK's Royal Mail pause delivery for much longer, for a fee. Other countries likely have similar options. In all cases you'll need to set the service up several days ahead of time.

You can also set a forwarding address, usually a parent or other family member's home. Someone you trust to sort the junk mail from the mail that's junk. Usually, this works for a limited time, up to 18 months in the case of the USPS. In many places you can rent a mailbox, which could help if you're planning to be in one place for a few weeks or months.

Most likely, though, you'll only have a few regular items arriving by mail. You'll probably have to cancel subscriptions like your cell phone, streaming services, and so on, as they often don't work outside the country you're from. Health insurance, for Americans, is a big one not to be overlooked. If you're staying in your home country, that makes things a bit easier. Most services are set up to let you move around nationally, just not internationally.

Speaking of, you'll need to figure out health insurance. There are some travel insurance policies that are good for a year, but you'll need to read the fine print about what they cover. Even if you're from a country with national health care, you should investigate what it actually covers when you're abroad.

What about all your stuff now, and later?

If you're leaving for longer, you'll need to either sell off or store your stuff. If you know you're coming back, the latter is more expensive but possibly cheaper than buying everything new when you return.

You're not going to want to leave your apartment/house empty for the entire time you're gone. That's a bad idea for a lot of reasons.

My solution at first was offering my house to friends and family for weeks at a time. They got a place to stay for a vacation, and I got someone looking after my house. Eventually you'll run out of people who will take you up on that offer. My next fix was to get a roommate. They get to live by themselves while I'm traveling, and I have the peace of mind that there's someone at home.

If you have a car and you don't want to sell it, make sure you research what you need to do for long term storage. You can't just park it and expect it to work again after several months. At the very least you'll need a trickle charger for the battery. There are solar options if you don't have a nearby outlet. I also recommend a good car cover. Gasoline goes bad after a while, and tires can flatten and rot. Definitely read up on what steps you need to take.

Lastly, figure out your re-entry procedures. Which is to say, assuming you're coming back, what does that process look like? At the very least you'll need a place to stay. Will you have enough money for a deposit on a new place if you need one, and if not, how long will that take? If someone is subletting from you, how much notice do you need to give them, assuming that wasn't pre-determined. Also don't underestimate the shock of being home after a long time away. It will take some readjustment.

REMEMBER

All the above is all under the assumption that you'll be traveling, not settling down in one location for several months or more. That will require a visa, which I talk about later in the chapter.

When remote isn't an option

I understand this isn't going to be possible for everyone. Not every job can be done remotely. I'm not going to recommend you quit your job to travel. However, I will say that I've met a lot of people who have done exactly that. They saved up what they could, quit, and just made what money they could along the way. Crazy? Irresponsible? Not necessarily. Done right, with the right "reentry" plan, it's not as crazy as it seems.

If you've got three kids, a dog, and a mortgage, maybe this isn't the best idea. If your only dependent is a needy houseplant, you hate your job, your apartment lease is ending, and you have a place to crash when/if you come home, maybe a "gap" year isn't the craziest idea. Gap years are quite common outside the US Sometimes that gap year becomes even longer. Does a "gap" in your employment history look bad on your CV/resume? Hard to say. If in that time you traveled to a dozen countries and have a different outlook on life and the world, what's that worth to certain employers?

I certainly can't give you career advice. I'm neither qualified to do so, nor do I have any idea what your chosen career might be. All I can do is say that there is another option out there beyond the nine-to-five grind. That option doesn't work for everyone, but then, neither does the typical nine-to-five job. If you've read this far into this chapter, I suspect that might be you. This different, travel-heavy path could mean working remotely from some cool location, taking a year off to travel, or something I haven't even considered. The only person who can figure out what works for you, is you. Just make sure you have a plan in place if it doesn't work out, and then figure out your own path.

Changing Flights versus Canceling Flights

Unless you've fully adopted my love of minimal planning, you've probably booked at least some flights and probably more. If you've decided to stay somewhere longer than you initially intended, what are your options for the flight?

Without a valid excuse — and just wanting to stay longer is, sadly, not a valid excuse for the airlines — your options are either canceling, changing, or postponing. The specific costs and restrictions for each of these will vary per airline, per country/region, and often per ticket. The cheapest tickets are usually non-refundable for almost any reason. Others can be adjusted, either for free, or more likely, for a fee.

Keep in mind that you should be able to cancel or change your reservations within the first 24 hours of booking. Given that we're talking about extending your stay it's unlikely you're within that window, but it's worth keeping in mind.

Costs/fees/hassle

There's a calculation to be made here. How much is your time worth? Generally speaking, it's probably worth contacting the airline and trying to get some money back. You might be able to get the taxes and fees back, for instance. Some airlines might offer you a credit toward a future flight, which in this case is just about ideal. There might still be fees, but considering the alternative, that's okay.

If you purchased travel insurance, some have a clause for a "change of plans" that might reimburse you for some of the cost. However, these also usually require a specific reason. These reasons are often more forgiving than an airline, like a concert or conference you're planning to attend gets postponed. It's worth checking the fine print or giving them a call.

Can you postpone instead?

Instead of canceling a flight, perhaps just postpone it instead. Shifting the dates is often cheaper, and you can kick that can down the road quite a bit. If, after several months, you're still not ready to go home, kick that can again. Will you need to pay a re-booking fee again? Possibly.

I did this once with an international flight, re-booking it for six months later expecting to return to that country around that time. There was a small fee, but it was a tiny fraction of the overall ticket price. In other words, well worth it.

Canceling and getting a new flight

Worst case, you have to cancel your flight and get little, if any, of the money back. Is it still worth it? That's a calculation you'll need to make in the moment. Could those hundreds of dollars (or more) be better spent on a different trip down the line? The idea behind budget travel is being able to afford not just a single trip but making travel affordable enough to do it regularly. Essentially "throwing" away a ticket sure seems antithetical to that.

However, maybe not. If you've found the perfect place with the perfect people, that's worth something. There's no dollar value to that. Maybe staying in that moment is worth sacrificing another future trip which may or may not be as good as the place and time you're currently in. There's no right or wrong answer here. Looking back on own my travels, I can say there were many moments that I wish I'd extended but didn't because I'd already booked things I'd have needed to cancel. The money seems inconsequential now compared to the memories I could have made.

One-way tickets

I mention in Chapter 4 about my love for one-way tickets. Usually there isn't a huge price difference between that and 50% of a round-trip ticket. There are exceptions. Certain destinations have heavy fees, or deep discounts, for one-way and round-trip tickets respectively.

The benefit, of course, is the ultimate in flexibility. Want to stay longer? Want to leave early? Want to go somewhere new? It's great just having the ability to fly out of a different part of a large country because you ended up taking an unexpected road trip.

Once you're ready to be more flexible in your travels, it's worth pricing out one-way tickets each way as well as a roundtrip ticket. If there is a price difference, is it small enough to justify giving yourself the flexibility? On an extremely tight budget, probably not. With a slightly larger budget? It's definitely worth considering.

REMEMBER

As I've mentioned before, double check that the country your visiting doesn't require a ticket out (aka a return ticket or proof of onward travel). This is most common with island nations, but there are others as well. You can usually find out about this with a country's visa info. Don't rely on an airline to inform you. They're supposed to, but sometimes don't.

When Do You Need a Visa?

Trick question. You basically always need a visa. Many countries, for many travelers, have a "visa on arrival" program that automatically activates when you clear customs and immigration. Other countries, especially for some visitor nationalities, require applying for a visa before you arrive. Regardless, every country in the world has a limit to how long foreigners can stay. It might be as short as a few days or weeks, or as much as a few months. Beyond that you need to get special approval from the government that you intend to stay longer than is typical for a tourist. While some countries don't require a visa *per se* they'll still have restrictions on how long you can stay.

Don't assume you can just enter a country. A simple Google search for "Does [your nationality] need a visa for [country you're visiting]" should do the trick. That country's government's webpage should also have the info.

What's a visa?

A visa is not the same as Visa. It has nothing to do with credit cards. A visa, among other things, is an authorization by a country for you to stay for a time specified by the visa. You almost always need one to stay in any country for any length of time.

The process to get a visa, and how long they last, varies greatly depending on where you're going, and where you're from. Countries with "strong" passports, like the US, UK, most EU countries, and others, might not need to apply for anything in advance. You can just arrive, get a stamp in your passport, and you're free to go. Increasingly you don't even get a stamp, with the entire process simplified to a photo and a passport scan by a computer.

Countries with "weaker" passports may need to apply for a visa ahead of time, sometimes requiring a visit or at least mailing a passport to an embassy in your country.

There might be a fee to get a visa on arrival or ahead of time. This might just be the equivalent of a few dollars or much more. Bhutan, for instance, requires you to prepay a set amount, $100 each day of your intended visit as of this writing.

Most countries require six months validity on your passport. That means your passport "expires" six months before it says it does.

Some countries might still want to pre-approve you before you arrive, which isn't exactly the same as a visa, but is functionally the same. Australia, for instance, has an Electronic Travel Authority, the US has the Electronic System for Travel Authorization (ESTA), and the EU has European Travel Information and Authorisation System (ETIAS). The process for these is an online form and approval is often instant or at most a few days. You're often advised to get this approval before you buy tickets for a flight.

Usually, an airline won't let you board without the proper documentation. This is because they're usually liable for taking you back *out* of a country if it's deemed you can't stay.

Options for extending your visa

Tourist visas are often good for three to six months and are usually only good for that country. Europe's Schengen Area is a rare exception, where entry into one country gives you access to all the countries in the zone. You'll still want to carry your passport with you at all times. Don't ask me how I know that fact.

To stay longer, many countries offer longer stay visas, though these are often much harder to obtain. For instance, there can be student visas, youth visas, work visas, and so on. You'll need to apply, and often you'll only be allowed to apply from outside the country. New Zealand, for instance, has the "working holiday visa," which lets people under 30 years old (35 for some nationalities) live and work in the country for one to three years. Many countries around the world have these, but they're usually fairly limited in which nationalities can apply and are rarely available to anyone over 30.

TIP

There are an increasing number of "digital nomad" visas available from various countries. The restrictions vary, but generally if you can prove you're capable of supporting yourself as a digital nomad, you're free to stay for much longer than a typical tourist visa. These are usually only available to already-successful digital nomads. You might need to prove significant monthly income and/or a long history of working "remotely."

What other visas are available will depend on your nationality, age, and what you intend to do in the country. Generally they don't want you loafing around for a year unless you can prove you have the means to do so (read: a lot of cash in your bank account).

Some countries will "reset" your visa if you leave and then come back into the country. How much time has to pass between exit and re-entry varies. Some it could be that day, others it might be something like "three months maximum stay out of six months total." Then there are visa runs, which I discuss in the next section.

The perils of "visa runs"

A "visa run" is a day trip to a border, with the idea of crossing and then immediately crossing back, to "reset" a visa. Someone might want to do this to stay "legally" in a country for longer than the visa technically allows. When I was in Thailand several years ago, there were advertisements everywhere, in English, for this service.

How legal this is, or if not illegal how frowned upon it is, varies a lot per country. I met one traveler whose boyfriend tried to do this in a fairly strict country and on the third time the immigration officer said "I know what you're trying to do. I'm going to let you through, but the next guy probably won't." Other countries, including Thailand, have started to put restrictions on the practice, only letting you stamp in and out a certain number of times per year.

There are countries that don't care at all. It might not be tacit approval as much as it's just not caring enough to enforce. As long as you're spending money and not causing trouble, they'd rather have you than force you to leave.

WARNING

I've met a lot of travelers who are very casual about all this, and that's fine up until the moment it isn't. Best case you get kicked out of a country. Worst case can be a permanent ban or even jail. Having this on your record might even prevent you from visiting other countries in the future. Personally, it's not something I'm interested in testing. My longest stay in one country was Australia, and I left on my 88th day, two short of my visa.

Exploring different ways to stay

A far better option than trying to game the system is just do everything above board. Admittedly this isn't always possible, but it's worth considering. Options include going to (or back to) university, teaching English, getting a job, and so on.

Again, the specifics vary a lot depending on where you're from and where you want to stay. Many countries have specific visas for young people that aren't available to people over 30. Teaching English is a possibility in a lot of countries, though not as likely in countries where that's the official language.

Then there's full-blown citizenship, which is well beyond the scope of this book. I've known a few people who have done it, but it's a long, frustrating, and often expensive process. But hey, if you see the mountains and fiords of New Zealand and think "I never want to leave," it's worth looking into.

Volunteering (aka volunteer travel)

It's a normal and understandable sentiment to want to give back to the world for the privilege of travel. There are a variety of companies and services whose goal is to match you with an area that needs assistance in some way. The idea being, instead of spending your days relaxing on the beach or touring a city, you aid the locals in an area instead — travel that gives back, if you will.

There's a name for this kind of good-intentioned travel: "voluntourism." In theory, this seems like a great option. You get to travel and yet also help people who aren't as privileged as you. The reality is a bit murkier.

WARNING

I've tried to avoid being negative throughout this book, but this is a specific subject that can get dark very quickly. Before you get your heart set on something like this, please research the company, where you might be stationed, how exactly the organization and you will be helping, and to be brutally honest, think deeply about your intentions. Doing more harm than good is bad for everyone, even if your intentions were pure. Don't get me wrong, some of these programs can absolutely help a community. But sometimes they harm them and cost you money, only benefitting the organization.

That said, longer-stay volunteering, with organizations like the Peace Corps, are usually far more beneficial. Instead of popping in a for a few days, you're assigned somewhere for 3 to 12 months. Host countries offer positions they need. If your goal is to "do something good in the world" this is a far better option than a superficial few days or weeks.

REMEMBER

No matter what type of program you have in mind, reach out to people who have done it (social media can be a help for this) and read as many reviews online as you can find (*especially* the negative ones).

Becoming a Digital Nomad

One of the reasons I'm able to travel as long and as frequently as I do is because I'm a "digital nomad." The term has fallen out of favor in some circles, due to some of the negative stereotypes associated with some of my nomad brethren. I still like the name, though. With more and more jobs going remote, or at least "work from home," more people are realizing that if you don't have to go to an office, can you just work from anywhere? In my opinion, that answer is yes more often than not.

What's a digital nomad?

Broadly speaking, a digital nomad is someone whose job is done primarily via a laptop and an internet connection. The idea being, as long as you have those two things, you can work from anywhere. I'm a writer (obviously), and for the last ten years I've done my job from beaches of Fiji to the highlands of Brazil and on trains in Japan and ferries in Europe. I traveled extensively for years before I ever got paid to write about travel.

There are plenty of other options to work as a digital nomad. Web designers, graphic designers, coders, any number of consultants, analysts, and so on. If your job entirely entails clicking a mouse and tapping a keyboard, you could probably become a digital nomad. If you do all that but "have" to come to an office, the roadblock to extended travels is often your boss, not your job. Though unfortunately to deal with one you might need to deal with the other.

Working from "home" when home is anywhere

When so many jobs went fully remote because of the pandemic, I think a lot of people realized, "Hey, why do I need to go to an office at all?" I agree. Then the next step, making your home office wherever you want to be, isn't that much of a leap. Unfortunately, the corporate structure at most companies is going to resist this by any means necessary. Many companies required people to return to an office as soon as they could. Others delayed, claimed they'd stay flexible, and then changed their minds.

Convincing your boss that you want to permanently work remotely is going to be the biggest challenge to becoming a digital nomad. I'm lucky. I haven't had a real "boss" in over a decade. That's one of the many benefits of being freelance. I've had, and still have "bosses" that supervised my work, but none could dictate my time or location as I wasn't actually an employee.

It's important to keep in mind that your boss almost certainly doesn't want you to become a digital nomad. Even if they're fine with it now, they might change their mind later after you're already committed. They could also just let you go for no apparent reason. I mention earlier in this chapter about the steady gig I had with one outlet for years. A new boss came in and wanted to talk to everyone. We had a face-to-face, and he kept asking how I could do any work if I wasn't in an office. This is despite the fact that I had been doing the job to rave reviews for years and even had multiple people reporting directly to me, all while being remote. We ended the conversation seemingly on positive terms, only for him to essentially fire me the next day over email. So it goes.

WARNING

Is a lack of home address going to be an issue with an employer? And don't forget about taxes. An accountant to help with that could be a worthy investment.

While I am obviously a huge proponent of being a digital nomad, or at the very least not being required to go to an office, I'm the first to admit that it isn't easy. It does require discipline. When you can see some amazing location out the window of your hostel but you're on a deadline and need to work all day, it's a challenge. If you can't get your work done because you're too distracted, you're not going to be able to maintain being a digital nomad. It's not for everyone. I do think it's for more people than currently do it, though.

Downsides

The lure and glamor of permanently traveling often masks the reality, which isn't always as shiny and exciting as it seems from the outside. Don't get me wrong, I love it and wouldn't change a thing, but the reality is far different from how the flashy Instagram and TikTok content makes it seem.

For instance, you still need to, you know, actually work. Whatever your work is, you still need to find a time and a place to do it. This is certainly an enviable problem to have, but when you're on your fourth day in a row hunched over a very un-ergonomic table in a busy hostel, while everyone you've met is out exploring the amazing world, it becomes a lot more difficult. Again, this isn't a complaint, but it does take discipline to be able to work while there's enticing adventure just steps away.

There's also the timing aspect. If your job requires meetings, as mine occasionally does, you need to make that work with their schedule. I've had meetings at all hours of the day to match US-standard work hours. The worst was in Perth, where I had to get up at 3:30 a.m. to be presentable for a 4 a.m. meeting in my time zone. Of course, the meeting could have been an email, but then, can't they all? But I digress. A flexible location requires you to be flexible with time, and that's a valid tradeoff in my book.

Perhaps most frustrating is you can't complain. You might want to. You might have a bad day or week, feel lonely or lost, might want to vent about a bad hostel roommate or disappointing location, and you won't be able to. No one will understand. Instead, you'll be greeted by a chorus of "must be nice" or "but you're traveling" or the worst, "but you're on vacation." There's inevitably some variation of those by people who see that you're not at home and assume that means everything is perfect, always, and you should feel lucky to be doing any of it. Sure, you are lucky to be doing it, but that doesn't mean there aren't bad days, too. I've had this happen numerous times with even close friends who I thought understood. It can be a frustrating and isolating experience.

Don't get me wrong, I wouldn't change a thing. I love what I've managed to do with my life over the last decade, not least this book, but I caution anyone going into it thinking it's all sunsets and sushi bars. There are days that aren't great. There are days that are lonely. There are days where you're not sure it's worth it and you want to go home.

For me, thankfully, those days are rare. If you move slowly, stay aware of your needs, and know that it's okay to have bad days as long as they're outnumbered by good, you'll do all right. Most of all, it's worth remembering that at some point it's absolutely fine to stick a fork in your noodles and head home. Because there's a good chance you'll wake up the next morning and think, nah, let's keep going (especially if what you see that next morning is a view like the one in Figure 12-3).

FIGURE 12-3: The legendary Monument Valley, Navajo Nation, southwestern US, made famous by John Ford, countless movies, TV shows, and a certain book cover.

How It Works from Someone Who Has Done It for a Decade

I'd like to lead you through a day, week, and month of my travel life. It is not, nor could it be, a blueprint for your own extended travels. I figured out what works for me, based on my life, job, and interests. That's all going to look very different for you. I just want to lead you through it as an example of what the world looks like to someone who doesn't commute to an office, sit for eight hours, and then head home. If you're happy with that lifestyle, that's fine, but I'm guessing if you've read this far, that's not you.

A typical day

Awake. Nights in a hostel can be comfortable and quiet, uncomfortable and noisy, and anywhere in-between. If it's someplace I'm going to stay for more than a few days, I'm far more selective. Party hostels are fun but not conducive to work. My morning routine is typically checking email and messages, the amount of which depends which hemisphere I'm in. Sometimes the main working day of my clients starts when I'm asleep. Other times it starts in my afternoon.

It takes me forever to get going in the morning, so I'll usually start writing or whatever other work I need to do while still in bed. This has the added benefit of letting the room clear out of fellow travelers. Extra useful if there's an ensuite bathroom so I can shower and get ready at my leisure.

Eventually, I'll get hungry. I'm not a big breakfast person, so my first meal is usually lunch. I'll shower and pack my daypack with whatever I might need during the day. If I'm not particularly busy with work I'll just pack a camera, headphones, USB battery pack, and that kind of thing. If I've got a lot of work to do, I'll bring my laptop with the overly optimistic idea that I'll find a place to write.

I'll head out of the hostel with the goal of finding lunch. This varies depending on where I am. Sometimes a sandwich at a grocery store and other places a bowl of noodles — you get the idea. If my budget is particularly tight, I'll buy larger amounts of something and keep it at the hostel.

For the afternoon I'll explore. It's fun to have a destination or goal in mind, but it's also fun to just wander. Whenever possible I'll walk, but I love a good metro system. If it's a place that might have some good sunset photo potentials, I'll eventually make my way to wherever that is.

Dinner is either a repeat of lunch, or if I'm feeling flush, a restaurant that either looks cool or was recommended to me. Sometimes I'll work during dinner, though that varies depending on the type of place.

Evenings at the hostel are typically more work hours, usually staying in the common areas until after most everyone has gone to sleep. If there's an event at the hostel maybe I'll attend, depending how outgoing I'm feeling. Eventually, back to bed.

Now this was a typical day. There are also days where I never leave the hostel, working all day. I'm pretty sure not missing deadlines is one of the reasons I've been a successful freelancer for so long. If having to spend many hours inside hostels and hotels doesn't appeal to you, being a digital nomad might not be for you.

A typical week

A typical week will vary a lot depending where I am, but generally speaking, most days will look like the day described above. One day in the week I'll do laundry. That usually involves multiple trips to the laundry room in the building, or in rare cases, a few hours spent at a public laundromat. In the case of the latter, I'll just bring my laptop and work for a few hours.

Many weeks will have at least a day of travel. I tend to book travel that's as easy as possible, even if it's slightly more expensive. If it costs me $20 more to not have to get up at 4 a.m., then I'm going to do it. So let's say it's some ideal situation where I have a midday flight. I'll get up and shower. I'll have packed just about everything the night before when my hostel roommates were awake. If I can avoid being noisy while people are sleeping, I do so. I'll have figured out how to get to the station or airport the night before as well, so I know when I need to leave and how to get there. Before I leave, I'll quadruple check I haven't left anything in the bed area or locker, then I'll strap on my travel backpack and head out. Fully loaded, with my heavy camera gear and electronics in the daypack, there is a bit of a "tail wags the dog" aspect to travel backpacks, but with the straps adjusted correctly, it's not that bad. If you don't carry as many heavy things as I do, you likely won't have this issue. With any luck I don't have to walk too far.

A typical month and more

During my heaviest travel years, I'd set up everything so I wouldn't *need* to return home by a specific date. Many trips were open-ended. For me, however, I found that eight to ten weeks was the sweet spot. It was long enough that I never felt rushed, but not so long that I ever felt bored or burned out. Avoiding the latter is key.

It also speaks to my specific life. I have lots of friends at home, and I still wanted to see them when possible. Some might mention that they hadn't seen me in "forever," but the truth is we're all adults with our own lives. Before I started traveling, it'd be weeks or more between hangouts. In reality, I see most of my friends now with a similar cadence as I did before I started my travels. I just happen to be somewhere other than my home between visits.

There's a famous, and admittedly overused, section from T.S. Elliot's *Little Gidding*: "And the end of all our exploring, will be to arrive where we started, and know the place for the first time." Perhaps it's quoted so often because of how accurate and universal it is. Arriving home after weeks or months on the road, you notice things you didn't notice when you saw them every day. Everything is a little different. It's because you're a little different. You've changed, hopefully for the better. For me, travel has let me enjoy being home more because I appreciate it more.

That lasts about a week. Then I'm planning my next adventure, dreaming of roads and views like those in Figure 12-4. There's a big world to explore. See you out there.

Geoffrey Morrison

FIGURE 12-4: There and back again, Aoraki/Mount Cook, New Zealand.

Chapter **13**
Ten Things Worth Splurging On

The core idea of budget travel is saving money where you can, so you can afford to enjoy the best of what the world has to offer. There are some things worth splurging on, assuming you have the time and money to do so.

REMEMBER

The central theme to these splurge-worthy items is that they're more about experiences, not "things." With careful budgeting for the rest of your trip there might be some money left for these unforgettable moments.

Great Local Food

Saving money by cooking food at your hostel, surviving on simple sandwiches, and so on, is a great way to make travel more afford-able. You don't want to miss out on some incredible, and possibly unique, culinary experiences though. Keeping your food costs low most days should let you splurge on a meal or two at a great restaurant. That might mean a place with an epic view, or it might be a hole-in-the-wall place revered by locals.

Just because a place is expensive doesn't mean it's good.

Unique Local Activities

This is very broad, but I can explain. Everywhere you go you're going to find certain types of activities. There's going to be a zipline, a bungie jump, or a rope swing. I'm not staying avoid these things, but keep in mind that they're usually the type of thing you can do elsewhere, and often for less money.

That said, if you're caught up in the moment and want to add "bungie jump" to the story of your adventure, go for it. It's worth making sure that whatever that activity is, it's the best option in the area of your trip. You don't want to spend money on a bungie jump only to find out the world's tallest is one hour away.

What I will recommend, without caveats, are the singular activities that are bespoke to certain areas: A horseback ride past a herd of zebras, a scuba dive at the Great Barrier Reef, a hike to watch sunrise at Machu Picchu. Don't feel guilty about splurging on things like these. In fact, you should definitely make sure they're in your budget.

A Night to Relax at a Nice Hotel

The best way to save money for any trip is to stay at hostels. Even if the hostel is less than ideal, it's just for a few days and lets you afford the entire trip. For longer trips, and if it doesn't break the bank, pampering yourself with a nice hotel for one night can certainly "reset" the annoyance meter.

When I've been traveling for a few weeks, I try to have at least one night of quiet, air-conditioned comfort. Usually, I'll do this the night before a flight to a new location. Not only to I have a better

chance of getting a good night's sleep, but I'll have space to make sure everything's packed, I can use the hotel's towels instead of my own, and when I'm getting ready early the next morning, I'm not bothering anyone. The cost is often partially offset by the fact that most hotels near airports have free shuttles.

A Good Backpack

Luggage is expensive. The cheapest suitcases and roller bags are usually very poorly made. The most expensive suitcases and roller bags are wildly overpriced. There are decent inexpensive options, but I say avoid all of them.

Getting a good, but not too expensive, backpack can be a gamechanger for your travels. One that's not too big and fits you well can be a consummate travel companion for years.

A Decent Flight and Location

Flights are the single most expensive item of any trip. I am all for saving money on flights, but there's no hidden trick to do so. Flying on off days and during shoulder or off seasons, is your best bet. Within those times, there are usually a variety of similarly priced options.

Saving money is an important goal, but also consider that *time* is actually your most valuable currency. If you're losing an entire day to save a few dollars, or you need to get up at 3 a.m. to make a slightly cheaper flight, is that really worth it? Would it be better to spend a little more so you have extra time at your destination or so you'll have the energy to explore when you get there? There's no right or wrong answer here, especially if your budget is particularly tight. It's just something to keep in mind when you're doing your calculations.

Also consider that with a direct flight there's less or no chance of missed connections, delays, lost luggage, and so on.

Then there are accommodations. It's worth spending a little more for one in a great, usually central, location. It goes back to that ultimate resource: time. You don't want to waste significant chunks of your day just getting to the places you want to explore. If there's a better location that can save you that time, but it costs a little more each night, it's often worth the (slight) splurge.

Comfortable Sneakers/Walking Shoes

I'm going to be the first to admit I'm not one for style. I lack anything that would be considered "trendy." So take my advice here with a grain of salt. What I will say, though, is if your goal is to spend all day, every day, exploring some new and interesting location, having a comfortable pair of shoes is crucial. The last thing you want is to be three days into a two-week trip, and every step is painful due to blisters.

If you don't have sneakers/shoes you'd be willing to walk 500 miles in, or 500 more, it's worth finding a pair. I know some people can walk for days in simple sandals, but if you're not sure that's you, it might not be worth the risk.

USB Battery Pack

"Splurge" is a bit of a stretch for this one, as they're not that expensive and you don't need to spend a lot. These portable battery packs charge your devices when you're on the go. I know a lot of people have one already, but if you don't, they're a great purchase.

I find the best options balance size and power. A 10,000 mAh pack can charge your phone several times but is small enough to fit in any purse or backpack.

Good Noise-Canceling Headphones

Like the battery pack, you don't necessarily have to "splurge" on these. The best options, typically from Bose and Sony, are expensive. There are some good inexpensive options available, too, though, that offer better noise canceling than many expensive models and cost less than $100. You'll need to check out some reviews since what's best changes, but there should be several earbud and over-ear headphone options around that price.

Keep in mind I'm specifically calling out "good" noise-canceling headphones. Not all noise canceling is the same. The best noise canceling can greatly reduce the loud droning sounds that can make airplane and train travel so fatiguing. Bad noise-canceling barely does anything. So it's important to read the reviews to find the best options for a given price.

Literally Anything on Your "Bucket List"

I don't care what it is, if it's on your bucket list you should splurge on it. No regrets. If some "friend" or random TikToker says it's "cringe" to do it, *all the more reason to do it.* This is your life. Live it how you want.

Travel Itself

There are going to be people in your life who think travel itself is a frivolous expense. They think that spending money on something so temporary, so fleeting, so "irrelevant" is a childish and irresponsible endeavor. I've certainly met people who think I should be spending my money on a better car, or a bigger home, or just "saving for a rainy day."

Nonsense. Obviously, I'm biased, but I think travel is one of the best things to spend money on, period, full stop. I have memories and friends I'll cherish for a lifetime specifically because I didn't have a $600 a month car payment and $3500 a month in rent/mortgage.

Travel is not something everyone understands, but I'm guessing if you're reading this, you do understand. If you can't convince some naysayer about it, don't bother. That's on them. Go have your adventure.

Appendix
Travel Checklists

To help reduce the stress of packing, as well as hopefully minimize those pre-trip jitters, here are three lists. The first is what I personally bring on every adventure. My specific needs will be a bit different from yours, but it should give you a broad idea of all that's really needed for a multi-week or even multi-month adventure. The next is a checklist to help you organize what you need and limit that inevitable pre-trip anxiety about forgetting something (or worse, trying to pack too much). Lastly, I provide a pre-trip countdown checklist of some of the most important things to do leading up to your big trip.

FIND ONLINE

Check out some links to my reviews and recommended items, along with other helpful resources, at www.dummies.com/go/ budgettravelfd.

What I Pack

My typical kit (as seen in Figure 7-1 in Chapter 7) will likely be a little different than yours. For example, I tend to carry a lot of photography gear for my job that you might not need. In that space you could instead fit a makeup bag, prescription dive mask, additional hair/skincare products, hiking boots or heels, and so on.

Everything on the left fits inside the carry on-sized main travel backpack shown, everything on the right fits in the accompanying daypack which mounts to the main pack. While the exact items I bring change as things get worn out or replaced, in a general sense this is what I bring on every trip.

Left side, starting at the top:

>> Toiletry kit, shorts, Merino wool pullover

>> Hat, laundry bag, t-shirts (×4), long sleeve shirts (×2)

>> Merino wool socks, socks (×5), boxers (×6)

>> Laundry day shirt, swim trunks, rain gear, zippered pouch (shaving cream, soap, sunscreen/moisturizer), black box o' stuff (various camera gear and accessories)

>> Rain cover for backpack, pack towel, deodorant, plug adapters, water shoes

Middle:

>> Osprey Farpoint 55 main pack (center) and daypack

Right side, starting at top:

>> Action camera, with handle

>> Camera strap

>> Mirrorless camera with 135mm f2 telephoto lens

>> USB battery pack

>> Neoprene sleeve for lens, also containing a teleconverter and wireless mouse

>> 12-24mm f4 wide-angle lens and 50mm f2 prime

>> Laptop and e-reader

Not shown: Headphones, sunglasses, "Tell Your Dog I Said Hi" baseball hat, jeans, zippered hoodie, and sneakers (a.k.a. "running shoes"). These, along with one of the shirts shown, would be worn during transit days and therefore not "packed." The shirts, underwear, and socks go in packing cubes, also not shown.

Budget Travel Packing List

This list includes everything you'll need for any adventure (more or less). For more details about each item, check out Chapter 7.

- ☐ **Five to six tops**
- ☐ **Five to six pairs of underwear**
- ☐ **Five to six pairs of socks**

  Optionally, add one pair for transit days.

- ☐ **Two (or so) bottoms:** Shorts, pants, and so on

  If you wear dresses, you can count these as either tops, bottoms, or both depending on your style. Stick with around six total outfits for space, though. I recommend wearing long pants for flights, which can be one of these two or a third pair.

- ☐ **Sleepwear and/or something to wear on laundry day**

  Optionally, also a small laundry bag.

- ☐ **Toiletries:** Toothbrush, toothpaste, sunscreen (a must!), makeup, medications, condoms, and preferred period products

  Your favorite hair and skin products can go in travel-sized reusable bottles (unless you want to check luggage, then full size bottles in a waterproof bag is fine).

- ☐ **Outer layer:** Hoodie, zip-up, pullover, light jacket, and so on

  You don't need to "pack" this. Instead, wear it on the plane. For colder adventures, see the "Climate/trip-specific items" in this appendix.

- ☐ **Chargers, cables, USB power bank, and international plug adapters**
- ☐ **Microfiber pack towel**
- ☐ **Flip-flops, sandals, or water shoes**
- ☐ **Passport and/or ID**
- ☐ **Tickets** (saved on your phone is fine)
- ☐ **Apps and maps downloaded on your phone**

Optional items

The items in the previous list are your core kit. Following are items that may not be necessary for everyone or every trip but are worth considering:

- ☐ **Headphones/earbuds.** (ideally noise-canceling)
- ☐ **Sunglasses**
- ☐ **E-reader**

- ☐ **Tablet or small laptop**
- ☐ **Action and/or other camera**
- ☐ **Extra memory card or portable hard drive**

Climate/trip-specific items

Headed somewhere warm, cold, wet, or dry? Many typical tourist locations have fairly simple packing requirements, but sometimes specialized items are needed, such as the following:

- ☐ **Bathing suit**
- ☐ **Heavy jacket**

  Most airlines won't count this as a separate carry-on item, though that's worth checking ahead of time.

- ☐ **Merino wool socks**
- ☐ **Hat** (for sun or warmth)
- ☐ **Hiking boots**
- ☐ **Rain gear** (though not a bad idea for any trip)
- ☐ **Visa and/or vaccine documentation** (if required)

Countdown Checklist

Is your big adventure coming up? Are you excited or anxious? Excited AND anxious? Following is a checklist of things to do as your next trip approaches.

When you're buying tickets:

- ☐ **Apply for a visa or similar and check vaccine requirements.**

  This is likely required before you buy your tickets, but I'm adding it here to double-check if it's required.

- ☐ **Check your passport.**

  Most countries require at least six months *before* the listed expiration date. Rush replacements are possible, but they're expensive and rarely guaranteed.

- ☐ **Check the condition of your luggage.**

One month before your flight:

- ❏ **Check your seats.**

  As people cancel tickets, or airlines swap planes, the seats you chose when you purchased might change or a better option might be available.

- ❏ **Check you have the right international plug adapters.**

  Also, any other gear you'll need, like a better charger, longer cables, extra memory card, and so on.

- ❏ **Check lodging.**

  I'm guessing you've been doing this since you bought the flights, but it's worth seeing what's available since you last checked. Book what looks good whenever you're comfortable doing so.

- ❏ **International data?**

  Are you getting a local SIM or eSIM? Is your phone unlocked? If not, how bad are your provider's traveling data rates? See Chapter 8 for more info.

- ❏ **Check your prescriptions.**

  Will you have enough for your trip? Your insurance should allow extra if necessary, but the process to do so might be annoying.

One week before your flight:

- ❏ **Check your seats again.**

  Why not?

- ❏ **Start "pre-packing."**

  Start a pile of things you want to bring and add to it when you think of something. Doing so will be less stressful than trying to remember everything the night before.

- ❏ **Get your phone ready.**

  You'll have enough to do the day before you leave, so download whatever apps and maps you'll need for your trip. Make sure your family/friends are set with WhatsApp or whatever app you're using to communicate.

- ❏ **Request a mail hold.**

- ❏ **Purchase travel insurance.**

The day before your flight:

- ❑ **Put your ID and/or passport where you can't forget them.**

  Put them with your phone/purse/pants — whatever you know you won't leave without.

- ❑ **Check in for your flight.**

  Did a better seat open up?

- ❑ **Save your tickets to your phone.**

  A photo or screenshot will work. The airline's app works too.

- ❑ **Charge all your batteries.**

- ❑ **Finish packing.**

  With any luck, you'll have everything already together in one place. If you followed the earlier packing list, it *should* easily fit in one carry-on bag. (If you manage to fit everything in one bag on the first try, let me know how.)

- ❑ **Resist overpacking.**

  The urge to overpack will be *strong*. Resist! You don't need that eighth hoodie.

The day of your flight:

- ❑ **What's the travel time to the airport?**

  Unexpected construction or traffic can really mess with your schedule.

- ❑ **You definitely have your ID and passport, right?**

  Honestly, it's the only thing you absolutely need.

- ❑ **Adventure!**

Index

About the Author

Geoffrey Morrison is a freelance writer and photographer about tech and travel. He contributes regularly to *CNET*, *The New York Times*, and the *Wall Street Journal*. His work has also been featured in *USA Today's Reviewed*, *Forbes*, *Men's Journal*, *Business Traveler*, *Sound & Vision*, and more. His photos and videos have been used in a variety of content by other authors and creators including books, magazines, as well as in music and corporate videos. He was the original A/V editor of *Wirecutter*, editor in chief of *Home Entertainment* magazine, and is the author of two sci-fi novels, *Undersea* and *Undersea Atrophia*. He has traveled extensively through all 50 US states including several multi-month road trips, and to 60 countries across 6 continents. He spends four to six months each year "on the road" either traveling internationally or exploring national parks in a campervan he converted. You can find him on Instagram (Inveterate_Adventurer) and on YouTube (@GeoffMorrison).

Dedication

To my mom and dad, who gifted me a love of travel at a very early age, and to all the friends I've made along the way.

Author's Acknowledgments

First of all, I'd like to thank you. Thanks for reading my rambles about something I deeply love. Travel has changed my life entirely for the better, and I hope it does for you too.

I wouldn't have had nearly as much fun, nor as many stories, nor would my life be as full of love if it weren't for the many incredible people I've met during my adventures. Many of those stories I've written about in these pages, and hopefully they bring a knowing smile to those involved. Thank you with all my heart to Grace, Jelley, Kay, Mary, Thaynara, and the many more who check in, like my social media posts, and make time for me when we're at all nearby. Distance doesn't make us any less close, and you have all taught me so much.

I'd also like to thank my friends from home, who keep me grounded and are always excited to see me when I return. Alex, Art, Brent, Dennis, Carrie, Carolina, Courtney, John, Jonathan, Lee, Lauren, Maureen, Stephen, and Phil, you all travel with me always.

And lastly, my incredible editors, who have cleaned up and organized my words and thoughts into something cohesive. Thank you, Chrissy, Jennifer C., Kristie, Ria, and of course Jennifer Y., without whom none of this would have happened.

Thank you all. I hope we can meet on an adventure somewhere out there.

Publisher's Acknowledgments

Senior Acquisitions Editor: Jennifer Yee

Project Manager and Development Editor: Christina Guthrie

Copy Editor: Jennifer Connolly

Technical Editor: Ria Misra

Managing Editor: Kristie Pyles

Production Editor: Saikarthick Kumarasamy

Cover Images: Text: © procurator/ Getty Images

Landscape: © teddyandmia/ Getty Images

Luggage Tag: © RLT_Images/ Getty Images

PERSONAL ENRICHMENT

Staying Sharp
9781119187790
USA $26.00
CAN $31.99
UK £19.99

Facebook
9781119179030
USA $21.99
CAN $25.99
UK £16.99

Guitar
9781119293354
USA $24.99
CAN $29.99
UK £17.99

Investing
9781119293347
USA $22.99
CAN $27.99
UK £16.99

Beekeeping
9781119310068
USA $22.99
CAN $27.99
UK £16.99

Digital Photography
9781119235606
USA $24.99
CAN $29.99
UK £17.99

Meditation
9781119251163
USA $24.99
CAN $29.99
UK £17.99

Pregnancy
9781119235491
USA $26.99
CAN $31.99
UK £19.99

Samsung Galaxy S7
9781119279952
USA $24.99
CAN $29.99
UK £17.99

iPhone
9781119283133
USA $24.99
CAN $29.99
UK £17.99

Crocheting
9781119287117
USA $24.99
CAN $29.99
UK £16.99

Nutrition
9781119130246
USA $22.99
CAN $27.99
UK £16.99

PROFESSIONAL DEVELOPMENT

Windows 10
9781119311041
USA $24.99
CAN $29.99
UK £17.99

AutoCAD
9781119255796
USA $39.99
CAN $47.99
UK £27.99

Excel 2016
9781119293439
USA $26.99
CAN $31.99
UK £19.99

QuickBooks 2017
9781119281467
USA $26.99
CAN $31.99
UK £19.99

macOS Sierra
9781119280651
USA $29.99
CAN $35.99
UK £21.99

LinkedIn
9781119251132
USA $24.99
CAN $29.99
UK £17.99

Windows 10
9781119310563
USA $34.00
CAN $41.99
UK £24.99

SharePoint 2016
9781119181705
USA $29.99
CAN $35.99
UK £21.99

Fundamental Analysis
9781119263593
USA $26.99
CAN $31.99
UK £19.99

Networking
9781119257769
USA $29.99
CAN $35.99
UK £21.99

Office 2016
9781119293477
USA $26.99
CAN $31.99
UK £19.99

Office 365
9781119265313
USA $24.99
CAN $29.99
UK £17.99

Salesforce.com
9781119239314
USA $29.99
CAN $35.99
UK £21.99

Coding
9781119293323
USA $29.99
CAN $35.99
UK £21.99